Timinology:

by Tim Leach

This edition first published 2018

Tim Leach www.timinology.com

First edition

A catalogue record for this book is available from the
British Library.

ISBN: 978-0-9957690-0-7

Printed and bound in Great Britain by Clays Ltd, St Ives plc

Front cover design: Arigoldservices

Editing: Emma Close-Brooks

Typesetting: Ana Marija Meshkova

To Ma, Pa, Bex and Katie, thank you for your unending support and love for me throughout this extraordinary journey. I love you to the moon and back.

Contents

Timinology:

How to manage your thoughts, live a happy life, embrace mindfulness and learn to love yourself.

Timinology publishing

Introduction

A lighthearted, mindful lifestyle approach for the time-strapped observer

This book covers a multitude of daily habits that we, as humans, manage to get decidedly wrong. As someone who has, for most of his life, found himself on the wrong side of the happiness fence, in this book I'll show you how I learned to change these habits and turned my life around – through grit, determination and a lot of experience. It's what I call 'Timinology': my approach to leading a happy life, no matter what it throws at you. Whatever your demons, reading these first-hand experiences and learning how to apply this approach will give you an invaluable armoury with which to fight them.

Parts of the book may come across as a little controversial, or slightly close to the bone. You may not agree with or like everything that I say. However, I have vigorously researched almost everything that is encompassed herein – and that which I haven't researched comes from my own experience. So, whether or not you approve of a particular part, the routes to my opinions, at least, have the backing of a host of sources that can all be found in the bibliography at the end of the book; those that don't, I ask you to take as nothing more or less than the experiences of one human, shared with another.

Owing to my now unique memory (as you'll learn) and my love of (mainly incredible) music, a lot of the subheadings within this book have borrowed their titles from the wondrous canticles bestowed upon us by some of the leading artists in the musical world. The titles I have chosen were those that just so happened to be ripe for depicting the subject matter about to be discussed and which I felt brought things together in a way I could not better. In recognition of this quirky little feature, you can find a playlist named 'Timinology', on Spotify, including each and every subheading that makes this book such an Aladdin's cave of charm. www.goo.gl/4MzNVd

This, intentionally, is an easy read. It's written for the majority of people who don't have time to retreat and discover for themselves the hard-to-find things that can make life so simple. Wherever you stand, I can guarantee parts of this book will speak to you. They will help you to lead a happier and more fulfilled life. It's a domino effect, too; your happiness will make the lives of everyone around you better. After all, happiness is as infectious as its counterpart. Wanting to spread the happiness is at the core of why I have written this book. I'm not unrealistic; it won't transform you into a beacon of light, love and compassion. What it will do is help you become a happier and more grounded, loving individual. So, in that small way, we can make the world a better place.

I won't tell you that you will become a millionaire if you simply believe it. Nor will I tell you that writing your desires on Post-it notes and plastering them across your house will cause them to eventually materialize. Because they won't. Belief is imperative to achieving a goal but you have to put the work in to make it happen and believe in yourself, not just the outcome.

I will tell you about my experience of the power of the mind and how it can potentially heal a physical ailment. I will also share my experience of how belief in yourself, alongside modern medicine, can be a winning combination in returning to health from an apparent point of no return.

On the surface, I'm no different to anyone you might meet in the street. I'm young...ish, I'm fit and I'm healthy. I adore cooking and eating. I love skiing, tennis, cycling, meeting friends, watching great films and drinking good wines and whiskies. In the context of my friends, I had a fairly normal childhood but I will readily admit that my upbringing was wonderfully privileged compared to a large proportion of children around the world. But I was carefree, as many children are, and did what most families do with kids growing up; holidays, school, bickering, teasing and laughing. I have two sisters, with whom I *now* get on very well, and a fabulous set of parents, who bestowed upon me the fundamental basics of being a good person. I have a circle of close friends and I'll happily spark up a conversation with anyone crossing my path. But I wasn't always this way.

I spoke to a family friend and successful author, Mike Dickson, while I was working on this book. He asked me a very frank and pertinent question, which was simply: why was I writing it? It most certainly wasn't to make a lot of money, because, as you will find out, I should have carried on becoming a lawyer if that had been my wish. Well, the crux of the matter is this. I might only sell one book, to one person. If, as a result of reading it, that one person can tackle a part of their life that needs addressing, and go on to lead a happy, healthy and successful life, then all this will have been worthwhile. Of course, I want to help as many people as possible but this isn't a numbers game; this is a loving act. I know what it is to hit near on rock bottom – literally as well as mentally – and I want to help others make the best of what they have, and be able to go further than they ever thought possible.

The chapters of this book are ordered systematically, to make the transition from your current state of mind to your desired state of mind as easy as possible. Because I've based this book on my life experiences and with a process in mind – that's the 'Timinology' bit – even if a chapter title doesn't apply to you, stick with me and you won't regret it.

But who am I to tell you what to read? It's what you do with it that matters.

The Thought Theory Model

For there is nothing either good or bad, but thinking makes it so - William Shakespeare

Halfway through writing this, my mother gave me a book entitled The Inside Out Revolution by Michael Neil[1], which stresses that we have the ability to change absolutely any situation by thinking differently. It is almost entirely our thoughts that have the power to influence and define our every living moment. This isn't the first example of this idea; it's often been discussed in several books, although it seems like common sense. I'm calling this technique the Thought Theory Model for the purposes of this book.

She gave it to me after a close friend of hers, Janet, who suffers from chronic MS, is unable to walk and is in constant pain, experienced an almost immediate change in her train of thought regarding the illness. This change effectively transitioned her previously negative and fatalistic thoughts about the situation into a positive, serene and confident approach. She recognized that it had been her previous thoughts making a devastating situation intolerable and that through changing her mindset, life not only became bearable again, but joyous. Asking her about the transformative effect, she said that 'nothing changed, but everything changed'.

It is all about letting go and becoming aware that although our thoughts are whizzing away all the time, we can learn to mindfully recognize the bad thoughts and then systematically let them go, along with their negative influences over us.

Following her diagnosis thirty years ago, Janet couldn't cope with the stress and anxiety of living with a progressive disease, so she turned to Transcendental Meditation (TM) (described in the Kindfulness chapter), which helped her to overcome her chronic fatigue and gave her the emotional strength to live with the suffering that MS brought. She found that by following this doctrine, the stress and tension associated with MS began to slowly dissolve and her life improved, although she was still bothered by the thoughts and worries of the disease and her future. It was only relatively recently that she had been introduced to The Inside Out Revolution, describing how to manage your thoughts through the principles of mind and consciousness, with simple, yet powerful techniques to subdue senseless and damaging thoughts. Following the principles increased her resilience and wellbeing and coupled with the transformative effects of Transcendental Meditation, transported her from despair to calm and from fear to acceptance.

The long and short of the Thought Theory Model is simple: you have to slow down your mind. This will be explained in more detail in the Kindfulness chapter. Once you have taken yourself 'off-line' and stepped back from the crush, you need to rationalize your thought processing surrounding whatever issues are troubling you. These may be work problems, an unfaithful lover, a noisy neighbour or a disobedient dog. Whatever the confounding problem, however big it originally appears to be, you need to recognize that it is, in part, your thinking that is elevating it to such tremendous heights. Were it not for those negative thoughts, you would be in a substantially better place to confront the issue and deal with it from a position of strength, balance and calm, considering it for the problem it genuinely is, not the problem you have magnified it to be. Having slowed down your mind, allow and develop transient, peaceful thoughts to replace the malevolent ones.

A psychologist walked around a room while teaching stress management to an audience.

As she raised a glass of water, everyone expected they'd be asked the "half empty or half full" question.

Instead, with a smile on her face, she inquired

"How heavy is this glass of water?"

Answers called out ranged from 8 oz. to 20 oz.

She replied, "The absolute weight doesn't matter.

It depends on how long I hold it.

If I hold it for a minute, it's not a problem.

If I hold it for an hour, I'll have an ache in my arm.

If I hold it for a day, my arm will feel numb and paralyzed.

In each case, the weight of the glass doesn't change, but the longer I hold it, the heavier it becomes."

She continued, "The stresses and worries in life are like that glass of water.

Think about them for a while and nothing happens.

Think about them a bit longer and they begin to hurt.

And if you think about them all day long, you will feel paralyzed – incapable of doing anything."

It's important to remember to let go of your stresses, upsets and anything that doesn't feel good to you as early as you can.

Put all your burdens down.

Don't carry them throughout your day or even an hour or more than the few moments it takes to notice that you are feeling in a way you don't want.

Remember to put the glass down! [2]

The act of slowing down your mind and going 'off-line' will help you to naturally reach a placid place within yourself that allows you to neutralize the harshness of the outside world. It is, at the end of the day, the inner you that needs to be looked after. This method, coupled with meditation and mindfulness, will allow you to change your whole approach to life.

I didn't write this book to keep myself busy for a year. I wrote it because the approaches and techniques that I am going to share with you genuinely changed my life. They have made me a happier, more loving, empathetic individual; if I give you a boost in the same direction, then it has all been worthwhile.

Every chapter that follows, with the various accompanying techniques and stories, can be affiliated with the notion that it is our thoughts that control our lives. I will be exploring the benefits of the Thought Theory Model when the situations arise.

My Life

Before embarking on the Timinology approach and how it can apply to you, this chapter will get you acquainted with me and who I was, before everything happened. It is important that you understand the way I was, how I am now, and how I got here. A lot of my life before the events I'll share with you is incredible, and I wouldn't change it for anything. But my previous mindset, which I have since managed to transform, has only changed because I wanted it to:

You have to unconditionally and fundamentally want something, before any kind of development can take place.

***

I went to a school called Framlingham College, where I wasn't the most academic boy. I wasn't exactly the most popular either, so in a bid to while away my free time I joined the Combined Cadet Force (CCF), and established a love for rifle shooting. We were fortunate enough to have an indoor rifle range at school, which is where I could usually be found. I befriended the teacher in charge of CCF, Mr. Todd, who became my closest confidant, even though he was thirty-odd years my senior.

Another Brick in the Wall ♫

I didn't enjoy school, I saw no point in it. I hated any form of discipline, and I saw no value in exams and tests. I wasn't exactly a badly-behaved boy – apart from on one occasion when I managed to accidentally launch a firework through a top-floor dormitory window, where it exploded, causing the whole school to be evacuated. I probably would have got away with it too, if it wasn't for my innate tendency to tell the truth. I wouldn't say that the firework incident prompted my swift departure from the school but this, coupled with my extreme lack of drive to succeed in any subject, led to notice eventually being given.

I found myself leaving school at seventeen with no qualifications. In response, my parents sternly suggested I join the local agricultural college to embark on a two-year Business Studies course. I did this and although I had no genuine interest in the subject, I managed to sweet-talk a lecturer into mentoring me and somehow got into a university called Buckinghamshire Chilterns University College (BCUC) to study Music Industry Management, a subject which had recently tickled my fancy.

School's Out ♫

Until now, I had always lived at home. My parents had at one point petitioned for me to go to a boarding school halfway across the country but they, as most good parents would do, listened to my cries of protest against this ghastly idea. They allowed me to attend a similar kind of school much closer to home, although, as you've just read, I neglected to make the best of it. That aside, I had never really experienced life away from home before and it was with this naivety that I started my life at university.

As at school, I was never a bad person, I think mischievous would be the best description. The course at BCUC turned out to be about as interesting as watching grass grow so, in the absence of intellectual stimulus I built up a group of friends and became a social gatherer. I had, on arrival, been placed in university halls, a home intended to last for the entire first year. By the end of the first term, however, I was asked not to return back to halls after the holiday, for reasons relating to loud music, alcohol, mess and parties. I had built up a good group of friends, so I persuaded four of them to move into a house with me to see out the first year.

The following term, living in my very first house away from my parents and realising that life is not all about causing mischief, I was for the first time starting to grow up. It slowly dawned on me that education and work were fundamental to success. Owing to my unexpected lack of enthusiasm for the course, however, I didn't see a massive future within music industry management after all, so decided instead to seek a career in law. My father is a lawyer and as a family we have always been very comfortable, so it seemed logical that this path would lead me to success.

I needed a degree to reach my most recently revized goal, and so applied to numerous universities to study law. I brazenly applied to some of the top universities in England, and very surprisingly got accepted by Bristol university. On receiving a provisional offer, I was asked to go for an interview to guarantee my acceptance. However, it just so happened that I had planned to go away on a gap year over the interview date, so I called to say that I would not be available to attend. Yet more surprisingly, they subsequently guaranteed me a place anyway, without so much as a phone interview.

With the next stage of my university career booked in, I triumphantly boarded a plane with my close school friend, also called Tim, and started a six month voyage around the world. We travelled to Thailand, Bali, Australia and New Zealand, before finally returning home with invaluable life experience and three lifelong friends: Freddie, Dave and Ollie, who have each individually played significant roles in my life since.

Because of the different courses, colleges and a year-long travelling expedition, when I arrived at Bristol I was three years older than the majority of my contemporaries, which categorized me as a mature student. This didn't really bother me, so I applied to be enrolled into the best of the University's halls with all the other first year students. Thus, I began my fortunately acquired position studying law at one of the world's top universities.

Life at Bristol was incredible. I made a lot of great friends and fully engrossed myself in every activity that interested me, apart from my degree. By now you will be beginning to see a pattern. I joined the Wine Society and found myself utterly inebriated every Tuesday, having consumed copious quantities of wine, without a care in the world for its quality. I later became the Vice President of this society but even then my only intention was to get extremely drunk and have a lot of fun meeting other people.

Wasted ♫

Sadly, my love for partying outweighed my commitment to the course and I consequently failed my first year. Looking back on this, I see a hopeless layabout whose priorities were completely wrong. But back then I just wanted to party and have fun, so I did the minimum amount of work I possibly could to scrape by. I was awful. My parents had done so much for me and yet I had no inclination to demonstrate my appreciation for everything they had given me. Despite my appalling behaviour they didn't give up on me but instead bestowed another act of generosity upon me and bought me a house.

This house was arguably much too good to be a student house. It had five well-sized bedrooms, a large garden, two bathrooms, a massive open planned kitchen/dining/sitting room, and an extra mezzanine level to host guests. We even managed to climb onto the roof and had numerous parties up there. We all loved the house and arrogantly, though probably appropriately, named it 'The Palace'.

After I had passed my first year of exams a year later than everyone else, I did actually knuckle down to complete the degree, and although my grades were higher than those of some of my Palace-mates, it wasn't quite the first class honours result I had hoped for. My parents were ecstatic that I had been awarded a law degree at all – and from a top university – as was I. But had I known and lived by what I know now, I could have easily got a much better result.

Shortly after leaving university, I went on holiday with Sam, a fellow Bristolian. As we had not started working, we headed for the cheapest and most distant destination on offer. I had dreams of mainland America, however the travel agent crushed these with a pitying remark about student debt and suggested we try India instead. Four weeks later and after a whole day driving from Scotland to Birmingham and then to London to pick up a costly last-minute visa (because I had neglected to even think about needing one), we boarded the plane to Delhi. We only spent three weeks in India and it was a lot of fun. I mention it here because it also plays a very important part in shaping my life, as will be explained later.

On our return, we spent the remaining days of the summer in a rented holiday cottage in an attractive costal town near my parents' home. With the end of the summer came the time to apply for a legal training contract, to finally grow up and become a city lawyer.

Riders On the Storm ♫

With the realization that starting work would be the end of my carefree days, I decided to have one final blow-out and find work in a French ski resort for the upcoming season, before becoming, in my words, 'a corporate whore'.

Two of my university friends, Tess and Ru, agreed to join me and we started applying for work. Ru had always loved skiing and had enough experience to instantly find employment with a reputable ski hire company. Tess and I decided to go down the catering route and found work at a high-end chalet company. I spent the remaining couple of months before the season living and working in London with a friend called Bronya.

We touched down in Grenoble, greeted by surprisingly tepid temperatures for late November, from where we drove to Meribel, our home for the next four months.

A week into properly starting work here, life took on a whole new perspective. I was up at half past six every day, upon which I promptly made my way to whichever chalet was on my rota, where I would cook the guests breakfast and then transport them to the slopes. I then had 6 hours to amuse myself, usually skiing, before taking guests back to their chalets. This process took place every weekday. Saturday was my day off and on Sunday I would drive departing guests to the airport and pick up the new guests for the week. My evenings were normally spent at the local pizza restaurant and then the disco, except on Tuesdays when the restaurant hosted a Beatles tribute act, which never failed to entertain me. And in this manner my ski season played out week after week.

It's Not the Fall that Hurts ♫

One Saturday in February I got up early with a seasonnaire friend, Ewan, and embarked on a day of full-on skiing. I hadn't really been drinking for the previous week due to some generic plague or other and, having recovered from this, I was fresh and ready for an exhilarating day on the mountain. The snow had been pretty sparse for the majority of the season but the previous night had seen a massive fall of fresh snow. Even more surprisingly, owing to the night's apparent storm, we were blessed with a beautiful, clear and sunny morning.

What happened next changed my life completely and is the catalyst for eventually coming to write this book. I remember very little about this day, so I will be using Ewan's first-hand account to paint you as clear a picture as possible.

What I do remember is getting a chair-lift up the side of the mountain and then climbing up the final incline before skiing down. As unnecessary as it may seem for me to be writing this down, it is the only vivid memory I have of that day, where I remember [before stepping into my skis] relieving myself from my morning hydration and turning the beautiful white snow at my feet yellow. From then on, it's all up to Ewan to describe the day's events. At this particular point we were also skiing with another friend, Ryan.

Ryan says that he saw Timmy set off for his position, he then dropped down towards me. As Ryan came past the rocks I heard a shout (Ryan said that he was aware of something behind him and shouted 'Timmy'.) I looked up to see Timmy slide over the rocks on his back, head first. He must have fallen twenty feet or so. I did not see how he landed as the contour of the hill hid him from my position.
Ryan immediately headed across to him and I took my board off and ran up to them, calling to Ryan to find out how Timmy was. In the twenty seconds it took me to get to them,

Ryan had found Timmy at the foot of the rocks and shouted that he was blue.

Timmy was lying on his side facing into the hill, perhaps fifteen feet from the base of the rocks. There was blood on the snow by his head. I threw my gloves off and took a position kneeling behind Timmy's shoulders. I opened his airway, calling his name. Timmy was snoring loudly, so I knew he was breathing regularly. I opened his jacket at the neck, and his face was showing signs of circulation (he was not blue when I reached him). I was supporting his head with my hands using his hood as a compress, my knees were behind his shoulders and he was more or less in the recovery position with a clear airway.

I got Ryan to shout for help; we were about 100m to the piste above a small stream and level with the small hut at the bottom of the park. Ryan was strapping on his board to go when a couple stopped below us on a different section and Ryan was able to tell them that we needed immediate medical help. I tried to call 112 as I knew that they would have an English speaker, but was not able to get reception. With help on its way [from the couple below] I shouted for Ryan to come back and help me. We took off our jackets, covering Timmy, and I had Ryan take my position while I checked Timmy's body for deformities. There was no obvious out of shape bits and no blood from his torso and limbs. I returned to Timmy's head which had a bruise above his left eye, a small cut on his crown, and a ghastly wound at the back of his head.

I tried phoning again, this time to the office while Ryan set up our boards and Timmy's ski into a cross to make us more obvious. The visibility closed in [around] us so Ryan started shouting and whistling to guide the rescue teams to us. I made contact with Michael in the office and explained what had happened, and our location. Karen (our boss) used the other phone to contact the rescue services and tell them where to find us. I continued trying to [communicate] with Timmy but he did not respond to voice or touch.

The accident happened about 15:50 and by 16:08 Timmy was trying to move his legs and arm as if trying to rouse. I was talking to him telling him that he had had a fall, that he was with Ewan and Ryan and that help was on its way. I told him to lie still and not to try and move. Because he was moving his legs I had to shout Ryan to come back from where he was hollering to support Timmy's legs and stop his movement.

We heard a snowmobile below us and continued to whistle but the sound [moved] away from us. The visibility cleared once more around 1630 and we were able to stop lots of people on the piste below us with our yells and whistles. It took an age before someone started returning our signals and we knew that there was a spotter below and the rescuers must surely be close. The first guy to us arrived roughly 1645, and I hung up with the office.

I explained to the guy who Timmy was, how long ago the accident had happened and that he was unconscious but breathing regularly. This was in French but the guy was keen that I continue a dialogue with Timmy. This first guy checked over Timmy, feeling for breaks as I had done. He returned to me at Timmy's head and we moved his hood back as carefully as we could. The injury to the back of Timmy's head was horrific, the guy was trying to get gloves on but I told him just to pass the compresses to me and I used six between my hand and the back of Timmy's head. He wanted to remove Timmy's bag and was trying to tug it off but I made him get a knife and we just cut it away. Sorry about that Timmy.

A second rescuer joined us and it was unnerving the way they were sliding about in their ski boots as we tried to keep Timmy absolutely still. They gave me a large wound dressing and bandage to replace the dressings, and directed Ryan to scoop out a flat area just below Timmy. I again told them as many details as I could; Timmy had been unconscious for over an hour by this time. They said that they had been directed to the park first, which explains the snowmobile we [had] heard.

More rescuers arrived and we were able to get oxygen to Timmy, who was continuing to snore and trying to move his limbs, as though stirring. They were saying that he was O.K. and I kept talking to Timmy non-stop, telling him where he was, what had happened and that he was going to be fine. An inflatable bed and blood wagon had arrived and we lifted Timmy between us, inflating the bed and strapping him to it. We slid this down and on to the blood wagon.

Ryan and I then tried to grab ours and Timmy's stuff. I found Timmy's hat and goggles at the foot of the rocks. Ryan said that he had seen them fly off about half way down. One of his skis and his poles were there too. I grabbed his bag and ski and set off, catching up with the blood wagon. As we moved down I kept talking to Timmy. One of the guys with the wagon started to tell Timmy that he was O.K. and that the medical centre was twenty minutes away. I could not see Timmy's face, so I dropped round the other side of them, but he was still unresponsive as far as I could tell.

It must have been roughly an hour and a half from Timmy's fall to our arrival at Mottaret medical centre. We were met there by the pompiers and the doctors and nurses. We transferred Timmy to a gurney and took him inside. We removed his jacket, boots and trousers and cut away his T-shirt. They changed the dressing on his head and were able to get a drip in his arm. Timmy's eyes were open but I think that they had opened them his pupils were rolled back but of even size.

The doctor asked if Timmy could understand me as I was constantly talking to him telling him what was going on and reassuring him. He was not responding to my voice but was trying to draw his knees up, and moving his arms. He managed to spoil the IV in his left arm, so the doctor tried to get one into his right. He was moving his arm in response to the needle so we held him still and I kept telling him that he would be fine, not to try and move. I was holding his hands and he was squeezing my hands, so I squeezed back.

I was able to go into the room with Timmy once more. I saw them testing Timmy's soles for reaction, and his left toes not curling. I held his hand and talked to him as they prepared him for the journey to Grenoble. I was asked to leave the room, and met Karen as she arrived. Karen spoke to the doctors, and we ascertained that Timmy was stable enough to be moved down the hill. We collected his things and left shortly behind the pompier van. Unfortunately it was snowing so the roads were slow.

I have spoken with Mark and Lisa (who we had been skiing with earlier in the day) to get their views on the day and how everyone was skiing. They said that Timmy was skiing great, full of confidence and had said to everyone that he was having his best day skiing. We were not taking risks and [were] skiing within everyone's ability in a mutually supportive group. Returning to the area and skiing the same line, it seems like such an innocuous route. There is no obvious explanation but I can only guess that Timmy caught an edge and fell in the one place with such terrible consequences.

I ended up breaking my neck and my back, snapping my cruciate ligament, shattering my left ankle and hitting my head so hard that I was put into an induced coma for three weeks. Not your everyday sort of injury, but then again, not the worst injury ever endured. Although I didn't realise it at the time, because I genuinely believed I was the unluckiest person on earth, my injuries could have been significantly worse and I easily could have died. Which brings me to the age-old adage, 'what doesn't kill you makes you stronger'. It was very hard for me to see at the time but I now view the accident as a blessing in an extraordinary disguise, and something that has led me to a place I probably would never have reached had it not occurred.

People often ask me how it happened. Although Ewan speculated that I caught an edge, sending me off the side of the cliff, the injuries I sustained and the condition of the snow at the time give a more plausible explanation. Because the snow had been so sparse for the entire season, the dump we had the night before had only lightly covered the rocks, not actually submerged them. As a result, I presume that I might have accidentally hit the side of a lightly snow-covered rock at the top of the cliff, causing my cruciate ligament to snap and resulting in me losing my balance and falling off the cliff.

Half the World Away ♫

I spent five weeks in a French hospital and was then transferred to Addenbrookes hospital, in Cambridge, for a further five weeks. I remember nothing from France, even though I was awake for the final fortnight. It is sad not to be able to remember being flown back to England in bed on a private jet. Thank God the ski company for which I worked provided us with insurance.

Without going into too much detail about the multitude of physical and mental issues I had to face, there were and sporadically still are two lasting effects of the injury that I have had to learn to deal with and try to overcome.

The first, which is a pretty standard result of a brain injury, is reduced concentration. If I have no instant interest in a subject or can't see its immediate use, I will almost always switch off. I don't go to sleep but my mind will quite literally stop processing anything coming my way. For example, if someone gives me directions in advance to a particular location, I will happily nod understandingly as they are delivered. Yet when the time comes to actually find the place, I will invariably get lost and have to call someone to guide me in the right direction. I just turn off when it bores me, assuming it's just easier to be talked through it at the relevant moment than it is to put in the effort of properly concentrating in the first place. Concentration used to be a naturally achievable state, when circumstances called for it, but post-accident I need constantly to prompt myself to make the effort and motivate myself to do it.

The second issue that I have to deal with is a neurological disorder called prosopagnosia (facial blindness) the inability to recognize faces. I have very few solid memories of my time in hospital but there was one occasion when I was able to walk again, when I remember asking a nurse to direct me to the bathroom. She told me the way but also informed me that I had already asked her five times and that each time I did not recognize her. 'Why do you think I'm in hospital?', I said to myself. I thought all the nurses looked the same, so at the time, I wasn't too worried about it.

Thankfully I didn't have many issues recognizing my close family and close friends once I was fully conscious. I was told, though, that one of my dearest friends, Bronya, with whom I had lived with before embarking on the ski season, came to visit me in hospital in Grenoble. I don't remember this at all. She asked me if I knew who she was, at which I frowned, quizzically.

'I'm Bronya', she told me.

'Don't be ridiculous', I apparently retorted, 'you're much prettier than Bronya'.

On leaving hospital I remember having a few friends round for afternoon tea. Well, they had tea and talked to me in my bed. I turned the television on and started watching something. It was my favourite programme, Friends. After a short time, I asked why they were showing a spoof version.

'It's not', I remember Amelia telling me. 'Why do you think it is?'.

'Because they're different actors with the same voices'. I was mystified and convinced they were playing a joke on me. 'Seriously, guys, it's not funny'.

I don't know who felt worse at that point but there was a sudden realization that I had a long way to go before I could get back to living the way I had done before the accident.

The severity of suffering from prosopagnosia slowly dawned on me over the following months and years of my rehabilitation. I was fine with those close to me but if I met somebody new one week I would more often than not have no idea who they were the following week. People who were not close friends prior to the accident would also fall into the facially unrecognisable category, which often caused a lot of embarrassment for me even though I had no control over it.

A couple of years after the accident I remember visiting Johnny, a Bristol friend, in London. This was pre-internet film streaming, so we decided to go to a 'video shop' to pick up a 'DVD' (lots of old words there). Anyway, after making a joke to the assistant about the Liam Neeson film Taken, which was living up to its name by not being available (I thought this was funny), I noticed a beautiful girl enter the store, make eye contact with me and smile.

'Oh my goodness', I said to Johnny, 'hot girl just smiled at me, what to do?'

'Why don't you just go and ask her for her number?' He said, simply.

'Hmmmm, good idea, maybe I will'.

After lots of running around the shop and pretending to be interested in ballet DVDs, I motioned towards the incredibly pretty girl and started stammering.

'Ummmmm...' I paused for a bit. 'Hi, my name is Tim and I think you're beautiful, please can I have your number so that I can take you out for a drink?'

'Yeah, hi Tim, don't you recognise me? We were at Bristol together'. Ah, that'll be why she smiled at me, I realized. After explaining my situation, and after she told me how lovely it was to have been asked out but she had a boyfriend, we went our separate ways. As soon as she had told me who she was, I remembered her. I was fine with names and places and remembering situations involving people I met. It was their faces that were ghosts.

But it wasn't just faces, it was everything visually identifiable about a specific character, be it handwriting, the way they walked or the type of car they drove. I was not only blinded to faces but to all visually distinguishing features.

The accident was in 2007, and what an incomprehensible effect it has had on my life. It took me almost three years before I could confidently say that I had recovered. Because of the head injury, I sometimes still have mild repercussions from it. But these are nothing like I would have, were it not for techniques explained in this book.

(Not so) Dedicated Follower of Fashion ♫

After three years of recuperating from an experience that could have killed me, my life goals and desires had completely changed. I no longer wanted to be a corporate lawyer slaving away for a company with no aim other than making lots of money. I had nearly died. I had hit my head so hard everyone was surprized that I was still on the same page. This was the perfect reason to throw in the towel and duck out of the race that I had been working towards for the previous four years before the accident. I now had a golden ticket to do what I wanted, with the backing of everyone who cared for me. My life before the accident had only one direction, my life now had options, choices, and freedom. Or, to look at it less positively, I could use the accident as a tenable way to procrastinate. Obviously that wasn't a conscious decision but looking back at what I didn't achieve, it seems fairly evident.

I think that in my heart of hearts, I just didn't want to be a lawyer, working the majority of God's given hours at an office in the city. I remember speaking to Karen (my boss at the skiing company) a few years after the accident and telling her that I had decided not to go into law anymore. Her response was quick and frank. She simply said: 'you were never going to be a lawyer, Tim'.

My post-university trip to India now comes into play. It had been a great place to completely unwind and to see what the world had to offer. Amongst the plethora of activities, we both decided to have a few shirts made for ourselves – in order to look good in our upcoming corporate jobs. I had never done this before, and it felt amazing to wear a tailor-made shirt for a fraction of the price that it would cost in the UK. I also had a selection of shirts made on behalf of some friends at home. When we arrived back, the shirts I'd designed were all highly praised.

I didn't think much more about this activity until I found myself in hospital, unable to move for a few months. As the law was no longer my chosen career path, I made the decision to set up my own business: I was going to launch a new shirt brand.

Start Me Up ♫

I knew nothing about setting up a business. Yes, I had started a Business Studies course eight years earlier but, having taken so little interest in it, I did not remember anything useful. I had to start from scratch and build up my knowledge by trial and error. All I knew was that I could get amazing shirts made in India, at very little cost. Should I go over there, place an order and then ship them all back to the UK? Maybe I should set up a website first and then find a tailor to make them on demand.

I looked into transport costs and minimum order costs but the numbers did not add up. If it was going to be an on-demand service, I would have to have about 8,000 shirts made up and shipped at the same time before lowering the price to what I wanted to charge. That, or charge considerably more per shirt than buying from an established Jermyn Street shirt maker. There was no way I could get 8,000 orders for a business no one had ever heard of. Every option cost considerably more than the amount I wanted to charge.

After months of research and speaking to lots of start-ups and designers, I finally decided on a high-end manufacturer called Ringhart, based in London but with factories in India. The shirts produced by Ringhart were also of considerably higher quality than the ones that I had previously had made. I ordered roughly 1,000 shirts for both men and women in seven different styles and a selection of sizes. I made certain that the designs for both sexes were of an excellent standard and delivered exceptional quality. But what was I going to call my new label?

Though I hadn't been the most popular kid at school, by the time I was prompted to leave I had developed a strong friendship with two other boys, Ali and Tim. We invariably ended up causing mischief together and thus a strong friendship developed. The year after I left school, I bumped into an old friend, George, from prep school and we initiated him into our friendship group. We were so often together that at some stage, someone decided we should be named as a collective group. We put our young, obnoxious heads together and choose to call ourselves 'Tier One'. At that very moment, it was decided that if any of us was ever to have our own business, we had to name it after the group. Tier One Clothing was subsequently born.

Before that first order was made up, Dave, a friend from my gap year who now worked in graphic design, helped me with the logo and branding which needed to be integrated into the final product. We came up with a penny farthing for the logo, to be embroidered on the cuffs of all the shirts. A feature of every shirt was to be a contrasting lining to collar and cuffs, something I had done with my original Indian creations and which I felt gave the brand some character to distinguish it from all the other boring shirt-makers. The tagline was 'shrewd attire'.

I was given a three-month window before the shirts arrived, during which time I had to find someone to design and build a website. I managed to recruit my father to help with the legalities, Johnny to help with the accounts and a group of other friends to help with the abundance of tasks standing between me and the launch of the brand. My parents provided storage space and I chose to live with them during the start-up of the new company, which made sense considering I didn't have any money coming in. Inspired by my new commitment and all of the work that I had put in, my father invested some money in my new venture to help get it off the ground.

The first six months of running my own business was manic. I had to organize everything and had nobody to help me. I had the support of my parents but this was my venture and, in practical terms, I was on my own. I had to decide in which direction to go, how to get there and how to initiate every task. The website was up and running but I needed to market the brand. Marketing turned out to be a very costly exercise and so I decided to travel up and down the country in a large, cheap van that I had recently purchased, with a lot of stock, visiting as many Christmas charity fairs as I could. I ended up attending over forty fairs, travelling the whole length of the country in the process. I would arrive at each venue the evening before, set up my stand, either sleep in the van or at a committee member's house that night, get up early the next morning, talk the hell out of Tier One, trying to sell as many shirts as possible in the process, and then leave in the evening, to get to the next venue.

You can imagine that this wasn't exactly the life I was hoping to lead but it was the only way to market the brand at minimal cost, hopefully making a bit of money in the process. The charity fairs, surprisingly, went quite well at the very beginning and I was making a good profit margin. As the year came to close, however, and the closer it got to Christmas, I found myself actually losing money at some of these fairs. One in particular I didn't manage to sell a single shirt. I ended the year about £10k up, which was not great considering the profits a lot of the other stalls were regularly making. I couldn't see myself enduring another year of dull fairs, so I decided to focus on selling online and in pop-up shops, scrapping my only cost-effective way of marketing.

Barring a very successful advertorial featured in the Financial Times early on in the life of Tier One Clothing, it never really received the publicity that it so needed (and deserved, if the amount of work that I thought I had put in was anything to go by). There were high points and I expanded the product range to include jumpers, gilets and socks, some of which were popular. Tier One was something I embarked on to prove to my friends and family that I was still capable of success. It was also something that I thought would be an easy way to make money, because even though I had abandoned law, I still wanted to make lots of money.

If you speak to successful entrepreneurs, they have so much passion for their business or product that however long it takes for them to succeed, they will eventually get there, because making a success of that product or that idea was their goal, not money. Looking back on it now,

I didn't care about fashion, I never have. I love the shirts that Tier One produced but clearly not enough to push and push relentlessly, to help the company find its way out of the slump and become another successful clothing brand. If I'd had that passion, I would have achieved it. I thought I was passionate about Tier One and I genuinely worked my arse off for the first few years. The fact that it didn't make money didn't fuel my passion, instead sending me into a downward spiral of false hope, massive denial and regret. I never consciously acknowledged the reasons for my actions. It is only through deep understanding of my inner self, through meditation, that I now see where I went wrong. That said, without dragging you along the slow and arduous path that I endured for four years before finally realizing that it was probably not going to be quite as successful as I had hoped, I shall leave you in the knowledge that Tier One clothing is still awaiting its big break, though I'm not sure I will be the driving force behind its success.

Love is All Around ♫

I have so far not mentioned romantic love. Don't get me wrong, I wanted it, I pined for it, but I rarely encountered it. My childhood sweetheart had been Hannah, the daughter of my God-mother. She was a beautiful, slim, innocent brunette, with gorgeous brown eyes and the sexiest voice. We were together for nearly three years, during my time at BCUC, my gap year and the start of Bristol. The first year together was genuinely one of the best years of my life and to what I have compared every subsequent romantic involvement. We shared what I thought was such a deep love that I genuinely didn't believe anything could ever break us up. We did eventually part company and by the end we argued incessantly. Although I am sure we were both partly to blame for the demise of our relationship, I know that I was the catalyst for its collapse. My whole mindset was in completely the wrong place and I honestly thought that the world revolved around me and that I was always right. Why? Why did I act so egotistically with the most incredible girl that I had ever met? Why would I let narcissism destroy my greatest ever achievement? It's been over fifteen years since we broke up, which is a long time. I'm over her, I don't still pine for her or want her back but because I have never experienced a love that came even slightly as close to what we had, I was constantly on the lookout, searching for something similar.

In the summer of 2013, with many of my friends getting married, I began to question my role in the sexual game of life. I hadn't had a serious girlfriend since Hannah. I'd had flings along the way but the big love thing was still to show itself. I began to question my looks and apparent lack of charm. What was I doing wrong? I occasionally went out partying, where I hoped to benignly bump into 'the one' but maybe I needed to go out more in order to find the girl of my dreams. I scoured the internet for answers and eventually landed on a website whose owner appeared to know the secret to getting into every girl's pants (I would like to have said heart but apparently that wasn't what red blooded males should be after). I was bewildered. Was I really just missing a simple trick, which all my other friends had found but neglected to tell me about? I was desperate, I wanted to find a girlfriend and this had to be the answer. In a funny kind of way it was, but not quite how I was expecting.

I enrolled on a day long course with this company and tentatively approached its location, a grand hotel on one side of Hyde Park. I was directed to a room where I met a charming young man who briskly took the day's fee of £300 from me and then ushered me into the melee. While the other 'clients' continued arriving, I surreptitiously scanned the roomful of men to see what a whole bunch of losers like me really looked like. I say losers because that's what I thought we must be. We couldn't find girlfriends and had to pay an inordinate amount of money to be taught how to change this. The majority of them seemed similar to me, average-looking, with no visible impairments or alarmingly obscure personalities. There were a couple of chaps who looked like they might have misread 'pick up course' for 'church choir practice' but then first impressions can be very deceiving; I'm sure they're probably now lying on a beach in the Bahamas, with a trail of hot girls in bikinis pandering to their every need. I digress; the day was about to begin.

The organizer made a fleeting guest appearance at the very beginning, said a few reasonably narcissistic words and then made her exit, after introducing us to some 'highly trained' pick up artists (PUAs). I did manage to have a few words with her and after explaining that I wasn't actually after a one-night stand and that I wanted to develop my ability to meet and talk to my perfect match, she said that the final speaker, Luke, would be able to help me. I was intrigued.

We spent the morning being lectured on how to pick up girls in the daytime ('day-game'), and then set off into Hyde Park before lunch, to put the theory to test. We split up into groups of three, each with a PUA. I was actually paired off with both of the 'choir singers', David and Graham, so I had a feeling this was going to be interesting. Ali, our PUA, instructed us to banish all fears of approaching women ('approach anxiety'), by commanding us to just go up to the first girl we see and ask her where Oxford Street was. Easy enough, I managed that without a problem. Wow, I was almost a player. Not so fast. We then had to do the same thing again but this time compliment some lucky lady. I managed to complete that task by telling a very attractive young woman what a lovely hat she was wearing. This was going well. Ali then added to the directions and compliment by getting us to tell them our names, too. This was getting hairy. I felt that I wanted one of the 'choir singers' to attempt this gargantuan task, so I prompted Graham to give it a go. He was a little bewildered by what he was about to try to do. I noticed a slight young lady with blonde hair and unusually large breasts walking towards us. I pointed her out to Ali, who commanded Graham to complete this task.

Graham stepped away from us and approached the woman. Oh dear, his head was down and he wasn't making any eye contact. He kind of shuffled himself into her pathway and then after some hesitation while she attempted to step around him, speedily blurted out:

'Hello, do you know where Oxford street is?' He was facing the ground and used this to his advantage, making some remark about how good her shoes looked for walking in – directions and compliment both achieved.

The woman didn't seem fazed by any of this and quite candidly pointed him in the direction of Oxford Street and continued on her way, without responding to the compliment on her footwear.

'My name is Graham, what is yours?!' Graham articulated alarmingly to her back as she strode away from the now rather awkward situation, not acknowledging the fragile cries beseeching her.

'And that's what you shouldn't do!' exclaimed Ali, who then gave Graham a pep talk in confidence-building and led us further into the park for more 'day game'.

Graham and David had been instructed to work together on their 'approach anxiety', while I had the genius of Ali all to myself. We arrived at an Information Point in the park, where hordes of people were acquiring the relevant material to help them on their way across London. Ali asked me to pick out the most attractive girl I could see. I pointed to a beautiful young woman, who unsurprisingly had brown, shoulder length hair, was of a slim build and who looked fairly similar to Hannah.

'Very pretty', Ali approved. 'Now, stay close to me and watch this'. I was about to watch a real-life Lothario in action. He sidled up to my unsuspecting victim and very gently brushed his hand against her hip, then patiently waited for her to turn around to face him, whereupon he quietly asked her if she had the time.

'Yes, it's half twelve', she told him, after looking at her watch.

'Thanks', he replied, 'to be honest, I could have looked at my phone but I really wanted to talk to you'. She giggled and turned to face him fully. 'Can I just say what a beautiful necklace you are wearing'.

'Why thank you', she dutifully responded.

'I noticed it when I first saw you and wanted to compliment it'. He eyed the solid silver pendant around her neck where it clasped a silver letter E. 'I presume the E is for your name?' he asked. 'I don't want you to think that I am looking at your breasts, which are fantastic, by the way, but I genuinely love the necklace'. She giggled again and brushed his shoulder.

'It's Ellie,' she smiled at him.

I was incredulous. Ali had just gone up to a completely random girl and within the space of about thirty seconds had managed not only to get her name but to compliment her on her breasts and be basically thanked for it, not slapped.

We left that area and found a bench, where we sat while Ali proceeded to explain to me that so long as you do not come across as creepy, you can say virtually anything you want to a girl. 'It's about confidence and presence', he explained, before we walked back to the hotel to pick up some lunch, picking up the choir boys, on the way. I was impressed but unconvinced. Even with my less-than-perfect mindset at the time, I was sure there was more to a happy relationship than what Ali would have us believe.

That afternoon we proceeded to work on more 'day game' techniques, before moving onto 'night game' approaches and how to woo our way around a club. Throughout the day we received presentations from four separate PUAs. As the day's teaching drew to a close, before we ventured out to a restaurant and a nightclub to put all of our new-found wisdom to the test, we had one final presentation.

A young man, roughly my age, entered the room and introduced himself as Luke. Straightaway he seemed different from the other PUAs. For a start, he didn't come across as arrogant in the slightest. Confident, yes, but not up his own arse like the others had been. I was excited by what he had to say, especially as the course leader had informed me that he had the ability to help me achieve my goals.

'None of you will successfully find your perfect match until you completely understand and find yourself', he announced.

Hmm, that was not what I was expecting. I mean, I am who I am, I knew who I was, I most certainly wasn't lost, so why did I need to find myself? I looked around the room to see what kind of expressions my fellow wannabe PUAs were making. They all seemed pretty enthralled by this Luke character, so I refocused on his presentation and carried on listening.

'I want you all to close your eyes', said Luke.

Okay, this was a bit weird, but I was willing to go along with it. I closed my eyes and carried on listening.

'Now, concentrate on your breath and very slowly breathe in', he paused for a few seconds, 'And now breathe out. Breathe in...breathe out', any more of this and I thought I'd pass out. 'Breathe in...breathe out'. This was a room full of fifteen red-blooded males currently in the process of some weird sort of namby-pamby-meditation-type-thing. This wasn't what I signed up for, I thought to my judgemental, pre-enlightened self. Where are the girls?

After about five minutes of listening to Luke telling us to breathe in and out, over and over again, I became quite transfixed by his words and began to feel a strange kind of tranquility. As the meditation continued, he quietly explained how we should live only in the present moment that we mustn't live our lives in the past and we mustn't live our lives thinking about the future. The only thing that actually matters is the here and now. I thought about this for a moment and actually saw some sense in the madness I was submitting myself to. The meditation lasted for fifteen minutes before he asked us to open our eyes again. I felt a really strange feeling of contentment and calm. What was happening?

I opened my eyes to see Luke, still very quiet, telling us that to begin this journey of self-discovery, we need to fully embrace our inner selves. Only then would we be able to develop and find what we are truly looking for. He then said he wanted each and every one of us to try to meditate every day in order to achieve this goal. Using a method of self-imposed targeting, he asked us all to commit to how long we were going to meditate for each day. The roll call started at the other end of the room, so I at least had time to think of an answer.

'Twenty minutes', the first person said. What! That's ridiculous, you can't meditate for that long, I thought.

'Ten minutes', was the next. Well that's a bit more like it; still a little overly keen.

'Thirty minutes'. Whatever, I thought, seriously, go back to the pub. The answers got closer and closer to me, until eventually it was my turn.

'Um...', I stammered. 'Five minutes every day – but not at the weekend'. The weekend was my party time, so, I didn't want to meditate then.

'Very good', Luke said, 'you have now given your word to everyone that you will do this'. I didn't know any of these people, so I didn't really care about doing it for them but I had said it out loud and I had also set myself a very achievable target, so I was happy to do it.

Luke then gave us his email address, and told us to message him at the end of every week to tell him how the meditating is going. He then finished his presentation by saying that statistically only 1% of us would fulfil the requirements, which was not a lot of us, but that he wanted us all to be 1%ers. Virtually everyone in the room murmured some sort of anti-statistician stance and, I think, meant it. I, however, to my own surprise, kept quiet and silently contemplated achieving it.

We headed to the restaurant in Leicester Square, where we all had the chance to wind down a little and chat about the day's events over pizza. I managed to sit myself next to Luke, who explained the whole meditation concept to me and advised me to Google it to find out as much information as I needed. We headed to a rather shady club, where I had

Luke as my 'wingman'. He coaxed me into chatting up a lot of beautiful young women. I managed to meet one who I had a great chat with but foolishly walked away from before taking her number ('number closing'). Luke wasn't overly impressed by this and so set about getting her number for me. He supposedly did but I never got a reply from the number he gave me (after reading the draft of this book, he still insists that it was real!).

The days and weeks after the PUA course saw me keeping to my daily meditation target and even expanding it to include the weekends because I was getting so much contentment and peace from it. I was still living at my parents' house trying to make a success of Tier One. I had a pop-up shop booked in London that September, so I emailed Luke to see if he wanted to meet up. He did and we had lunch. It was great to see him again and discuss my progress with the meditation. I had managed to email him every week with my progress report, so I asked him how many others from my course still did. 'You are the only one-percenter', he proudly told me, which genuinely helped to give me and my newly-found meditation real meaning.

You now know about my life up until the PUA course, the point at which my life fundamentally started to change. It has now been nearly five years since I was introduced to meditation and the lessons that I have learned have been invaluable. The remainder of this book will teach you the techniques and the theories that have either helped me personally, from scenarios that occurred before and after the accident I had, or that have helped people I have met and talked to along the way.

(I've Got) the Power ♫

We have all heard it said that the brain is like any muscle in the body and, as such, can be exercised and trained. The more you enact a particular routine, the more your brain will become accustomed to it, until it eventually becomes an apparently natural trait. You can use this for absolutely anything in order to become good at something – be that learning to play the piano, in conjunction with training your fingers; learning a new language, in conjunction with training your tongue; or developing your tennis skills, alongside your whole body. Throughout this book I will encourage you to partake in a variety of different exercises to recondition your brain to help you achieve your aims. Some things may be harder to achieve than others, or you may need to stop yourself from overindulging in counterproductive activities (as will be explained in the self-control chapter) but when it comes to how we cope with day-to-day life, there are few things that are hardwired permanently into your mind. By taking advantage of your brain's natural neuroplasticity as a coping mechanism, you will be able to evolve it to help you achieve the best of your potential.

I want to end this synopsis of my life as it was by putting to rest a belief that many people hold regarding the concept of adopting a new lifestyle approach. Contrary to common belief, you do not need to have experienced a catastrophic, life-changing event to alter your perceptions on life. We see many people become devoutly religious following a life-changing accident, a mental breakdown, or a bereavement. It is clear that in these circumstances turning towards a doctrine or practice that can provide a sense of reassurance and control can be beneficial.

You will have noticed however, that after my accident, I didn't get into meditation for over seven years. During this time I had managed to slowly, although insignificantly (compared with now), restore my concentration and facial recognition. As you'll see, I can't stress to you enough how important my unexpected meeting with Luke was, at the PUA course, and I am still so thankful for having done it, even though its resulting benefits were completely different from those I expected. When I explain how lucky I was to have met him, he does tell me that everything happens for a reason, which I guess means that I was meant to write this book and you too were meant to develop profoundly as a result. If anyone reading this has recently suffered head trauma, I urge you to steadily get your life back on track as your doctors will have advised. I also urge you to try out the meditative methods I will teach you, before launching your recovering brain into something for which it is not yet ready.

I didn't get into meditation for the reasons you might expect. I have been the person recovering from a life-changing event and the person who chose to take control from a point of comparative calm. Yes, in the aftermath of the accident I would have benefited immeasurably from clearing and slowing down my mind through meditation. Life-changing events aside, it is possible to take control and gain that reassurance before crisis point and, in this way, to avert it. You cannot control what life will throw at you, as I well know, but you can control the way you respond to it. The following chapter will help you begin your journey.

Meditation and mindfulness is the bedrock of 'Timinology' and to get the best out of it, it is important to keep in mind two key things:

You don't need to change your whole life to suit a certain practise. You can create a practise that suits you

If you are lucky enough to be able to enter into a new approach to life with a clear mind, you are even more likely to reap benefits than if you are recovering from a life-changing injury or experience.

Kindfulness

'Kindfulness' is exactly how it sounds, being kind to yourself and others in a mindful way. Using your ability to analyse, accept and trust the feelings and emotions with which you are presented, in the most loving way as possible, without expecting in return anything other than loving kindness.

It concentrates on dealing with a more natural approach to meditation and compassion, without bogging you down with a lot of the spiritual elitism that many hardcore meditation and mindfulness disciplines can seem to entail.

Having explained to you the effects the head injury had on my concentration and facial recognition, I shall now tell you how I learned to overcome them. As you can well expect, my mind was pretty messed up. I lacked the ability to concentrate on any particular situation for more than a few minutes at the most, which made even normal activities like watching movies incredibly difficult. Coupled with not being able to recognise anyone famous in the movie, I eventually lost all desire to go to the cinema. It wasn't just movies, though, it was any television programme, reading books, or any conversation with friends or family that went beyond what we were having for lunch. My life had been whittled down to minute long episodes of disinterest.

I can remember the night of the PUA course, leaving the sordid club in which we had been practising our 'night-game' and heading back to where I was staying. After being bombarded with so much information about chatting up girls and trying to become an overnight sex god, the only thing that really stuck with me was what Luke had to say about meditation.

My life wasn't exactly at its peak of success on any level. Tier One was rapidly becoming a lost cause, I had been out of mainstream employment for pretty much all of my working life, and it was becoming clear that I wasn't going to make an overnight success within an industry about which I knew nothing. The majority of my friends had been working for nearly ten years by now and were all receiving reputable promotions within whichever field of work they had chosen. Not only did they all seem to have well-paid, responsible, respectable jobs, they also had spouses or long-term partners to add into the mix, and some had even started to procreate – shocking.

I was at the bottom of this ladder known as life, and I had no excuse for being there. It had almost been seven years since the accident and, as easy as it was to use it as a viable excuse to procrastinate, I was no longer able to justify this. I felt I had fully recovered and was sure that people had got bored of hearing about it. I wasn't going to feel sorry for myself, that helps no-one. So, I decided to properly research this practise about which Luke was so positive and see if there was any justification for his apparent madness.

Although I was aware that Tier One wasn't going to be quite as successful as I had originally hoped, I managed to get it into a pop-up shop on Fulham Road in London for six weeks. This was a great opportunity for me to properly make a mark in the big city and hopefully plant some seeds in a new industry. Days in the shop were mind-numbingly boring, so I set about researching meditation to further my understanding of it.

As with everything, there is no shortcut to educating yourself. I committed myself to methodically digesting as much information as possible. This became my main occupation outside the shop. I socialized a bit in the evenings but didn't really sell enough stock to fund being in London, were it not for a selection of very kind friends who let me stay with them. I just didn't know how to make Tier One a success but on the plus side, I was slowly learning about meditation.

Give Peace a Chance ♫

The general idea of meditation is to harness the ability to clear your mind of the everyday thoughts that constantly pester us, by utilising techniques designed to help focus our attention away from them. This in turn frees our psyche from inhibiting thoughts and allows space for the birth of new, more positive ones. This is the emphasis of the Thought Theory Model.

Although I didn't get into meditation as a direct consequence of the accident, it was only after many months of practising it that I started to realise just what an effect it was having on my mental well being, which had definitely been affected by the trauma. I didn't get into meditation with any specific expectations but found the immense peace that I was achieving enough to build up my mental strength and happiness. When your mind is in the right place, you can experience a profound sense of peace through meditating. How you cultivate and develop that peace is up to you but if you are using meditation as a way of gaining instantaneous results, then you are not in the right place for it. I think the wisest piece of advice I was ever given when it comes to meditating, is to expect nothing (other than time to yourself).

It is how you utilise your alone time through meditating that will develop you as a person. You will have noticed from my back story that I was never a very grounded individual. Even before the accident, I had no real direction and no particular sense of pride in myself. Yes, I did have the intention of going into law but even if I had, I would have been doing it for completely the wrong reasons how much money I could make, how many possessions I could own and what people thought about me.

Work aside, having started meditating, I was slowly starting to notice small changes in my previously staunchly capitalist stance on life and everyday living. If you had known me at Bristol University, unless you were one of my close friends, you would have easily mistaken me for a bigoted hedonist who only cared about himself. I wasn't, but that was definitely the impression I projected. These days I am very close to both of my sisters, (Bex and Katie) but I have vivid memories of their profound disapproval of my general choice of words and extremely inappropriate jokes. Even my parents used to question my humour. My father, being male, sticking up for his only son, used to sometimes laugh at what I came out with but I could always see a tinge of disappointment in his wry smiles.

I thought I was funny and a lot of my friends certainly laughed at my often incredibly inappropriate jokes. Looking back on it now, it wasn't funny and it most certainly wasn't how I needed to act. I was never agonisingly offensive but there were certainly a lot of sharp intakes of breath from a few people when I came out with one of my 'classic Timmy' lines. As this whole book will tell you, until you are ready to see that you need to change and then make that change, there is nothing in the world that can help you. You have to see what's wrong before you can fix it. It is through meditation that I stumbled across my errors and became conscious of them; became aware. If I could change anything now, it would be for the world to do the same. Developing your mindfulness costs nothing, it doesn't have to take up lots of time and it will make you, and everyone around you, happier.

By familiarising yourself with the techniques used to empty your mind of constricting thoughts, you will gain the power to regulate the thoughts you are able to process and give yourself free rein over your life, through how you are thinking. So think positively, give it a go and watch your life transform.

I am not a doctor, so I am not going to tell you to do anything that contradicts what a professional has to say. When it comes to conditions such as depression, which is being diagnosed more and more in this day and age, I cannot overrule any doctor's prescription for drugs. What I will say, having read the research and from speaking to my own doctors, is that if your mind is currently fit and healthy and if you decide to seriously get into meditating and mindfulness, you are scientifically proven to be far less likely to be diagnosed with mental illness in the future. According to neuroscientists, as you continue to meditate your brain will physically change.

Meditating is therefore like exercising the muscle that is your brain. The more you do it, the stronger the muscle gets and the easier it becomes for it to perform, which is when the changes you didn't expect to occur, will start to happen.

Hippy Hippy Shake ♫

Transcendental Meditation (TM) was one of the first New Age practises to hit the western world, back in the 1950s, and it gained a lot of media and celebrity attention at the time, with The Beatles bringing its existence to the mainstream. Being a huge fan of the band, this discovery was probably the main reason I decided to give TM a go, signing up to a course in London after the Tier One pop-up ended. Quite a few prominent celebrities practise TM, the most notable of which is Russell Brand. Although he remains a very opinionated individual, he has managed to completely revolutionise his previously hard core, drug-fuelled, sex-addicted life as a result of practising TM and now leads a completely clean existence.

In TM, each individual is given a unique mantra on which to focus. This is then repetitively chanted over and over again in your head, with your eyes closed, for the duration of the meditation session. The TM course on which I enrolled had us do this twice a day for twenty minutes at a time, allowing for five-minute warm-up and cool-down periods either side. The course took a whole weekend, with a follow-up the week after, so there was a little bit more to it than simply being instructed to engage in some chanting twice a day. It did give me the desire to persevere, and for two years I did it everyday, except at the weekend, when I would only do it once, because I felt that even my meditative mind needed a rest.

Although I became fully engrossed in TM after the course, I knew that there were many other styles of meditation and I wanted to research other avenues. I wasn't bored of TM, I just wanted to experience other practises and techniques to help guide my attention away from obtrusive thoughts I was experiencing during meditation. There are no rules stipulating that you can only practise one form of meditation, and what better way to become as enlightened as possible than to try several techniques? I've never been the sort of person to just stick to a single form or practise without researching all the other available options and, when it came to meditation, finding a suitable style with which I was happy and comfortable was of the utmost importance to me, considering the amount of time I was proposing to commit to it. It was this exploration that led me to mindfulness.

Got My Mind Made Up ♫

I watched an insightful programme recently, entitled *Trust me, I'm a Doctor*[1] which, in a bid to discover the most effective ways to tackle the symptoms of stress, recruited seventy-one volunteers, and allocated them into four different groups, each of which was given a different activity to pursue, over an eight-week period.

The first group, which got together every Saturday, was given gardening and conservation activities to complete. The second group was given a yoga course. The third group implemented ten minutes of mindfulness every day, focusing on the present moment. The remaining volunteers were the control group.

Levels of cortisol, the stress hormone released by the adrenal gland, were measured in all the participants both at the start of the experiment and at the end. Our bodies naturally release a big burst of it in the morning, known as the cortisol awakening response (CAR) and then the levels lower throughout the day.

Professor Angela Clow and Dr. Nina Smyth of the University of Westminster found that, compared with the control group, everyone who engaged in any of the activities had an increase in their CAR, so lower levels of cortisol throughout the remainder of the day.

Individually, the yoga group saw a healthy reduction of cortisol during the day and a small increase in CAR. The conservation group's CAR rose by 20% and the Mindfulness group's CAR rose by a staggering 58%. Interestingly, for the people who actually enjoyed their activities, they saw an even bigger rise in their CAR, with the mindfulness group raising it to an astonishing 78%. So mindfulness is scientifically proven to reduce stress and even more so if you enjoy it. Let me explain a bit more.

When it comes to mindfulness, although meditation is a prominent but not necessarily essential part of this doctrine, the following foundational characteristics of it create a practice that instils a whole new sense of wellbeing within the participant, something that sets it above the rest.

This may be the first time you have thought about mindfulness, or you may have heard about it long ago and just dismissed it as another 'namby-pamby, hippyish' pastime, but whatever your thoughts, as illustrated through the Thought Theory Model, you can only begin to benefit from it by having the correct attitude.

If you think it is a waste of time and a pointless exercise, then it will be: it's as simple as that. If, however, you firmly believe in the foundational powers it can have over your wellbeing and frame of mind, it is only a matter of time before you start to benefit from the wondrous gifts it can bring.

Attitudes, much like habits (as you will find out in the self-control chapter), are not easy things to regulate. They develop over a matter of time and take a certain amount of willpower to instil or change, if you make the decision to do so.

When it comes to mindfulness, think about how your attitude towards stillness, acceptance, peace and 'being' mode (which will be discussed in a bit) resonate within you, and then decide whether or not you are ready to welcome it into your life. If you're still on the fence, try some of the techniques I describe a little later on to help you to develop a mindful attitude.

As I will keep telling you, the positive effects of mindfulness are breathtaking (or giving), and with the right attitude are likely to help you in numerous ways; from learning how to deal with difficult sensations and emotions, quashing feelings of lethargy, anxiety, stress and pain, and developing the will and the power to confront your own demons.

It is attitude that will give you the strength to persevere and persist with a mindful lifestyle. Attitude is absolutely paramount to successfully taking it on board. We've all heard the cliché that practice makes perfect and it could not be more relevant here. Let's say you want to beat your long-standing rival at a game of tennis, which hasn't happened yet. You practice, I presume? In fact, you practice and practice and practice until the mere sight of a tennis ball raises your pulse every time you see one, because you are now a pro (well, a keen novice). The match day arrives and you whip his ass because you've devoted the last however many weeks to making sure it happens. This is exactly what you need to do with mindfulness and the more you do it, the better you get and the more results you see.

What exactly is being mindful, though? In the 1980's, Jon Kabat-Zinn, a prominent mental health doctor, became heavily involved in meditation. Inspired by the successful and positive results it has on mental health, he redesigned and westernized the practice, stripped it of the Buddhist connotations and created the version of mindfulness that is widely taught today. It boils down to a quality or state of conscious awareness of everything around you. 'Mindfulness means paying attention in a particular way; on purpose, in the present moment, and non-judgementally.[2] So let's break that down a little.

What is paying attention in a particular way? It is exactly what it says it is: purposefully making a concerted effort to devotedly observe and witness the workings of whatever situation you face. You don't need to understand it (although that might come as a pay-off); you just need to observe and accept.

Being in the present moment means that you are willing to accept whatever situation you may be observing, exactly how it is, which leaves little room for you to judge it, because it is what is happening and it needs to be accepted as such; there are no other logical options.

I've had issues trying to come to terms with this concept, I mean what if you're suffering from an illness that is making your life unbearable? It's all very well accepting it but that's not going to make it go away, is it? And surely looking into the future and hoping it will get easier is going against the whole present moment principle? But that's where I was wrong. Interestingly, in the context of physical pain, I read an incredibly insightful article[3] indicating the direct link between pain and emotions. For example, if you have recently started to experience a bad upper back, there is a strong chance that this could very well be linked to feelings of emotional rejection and lack of love; so instead of nipping to your local chemist for a box of painkillers, try mindfully assessing the whole situation. Start by noticing and accepting your physical discomforts and then your emotional discomforts. The pains are both present, as are you in this very moment, so instead of lamenting your situation, the idea is to learn to accept it and then work on loving yourself enough to ease the woes, correspondingly easing the physical pain. (There is a later chapter on self-love which will explain how to learn to love yourself in more detail).

Mindfulness isn't always easy, and this is where you need to put faith into it. By accepting the negative situation, you are leaving little room for your body to fight against it, because it has nothing to fight (you've accepted it, remember?). You have devoted yourself to the present moment and by doing that, you've had the freedom to realize that the exact moment you are currently living through will pass, with better experiences around the corner. Through your forthright acceptance of the situation, and with nothing to fight against, you are leaving little room for negativity to flourish and it will slowly start to ease its grip on you.

Having this attitude and mindfully carrying out your life in this way also leaves little room for situations to overcome you. I get that it's near on impossible to be mindfully present 100% of the time but, as I mentioned earlier, the more you practice it, the easier it becomes and the more likely you are to persevere with it.

If you find it hard to accept whatever situation is troubling you, try to mindfully acknowledge your feelings associated with it and note down the thoughts that accompany it. For example, 'I am feeling frustrated and out of control'. By noting it down you are halfway to accepting it. Now try to sense where in your body you notice a physical sensation of whatever it is you are finding hard to accept and be as curious as possible in questioning and observing its presence within you. This will help you to understand it properly in order to accept it.

I have found it easier to be mindful of situations if you change them around a little in order to concentrate more on it to get it right or to notice the difference, which is exactly what mindfulness is. Brush your teeth with the opposite hand that you normally use, for example, or stand on one foot when you're having a shower (just don't slip over and then sue me). Maybe take a different route to work, or wear some crazy underwear (secret mindfulness). Try talking to strangers, listening to different music and watching different films – while all the time observing and accepting things in the present moment. You may not like the music you've just listened to– I'm not asking you to – but by accepting it for what it is you're immediately taking a mindful step in the right direction.

Don't Let Me Down ♪

We've all been let down at some point or another in our lives, be that through an individual's failure to carry out a promised task or a situation turning out to be different from what was described; whatever the misrepresentation, we've subsequently lost our trust in the people involved. Trust is an imperative factor when it comes to welcoming someone or something new into our lives, so it is of utmost importance you can knowingly trust the principles, sources and ideas surrounding it, before committing your time and life to mindfulness.

Mindfulness is not something you can suddenly trust on the whim of my writings, especially as it is something that (I hope) is likely to become heavily entwined into your life.

It is also, as I mentioned at the start of this chapter, not something you can expect to give you instantaneous results.

You might find that although you had a great meditation session yesterday, today's session saw your mind wondering back to your first kiss, which had nothing to do with the present moment, and subsequently left you feeling unsure of the whole process. But, believe me, it happens to everyone and the sooner you learn to accept that it will keep on wandering, the sooner you can build up your trust and, although it seems illogical, the less it will wander.

You're not always going to get instantaneous results with any aspect of mindfulness. Curiosity, observation and acceptance may not grant you the serenity to understand why your head is aching beyond all proportions today but, by trusting it won't last forever and then carrying out a variety of meditations, including some quiet time to cultivate a love for yourself, the pain will slowly ease.

If you need proof to initiate trust, there is plenty of scientific evidence to put your mind at rest, so all you need to do is google it to find some reputable sources. If you need reassurance from mindful friends or colleagues to help you cultivate your trust, I can guarantee they will be more than happy to lend a hand. If you don't know anyone, by all means contact me directly (www.timinology.com) and I will happily talk things through with you. Give yourself and your new practice time. It won't happen instantly but by just trusting your own experiences in the present moment, you will get there.

Alongside trust you also need to develop and mature your curious side. As briefly mentioned earlier, you can only learn to completely accept a situation, however good or bad it is, by cultivating a curiosity for whatever it is; and don't just be curious of the situation, itself, be curious of everything. Be curious about mindfulness, be curious about this book, be curious about Timinology, your thoughts, your emotions, your feelings. Curiosity is the fastest way to learn about, befriend and accept whatever it is that is biding your time, instead of trying to cover up or forget about it. Be curious.

I've explained how mindfulness can help you to observe and tackle a variety of different problems we all encounter at certain points in our lives but the beauty of this practice is that looking after yourself makes you a kinder, more lovable person to be around. That's the joy of it, you benefit and so does everyone you meet. It's a never-ending cycle of positivity.

As humans, there are two states of mind that we can inhabit: the 'doing' mode and/or the 'being' mode.

Doing: This is the goal orientated, ruminative way of thinking, that compares your actual situation to how you think it should be, an assumption gleaned either from past experiences or future predictions. We formulate targets to achieve a desired goal and consequently suffer if the target is not met. This is not an inherently bad state of mind to be in when trying to get things done, like working, doing the weekly shopping or going to the dentist, but being in this mode means that when things don't go the way you planned them to go, shit hits the fan.

You can still be in the 'doing' mode even when you're not trying to complete a task or run an errand, which sees your mind constantly attempting to cover up or run towards feelings and emotions that it thinks are better suited to how you should feel; the 'doing' mode thinks it has your best interests at heart but its only real goal is to put the problem aside and move onto the next.

How many times have you driven from point A to B, arrived at your destination and then realized you can't actually really remember much of the journey at all? Or been to a drinks party, chatted to the chap from next door's brother for half an hour and then realized you didn't listen to a word he said. Or gone to the shop to pick something up and then completely forgotten what it was you went in for? This scenario happens to a lot of people and can be described as running on autopilot. It's when you spend your whole life in 'doing' mode and everything happens automatically. You have goals to achieve but miss the beauty of life around you; birds singing, children playing, the sun shining or the wind rustling in the trees. The things that give life colour and music.

Autopilot can also be transferred across to your thoughts and emotions, leading you to automatically generate presumptions that you are a useless, ugly, lazy waste of space, causing your state of mind to dwindle into the depths of your lowest points, provoking anger, resentment and shame.

Luckily, the aforementioned states of mind can all be remedied, accordingly.

Being: This mode is almost the complete opposite of the 'doing' mode. Whereas goals and targets are the objective of 'doing', accepting and allowing are the basis of 'being'. There is no emphasis on completing certain goals and there is no need to constantly monitor your progress to ascertain whether or not you are on the right path.

The aim of 'being' is to connect with the present moment, the here and now. To be fully aware of everything around you; be they sounds, sights, tastes, colours or feelings. Unlike being stuck on autopilot, you are fully aware of all your thoughts and emotions and never get caught up in ruminative reflections of what happened last night, or what might happen tomorrow.

Unlike 'doing', you accept things the way they are. There is no goal or target to be met and you don't need to evaluate your feelings to coincide with or match any preconceived ideals. Likewise, if things aren't going to plan, instead of fighting it, accept it wholeheartedly and willingly allow the unintended circumstance to play out, vigilantly observing your thoughts and feelings throughout the process.

'Being' grants you a whole new dimension of vigour and opportunity. No longer are you stuck in a void that plays out the same instinctive reactions every time something doesn't go your way. Every outcome is a brand new situation for you to develop from and, by allowing and accepting the circumstances that come your way, you will learn to respond to the affluent intricacy that each new moment brings in the most welcoming way possible.

In addition to the impressive benefits mindfulness has on mental health, it's transformative effects can help to 'dissolve negative mental patterns, increase happiness and encourage profound wellbeing'.[4]

So, as you'll probably have gathered by now, my meditative approach, which I've christened 'Timinology', is a combination of several meditative techniques but primarily mindfulness, with some special techniques (some learned, some devized) mixed in. The idea was that I could create something for myself, that allowed me to make use of the parts of established techniques that suited me and my lifestyle but didn't require me to use those that didn't. I will be sharing these methods with you as we go on but for now I want to tell you a couple of specific ways in which Timinology has helped me overcome some of my own issues.

Wild Thing ♫

What annoyed and upset my family the most, was my dislike of animals – cats, in particular. I know that a lot of people don't like cats, they are arrogant little pests and seem to convey a level of superiority over every human they encounter. But I was more arrogant than them, and selfish, and I took it too far. I wouldn't even let the family cat, 'Ickle', be in the same room as me. I hissed at any cat that I came across and would have happily culled the entire population of them if it wasn't frowned upon and illegal. When it came to dogs, I was okay with them until they either stared at me for more than a couple of seconds, barked, or made stupid sounds. My fuse was pretty short. I just couldn't tolerate the personification of animals, yet I was guilty of the same 'crime' by thinking about their presence and mannerisms in the same way as I thought about humans, attributing their actions with motivation and malice.

Katie, my youngest sister, is a massive animal lover and her reaction to my innate hatred of cats was totally justified. She never laughed at my hissing and taunting and would chastise me for treating animals with such disdain. I used to have personal battles with Tilly, my parents' dog. She would unrelentingly stare at me for what seemed like hours, winding me up no end. In retaliation I would stare back at her, approach her and then lurch forward, making her run out of the room and avoid me for the next few minutes, before doing it again. She knew when I was especially frustrated with her and would move away from me when I was in the same room, even if there were other people present.

I knew it wasn't normal to behave like this, so I made sure that my parents never witnessed it when I was living at their house. On one occasion, however, when I walked across the kitchen to the oven, Tilly ran away from me when I approached where she was resting, which prompted my father to question why she reacted in such a terrified way. I did not acknowledge the incident and carried on cooking but my father could see what had just happened and told me that if he ever saw me mistreating her again, I would be out of the house.

In the early stages of my practise, I didn't know what to expect and I was merely meditating to calm my agitated mind. I was doing it every day and very slowly I started to see myself in a different light. I think the first time I recognized a change in my mindset was when Ickle was reaching the end of his life.

When I walked into my parents' kitchen and expected to see him scurry away, he merely lay on the floor, next to the range and looked at me pitifully, visibly shaking. For the very first time ever, I not only felt remorse for the way I had treated him for most of his life, I also felt compassion. Only when he was a kitten had I tenderly touched him but in this moment of benevolence, I sat down beside him and stroked his entire body. Never before had I heard a cat purr so loudly and it was in that moment that I suddenly realized the misguided path that I had been following for so long.

Having had a thunderbolt of compassion run through my veins, my attitude towards animals changed in an instant. I felt a tremendous amount of guilt when Ickle died but I at least reached sanctuary in the knowledge that I had helped him see his final days out with a bit of dignity – and he had helped me to regain some, too.

By this stage I had ceased partaking in staring competitions with Tilly and we were building our relationship. A few months later, my father and I took Tilly out on a country shoot, where they were using a tractor and trailer to transport us around. Tilly was kept on a lead to ensure she didn't jump off the trailer, but unfortunately there was too much slack in the lead and she jumped off when she spied a deer. Hurtling through the air, the slack in the lead quickly reached its limit, pulling Tilly to the ground and then, much to everyone's horror, under the wheels.

There were 12 of us on the trailer and the face of every person turned a ghostly white as we all felt it run over Tilly's head with both sets of wheels. Shouts of 'STOP' promptly brought us to a standstill, at which point Tilly shrieked the most heartbreaking sound I have ever heard and then tried to run away. My father and I hastily followed her on foot, until she couldn't take any more and collapsed to the ground.

She was clearly in absolute agony and growled at my every touch. After a few minutes she gradually calmed down and lay quietly, murmuring and yelping every so often. My father called for help and Tilly was taken to veterinary hospital. She was in intensive care for the next two weeks and was back home in time for Christmas.

My recently established benevolence for animals was being clearly put to the test here, having to contend with a dog that couldn't really do anything other than stare at me or yelp constantly. I felt no annoyance, though. I know I would have done mere months before, and felt only compassion and love for this dilapidated black hound that was in need of a lot of attention.

In a funny sort of way, I felt I could understand what she was going through better than anyone else.

Road Rage ♫

I have always driven a great deal and with Bristol being so far from home in Suffolk, it was necessary for me to stay mobile. Wherever I have lived since then, I have always seemed to need a car to fulfil my everyday activities. But being in the driving seat of a car transformed me into a complete control freak. The roads were mine and if anybody got in my way, all hell would break lose. Lots of honking the horn, gesticulating and shouting the high heavens down. I could not tolerate anybody pulling their car out in front of me, traffic lights turning red or the look of anybody who thought that they were better than me. I was a full-on road rage psycho.

I understand that a lot of people suffer from this affliction and I am well aware that if two such drivers encounter each other, there's not going to be an amicable ending. As with most road rage perpetrators, it is mainly verbal abuse that ensues from an incident and fortunately very few people actually intensify the abuse to physical violence. I was in the mouthy camp and would have probably apologized profusely if somebody had actually got out of their car to remonstrate against my driving and maybe even cried a little, for added effect. The long and short of it was that driving around other cars (a very likely scenario) was not pleasurable in the slightest; especially not for anyone unlucky enough to be a passenger in my car.

Combining the inappropriate humour that used to flow from my lips with my detestation of animals and my road-rage, you would probably assume that I wasn't a particularly affable person to be around. That wasn't true and I can honestly say that I was always pretty likeable. I just managed to separate all of the traits from each other and incorporate them within my charming personality without causing too much upset. I definitely went too far on the odd occasion and have memories of upsetting friends and family along the way. I think Katie was the one person who saw through the dissimulation, as she used to often remark on how spiteful and evil a lot of my mannerisms were. I never meant any harm to anyone but I also didn't realise the effect that it was having on me.

Having described several of my idiosyncrasies with which I used to function, you can now see why I needed to take action. I had no idea what I was dragging around with me for all those years and it was only months after taking up meditation that I realized how much emotional weight I was carrying and could observe the ways in which it was manifesting itself in my behaviour. To be consumed by an overwhelming amount of spite and hate had an incredible effect on how I psychologically functioned and it wasn't until I started to release all of the venomous thoughts that I began to eventually feel free for the first time in my life. I was genuinely happy with myself, which I had never felt before. I am evidence that it works.

Since beginning my meditative routine there has been a real change for the good in my capacity for empathy and in my ability to respond and contribute to the world in a more balanced, positive and effective way. When it comes to driving, I'm afraid I can't say that I have miraculously become a shining beacon of empathy but the anger and frustration that I previously felt have diminished considerably. As for my humour and animal resentment issues, I found a considerable amount of solace in observing the peace that meditation was bringing to me.

Surprisingly, I think that my enraged driving has been the hardest of my personal transgressions to reconcile. I know that a lot of people have anger issues when it comes to driving, so here's a brief exercise for you to try if you too struggle with road rage, or even just road frustration. I found the following points helped me a lot and I hope will help to calm even the most agitated of drivers among us. In order to dissipate and defuse the anger you instinctively discharge, you need to first mindfully observe the situation, before being able to substitute it for the peace you experience through meditation. As soon as you have acknowledged and accepted your state of mind for how it is, you have the opportunity to knowingly alter it appropriately in the present moment. If you can achieve a harmonious driving experience, you have every right to be incredibly proud of yourself for edging away from the poisonous thoughts that motivate road rage, so take PRIDE in yourself and in the way you drive.

Positivity – Manifest feelings of peace when you are driving and stay as calm as possible

To help you to achieve this, recite these affirmations until you feel a sense of harmony within yourself:

I am peaceful and relaxed.

I can experience peace whenever I choose.

I am an intelligent adult, capable of taking care of myself.

I am comfortable in myself.

This activity calms me.

Realism – Don't expect other drivers to be courteous

If you drive with the expectation that you you have the right to be let into the other lane by the first driver you see, then you are likely to be disappointed. Experience has taught me that having our expectations shattered is one of the main causes of road rage. Learn to realistically assume that there will be rude, pushy and aggressive drivers and accept them as a problem for themselves, not you. Expect that others will treat you courteously where they can but, if they don't, perhaps there is a reason other than those you can see (see E).

Inner Peace – Harness your inner peace whilst driving

This will protect you from your own rushed reactions. It will conserve your emotional, mental and physical energies, saving you from anger, stress and anxiety. Even only partially realized inner peace will help you arrive at your destination happier, calmer and more safely than a nervous, stressed driver who lacks it altogether. By reciting the positive affirmations and nurturing them during and after meditation, you have a far better chance of achieving your inner peace.

Disassociation – Distance yourself from other people's bad driving

If you drive courteously, other people's poor driving is not related to you. It is very important, therefore, to disassociate yourself from their driving in order to feel calmer. Take the attitude that it is their bad driving, so it is their problem, not yours. You didn't cause it, so you are not going to worsen the situation by giving way to feelings of road rage. You choose which of your emotions to give way to and which to resist, so take a proactive stance and remain calm.

Empathy – Ask yourself why the other driver might be distracted

They may have recently received some bad news, compromising their ability to function. Perhaps they shouldn't be driving under those pressures but maybe they had no other option. Maybe their partner had been rushed to hospital and there was no other way for them to get there? There are countless reasons why some people might be driving erratically, so shift your viewpoint from 'they are inconsiderate, selfish drivers who need to be taught a lesson', to 'I don't know why they are driving so badly, so I will give them the benefit of the doubt'. They may be going through a situation that is out of their control and, if you were in their situation, you might very well be driving in the same way. Help spread your inner peace by making their journey safer through your response, not adding to their problem by creating your own.

Through following the PRIDE guidelines, you can make a concerted effort to drive mindfully. Become mindfully aware of other people and scenarios that could easily cause an accident. By being mindful you are effectively one step ahead of the game and will not only be calmer but safer.

The Peace Within ♫

At the end of the day, everything that I have achieved and recovered from has been accomplished through observing and accepting the situation I am in, and then knowingly allowing myself to change it. You can't expect anything to happen until you see your own misdemeanours in the present moment. Then, knowingly, kindfully and lovingly, quieten your mind enough to allow the peace to take over. As I said at the very beginning, you can only start to change your ways if you want to, unconditionally. You will never change your inner self until you can observe the issue, at hand, and then fundamentally act accordingly to make it happen, NEVER. It is all up to you.

So, there are countless benefits of mindfulness and meditation. Now the question: how the hell do you go about it? Before I start, it's very important for you to know that it is NOT hard and it does NOT take up a lot of your time. If you have never done it before, start small. I did. Work your way up to doing longer sessions. It's also not something to be embarrassed about or frowned upon. One of my friends got into meditation about five years before I did, but he only told me about it after I told him that I was doing it. I'm not saying that he was embarrassed by what he was doing, I just don't think that people knew enough about it to not question his peculiar pastime, so he just kept quiet. He also (probably rightly) expected my pre-mindful self to be harshly judgemental about it. But I urge you not to align with that stereotype. The recent resurgence and popularity of mindfulness has made it a very acceptable pastime, which is no longer seen as an activity exclusively engaged in by hippies. What's wrong with being a hippy anyway? Maybe I should let you find some peace within yourself before asking such a challenging question. Anyway, work your way through all of the different techniques to help you clear your mind and then stick to whichever works best for you.

Start with a short period of time to be with yourself. Perhaps try it in the morning, as soon as you wake up. Five minutes is fine, or even two minutes if five is too long. But make it a habit and do it every morning, before anything else.

Now that you've decided a time for this, find a comfortable place to just sit down, and then relax. If you're not a yogi, just sit in the most comfortable position you can find. Cross legged on the floor, or lying on your bed, maybe on the sofa, or on a kitchen chair while your morning cuppa cools –

it doesn't matter where you do it, just as long as you are devoting time to yourself.

It will slowly become natural for you to devote that little bit of time but until it does, set alarms and write yourself notes and leave them where you will see them, to remind yourself to meditate and be mindful. It takes any time between eighteen and sixty-six days of doing something every day for it to become habitual – everyone is different. I was one of Luke's one-percenters so here's hoping you lot are all eighteen-dayers.

How do you feel right now? Check in with yourself. Shuffle around wherever you are sitting and get as comfortable as possible. What is the state of your mind? Are there frantic thoughts buzzing around, or are you relaxed and content? Busy, tired or anxious? Just notice the state of your mind but know that whatever you bring to the session is completely okay.

When I was new to this, I closed my eyes, which I think can help you to focus on the task at hand far more efficiently. So, if you haven't ever done this before, feel free to close your eyes during your meditation sessions – but not before reading the following guide. Later on in this chapter I will give you an insight into meditating with your eyes open (so be excited. No, be calm!).

Once you are settled and your eyes are closed, slowly (anything between 3-10 seconds for each inhalation and then exhalation) breathe in and out through your nose (unless you have a cold, in which case breath in as comfortable a way as possible). Noticeably pausing between each breath and then observing the stillness and calm. Slowly in through your nose, pause, and then out through your nose, pause. Try to make it as relaxed and calm as possible. Pay close attention to your breath and then start to count. 1 as you breathe in, 2 as you breathe out. Do this until you reach 10 and then start again from the beginning.

Your mind will wander, this is a certainty. Everyone's mind wanders, you're human. Our brains are thought factories, so do not let it bother you that you forgot to put the rubbish out. The goal is not to clear your mind completely but to practise focusing on your attention, practising some more every time you notice it has wandered. When you notice it has strayed, smile and then start again, counting your breaths starting from 1. Don't let it bother you, you are new to this game and it will improve over time. Every time you focus your attention back to your breathing, you are effectively strengthening your meditative state, so it is actually a positive transition.

When you notice thoughts and feelings that pop up, accept them as part of you, because that's what they are. Be friendly with them and allow them time to come and go as they please.

Don't worry that you're doing it wrong. You're not, so smile and concentrate on your breath. In through your nose, out through your nose. See your breath as an anchor to the present moment, every time your mind wanders, you're only a few breaths away from coming right back to the here and now.

If a particular thought keeps returning to you, allow it to stay for a while and give it some attention. It is not a bad thing to do and will help dampen your curiosity. When you have given it enough attention, bring your thinking back to your breath and start counting again strengthening your meditative state.

Become your own best friend. The more you continue to meditate, the more you will get to know and love yourself. As you will find out in the following chapters, this is the second fundamental requirement of Timinology.

I have now explained to you the best way to get started with meditating. It's easy and I know that you will start to benefit from its peace as soon as you begin practising. Now it's time to show you some techniques to help stop your mind from wandering.

Just Breathe ♫

Alternate nostril breathing is something which I was introduced to during the TM course, linked to pranayama, a technique associated with yoga. Place your right thumb on your nose, your index and middle fingers in-between your eyebrows and your ring finger on your left nostril. Press the thumb down on the right nostril and breathe out gently through your left nostril. Inhale through the left nostril and then gently close it with your ring finger, before releasing your thumb and exhaling out of the right nostril. Breathe in from the right and exhale. Continue inhaling and exhaling through alternate nostrils, complete 10 rounds in total or until you start to feel a deep sense of calm.

Supposedly, breathing in through your left nostril invigorates the right 'feeling' hemisphere of the brain. Breathing in through your right nostril invigorates the left 'thinking' hemisphere of the brain. Left nostril for calming, right nostril for energising. Interestingly we predominantly breathe through one side of our nose in a cyclical fashion, changing every couple of hours - try placing your finger under your nose now to notice which side is currently more dominant. If you want to find out about the multitude of other benefits of this practise, there is a great website called thehealthylivinglounge.com, which gives more information on these and other techniques.

The Name of the Game ♫

As I was taught with TM, use a mantra on which to focus. Mentally speak it out to stop your mind from wandering. I was given a unique phrase which amalgamated a sequence of syllables to create words that have no meaning in our language. The purpose of this is that we don't then visualise any other meaning of the words we are saying but associate them only with our sense of love, peace or calm.

The mantra may change in different ways. It can get faster or slower, louder or softer, clearer or fainter. Its pronunciation can alter, lengthen or shorten, appear to be distorted, or it may not change at all. In every case, take it as it comes, neither anticipating nor resisting change and without judgement.

Create a word for yourself and then visualise peace, love and calm with it throughout your meditation. Make it your own word. Here are some potential mantras sounds that you could use to form your phrase: eng, em, enga, ema, ieng, iem, ienga, iema, shirim, shiring, kiriz, kiring, hirim.

I Can See Clearly Now ♪

Open your eyes and concentrate on a visual stimulus. This could be anything – a lamp, a flame, a small object, a crack in the wall, maybe a picture? Anything you like. Whatever you focus on, take note of the light and the energy that surrounds you.

As you focus on this object, take note of how your body feels and the position you are sitting in. Feel the weight of your body pressing down on your seat, then notice how your body feels against the surface on which you're sitting. Notice the sensations from your clothing on whichever part of your body it is stimulating.

For this exercise, don't count your breaths or visualise the light in your body, just breathe regularly and deeply to the rhythm of your heartbeat and concentrate on the object you've chosen, imagining and feeling the energy of the whole world emanating from that very spot. With your eyes open, you have the chance to rationalise and experience fully the present moment, the here and now. Feel and understand that the whole world is revolving around this very point in time; don't think about past experiences and don't think about hanging your washing out. You are the master of your own destiny and this very moment is only for you. Gain as much peace, harmony and love as you need. These are ever-present and available to you whenever you choose to call on them.

Love in the First Degree ♪

I read about this method a while back and it gives me such a sense of heart-warming peace. It involves recalling your most vivid recollection of love. It can be a love for whom or whatever you were cherishing but this exercise does not involve reaffirming your love for any person or situation, this is about reactivating that feeling that you had (or may still feel).

For me, it was a Sunday afternoon in early January, in Scotland, with my then girlfriend, Hannah, about three weeks into our relationship. We were on a walk before I was due to head home. We found a stream flowing down the side of a steep hill and noticed that the pool of water into which it was flowing had completely frozen over, with snow dusting the entire area. It was so cold but all we could do was stare lovingly into each others' eyes, absorbing the beautiful surroundings. I can still feel the shooting sensation of pure love streaming through my body and the realisation that she was the only person I wanted to spend the rest of my life with.

This is about recollecting a past feeling of pure love and using it to evoke the perfect love, for yourself. Even if you have felt it on another occasion, you can use whatever memory you find easy to summon. This is about using the feeling of love that you had, to strengthen and develop love for yourself. When you are meditating, breathing steadily and noticing the sensations running through your body, encapsulate that pure love and reinvigorate it, refocusing the feeling on yourself.

The Final Countdown ♫

This technique is something I developed after reading a fantastic book called *Moonwalking with Einstein* by Joshua Foer[5], about improving your memory, something I was having problems with after the accident.

Similar to the practise of numbering your breaths from 1 through to 10, in this exercise you need to visualise each number as an object or character. If you also have memory difficulties, replacing each number with it's corresponding image will help you to visually retain it. You can change the images to whatever you like but it actually helps if they are as incongruous as possible, you will remember something that is out of place more easily than something that is logical.

So you're sitting, cross legged, on a beautiful sandy beach on a gloriously hot, summer's day. Behind you and to your sides stand a surplus of palm trees that silently rustle as the wind calmly passes through them. Bird song fills the air, and the fresh, freeing smell of the sea encompasses your airway.

On your first inhalation, visualise running your finger through the sand you're sitting on, resembling the number 1

On your next breath, you notice a magnificent swan swimming towards you, its neck resembling a number 2.

As the swan gets closer, it opens its wings and releases an abundance of loving hearts, which resemble a 3 taking you back to the strong feeling of love that you summoned in the previous exercise.

You look past the swan and notice a sleek sailing boat coming your way, which looks like a number 4.

As you take another breath, you board the sailing boat and notice a door knocker resembling a 5.

You knock on the door, and as it slowly opens you notice a baby elephant, whose trunk is shaped like a number 6, which breathes out a mist of loving happiness, joy and laughter.

You look to the side of the boat as you take your next breath and see a diving board, which looks like a number 7.

You go over to the board, jump up into the air and propel yourself into a large hour glass timer, resembling a number 8. It is using love and laughter, instead of sand, to track time.

You get whisked down to the bottom of the hour glass timer and notice a large helium balloon with a rope attached to it, looking like a number 9.

You grab hold of the balloon rope and it whisks you into the air. As you rise above the number 1 you drew on the beach, you notice the swan and all the hearts surrounding it, you see the majestic boat sailing in the water beneath you as you catch a glimpse of the door knocker. You then see a baby elephant stepping out on deck, in front of the diving board which is now next to the hour glass timer floating in the water, you look up to see the balloon you are dangling from expanding beyond all proportions, and then suddenly exploding in magnificent style as you breath out, covering everything around you with love, joy and happiness, culminating in a number 10. You then visualise yourself from above, wherever you may be sitting, and then start again, with a massive smile on your face.

(Don't) Scratch that Itch ♫

This next technique is something that suddenly came to me one day. While you're meditating and focusing on sensations, or breaths, or your own love, you suddenly get an itch on your left ear. Your natural reaction is to scratch it to alleviate the annoyance. Do not scratch it. Instead, focus on the itch and notice how aware it makes you feel of that tiny area of your body. Your mind is now directed at this irritation, which is increasing your awareness and helping you to be as fully present as possible. Keep this up and remind yourself not to relieve it. You will find that within a short time the itch will subside and you have consequently invigorated your awareness as a result. Bless the itch.

Smile Like You Mean It ♫

The final chapter is on Happiness but before I show you its importance I will briefly mention some meditative happiness techniques.

Smiling, nine times out of ten, means you're happy, unless it's a sarcastic smirk. Generally speaking, smiles activate peace, joy, love, laughter and happiness. Using the methods I have just shared, visualise a massive smile, from cheek to cheek, in the front of your mind the next time you meditate. You will find that even imagining a smile will make you feel happier and more positive.

If a smile isn't enough I quite often do the following to actually make me laugh during meditation. It might not work for everyone but I have quite a simple sense of humour, so we'll see if it works for you. When you're next on the internet, google search for 'meerkat Alan'. Lots of people have seen this but if you haven't, you'll have to follow my advice and look it up. It's a simple image and I can easily see the video in my mind, which makes me laugh every time I think of it. If that doesn't amuse you, I'm sure you know of other sketches that make you giggle every time you think of them, so experiment with whatever makes you laugh next time you are meditating. 'Alan'!

My Way ♫

I hope that the above techniques will enable you to make a proactive start to meditation. Feel free to alternate between the methods, or even combine them all during the same session. During my meditation earlier this morning, I decided to do just that and moved through all of them. If you find that your mind is particularly restless one particular day, have a go at this.

Sit cross legged on your bed and, with your eyes open, focus on a prominent but relatively innocuous part of a picture, poster, or part of the view from the window, in front of you.

Slowly take a deep breath in through your nose, pause for a couple of seconds and then breathe out through your nose. Continue to do this until you get into a natural rhythm.

If your mind is focused on your breath and doesn't wander into thoughts about the party you had last night or how many bags of rubbish keep piling up for you to put out, then continue with the breathing, and smile.

If you find yourself singing in your head a rendition of Don't Look Back in Anger with a bunch of your drunken friends and then see yourself downing copious amounts of vodka; breathe in through your nose but this time visualise a steady stream of warm light infiltrating and circulating around your body.

On your out breath, see your drunken misdemeanours leave your body and then dissipate into the wall in front of you.

Without focusing on the comic mishaps from last night that just flew into the wall, take another deep breath in and then allow the passive light to gently flow throughout your body again, before breathing out.

On your next breath in, notice the feeling of your whole body sitting on the bed and focus on how your thigh feels cross legged next to your foot.

On your out breath, start to turn the drunken mishaps into shady light and breathe more of it out. Use the next few inhalations and exhalations to listen to any sounds from outside, see them as different shapes, colours, smells and textures, and know that you are as conscious as possible in this moment and that you are present.

On your next breath in, you choose to visualise a massive smile in the front of your head, which consequently causes you to smile and feel calm and happy about how your life is going right now.

Then replay a comic YouTube clip in your head, on your next out breath, which causes you to laugh out loud. You're happy, smiling, present and meditating.

Over the next 20 breaths visualise each number from 1 to 10 as you breathe in and out, releasing feelings of relaxation and pure joy.

After a while you'll reach a point where you no longer feel the need to stop. You are perfectly content in this moment and you are at peace with the world.

Know that when you eventually stop meditating you are going to bring with you the peace, harmony and love that is currently enveloping you, and smile.

Teacher ♫

Near the end of writing this book, I met up with a business consultant and discussed the direction I wanted my career to take once it had been published. I consequently completed a mindfulness teacher training programme, giving me the opportunity to conclusively read up on and fully understand the workings of mindfulness; now allowing me to comprehensively teach it.

Alongside life consulting, I also conduct eight-week mindfulness courses (if you fancy it, info can be accessed through the website www.timinology.com) which also includes a selection of guided meditations to help get you started). Following this, I have written down the four core mindfulness meditations, in order to help get you started here and now, some of which can also be found as guided meditations on the website.

Rock your Body ♫

The body scan:

For beginners, this is a great starting point for experiencing the immediate sensations, throughout your whole body, of what meditation can offer you. Some people find it very daunting at first while others might switch off instantly, but by vigilantly observing whatever thoughts, feelings or opinions of it you encounter, you are doing everything right, whatever you think. So, smile to yourself and know that this is by far the most comprehensive way (certainly for your whole body) to begin your meditative journey. It is about noticing your breathing and allowing your mind and body to conjoin with each other. Your mind will wander, everyone's does, but every time you bring your attention back to your breath and whichever part of the body on which you are focusing, congratulate yourself for doing so, smile and then continue. Do not punish yourself for letting it wander, because by just noticing it, you are automatically strengthening your meditative state, so be happy.

You can perform this meditation sitting or lying down or even standing up. I personally like to lie down for this one because it helps with covering my whole body (as you will find out).

Whatever position you decide to take, settle yourself and relax your body into it. Close your eyes and begin by slowly breathing in and then out. On each in breath, feel the serenity, joy and love of life enter into you, and then on each out breath feel yourself sinking deeper into your chosen position.

Notice your left foot and all the sensations that accompany it: the weight of it, the feeling of it resting on the floor, maybe your blood pulsing through it or maybe even the temperature. Starting with focusing on your big toe, breath in slowly. On your out breath, move your attention onto the next toe and systematically guide your attention through each of your toes, slowly breathing in and out; to the sole of your foot, your heel, your ankle, your shins, your knee, your thighs etc., until you eventually reach the top of your leg.

Now move over to your right leg and foot and perform the same routine, slowly observing and feeling the sensations of every part of your body, moving up slowly with each breath until you reach the top of your leg.

Direct your attention now to the little finger on your left hand, again, slowly breathing in and out while moving your attention from each finger to your whole hand, your wrist, your elbow, your upper arm until you eventually reach your shoulder.

Move over to your right arm and perform the same routine that you just did for your left arm. All the time observing and acknowledging the sensations and feelings that occur, upon each breath.

Now move down to the top of both your legs and slowly notice the feelings and sensations of every body part from your torso all the way up to you neck, your chin, your mouth, your cheeks, your eyes, your ears, your hair until you reach the top of your head.

Be aware of your whole body as one now and, when you are ready, slowly open your eyes, smile and congratulate yourself for completing this meditation.

Sitting meditation:

Similar to the body scan, this meditation focuses more on managing your thoughts and helping you realise that your mind will wander but that this is never a bad thing, and can only help to strengthen your routine. The sitting meditation uses a variety of different scenarios that can all be experienced sitting down, with the sole purpose of helping bring your mind back to the present moment through seemingly obvious distractions.

First things first, you need to sit down. There is no right way or wrong way. Ideally it would be good for you to keep your back straight and unsupported but if you have a bad back, by all means rest it against the back of a chair because meditation is not meant to be uncomfortable in the slightest, so sit yourself in as comfortable posture as possible. Maybe try a meditation cushion or use some pillows to elevate your hips above your knees. I personally like to cross my legs and sit on my bed or the floor but do whatever suits you.

Like with the body scan, where the intention is to focus on each part of your body without letting your mind wander, this time you will be guided to focus on a variety of different situations and sensations, while all the time observing them non-judgementally, kindly and curiously.

Start by finding your posture with your back as straight as possible, allowing your hands to rest on your lap or by your side. Partially close your eyes or focus on a prominent object in front of you.

The Sound of Silence ♫

Sounds: Bring your awareness to all the sounds around you. The sounds in the room you're in or the sounds outside. Maybe your tummy is rumbling or the washing machine is spinning in another room. Don't make any effort to identify the sounds, just allow them to come to you.

If your mind suddenly gets distracted by a conversation you were having with your neighbour earlier, or by what you might be having for lunch, bring it back to a noticeable sound and non-judgementally observe it again.

If you become distracted by whichever sound has just arrived, perhaps you don't like it because it is just irritating, look past that emotional distraction and try to just observe it as it is.

Notice the silence between each sound and let it bring a unique quality to the variations of sounds heading your way.

When you are ready to bring your attention back to the room, stretch your arms up in the air, heave a big sigh, and continue.

Breath: Sit in the same position you were in previously, lowering your eyes and resting your hands. Allowing all distractions, thoughts and feeling to pass you by, take a deep breath in and feel the direct sensation of it entering into your body and then leaving on your out breath. Try not to be distracted by where the breath goes or what it is doing, just focus solely on the sensation of it entering and leaving your body.

Notice the way each in breath expands your abdomen and how each out breath lowers it. There is no destination for you or it to reach; you are solely experiencing the present moment with your breath.

If your mind wanders, bring your attention back to your breath, smile for noticing it and then carry on observing it until you are ready to come back to the room to stretch your arms and take another big sigh.

Thoughts and feelings: Resuming your starting position. Notice your breath every time it enters and leaves your body, focus on the sensation it creates as it enters your nose, and the sound of it leaving your nostrils. Feel the temperature difference as it passes.

Now notice any thoughts that are entering your mind and allow them to take a front seat. Observe the process of thinking. Notice how some thoughts are pulling your attention towards them more than others, and how you might want to follow them and get caught up in them, constructing stories to feed their desires. Whatever the thoughts, be they about the past, the future or some cognitive problem you are trying to solve, witness how your mind gets caught up in some stories and is repelled by others. Notice what interests you and what bores you without getting drawn into any of them.

Now practice letting the thoughts be. Observe them for what they are but don't get caught up in their cogs. If you find yourself being drawn into a thought, observe what is happening, take a metaphorical step back and then visualize thoughts as clouds in the sky, letting the one in which you nearly became entangled slowly breeze past you.

If you come across a disturbing thought that won't leave you alone, know that you can always go back to your breath, or find a sound that needs to be observed and then let it pass you by. The same can also be said for emotions, be they linked to anger, resentment, sadness, fear or anxiety, knowing that your breath will always be a solid and reliable grounding for you to revert back to if things ever get out of hand.

Mindful Movement:

As you will find out in parts of the nutrition chapter and the self-love chapter, movement, however strenuous, has the ability to revitalize a stagnant mind. It seems appropriate, therefore, that this very concept can be utilized to boost the benefits of mindfulness up another notch. What better way to look after your precious body than by kindly giving it a workout and mindfully watching over it at the same time. Kindful and Mindful.

I understand that yoga is a similar kind of activity but don't worry, I won't be asking you to do any downward dogs in this section. I am merely using it to emphasize the importance that movement can have on your meditative workings, and dispelling any rumours that meditation is only about sitting still, closing your eyes and thinking about nothing. (which I hope I have proved to you already).

Always focus on your breath, that's the bedrock of meditating but this time try stretching your body into a certain posture, noticing the stresses and strains throughout your whole body. How is it making you feel? If your mind suddenly wanders, that's okay, but bring it back to another mindful movement or posture along with noticing your breath.

Like with everything, the more you do it, the better you will get at it; and before long you might even take up a bit of yoga, also. Mindful walking is a key attribute to the eight-week mindfulness course that I am now running through my website, so if you want to learn anymore about this incredible technique, sign yourself up.

The Breathing Space: ABC

If you only pick up one thing from this book, I want it to be this. When you reach the Self-Control chapter you will notice that this is a technique that has the power to potentially retrain an addictive mindset at any given moment, and therefore something I am going to wax lyrical about. Obviously you will need to have developed your mindful self in order to benefit profoundly from this exercise but I hope my rather forthright comment and enthusiasm for it will be enough to encourage you to take everything from this book onboard in order to maximize your potential.

The breathing space is a simple, quick (three minute) meditative strategy that has the ability to relax and unwind a cluttered mind at any given moment. You can obviously make it as long or as short as you want but unless you're in the middle of surgery, realistically, if you're feeling overwhelmed, we can all break away from most situations – to maybe nip to the bathroom for three minutes to give this a go – so it's a no brainer.

The purpose of the breathing space is very simple. You are not trying to banish your thoughts, bodily sensations or feelings, you are merely observing them from a fresh perspective which will give you the ability to address them accordingly.

A, B, C: very easy to remember. Awareness, Breath and Belief, Choice.

Awareness:

You should be used to it by now, so after mindfully observing your bodily sensations at the start, during and after a specific bout of addiction, anxiety, stress, depression etc, you will have become acutely aware of how you are likely to feel at any of these given moments. For this part of the exercise, you need to become aware of the sensations you are likely to encounter at the very start of whatever episode you want to manage and, as such, knowingly understand what is likely to happen if you don't take appropriate action.

Breath:

You guessed it, you need to breathe. Make a concerted effort to mindfully breathe. Take a deep breath in and notice the sensation you feel as the air passes down into your lungs. Before you breathe out, notice the short pause between the in and out breath and then slowly release the air that has been briefly resting in your body. If you notice any other sensations within your body, acknowledge and accept them, don't try to change them, just let them be.

Belief:

Now question the strength and feasibility of whatever potential strain of addiction, anxiety, stress, depression etc, you feel is heading your way. If you have just felt the warning signs that you are moments away from smoking a cigarette or cracking open a bottle of whisky or about to have a panic attack, praise yourself for noticing its potential dominance over you before it hits and then question its authority. You are now fully aware of what might occur, you have taken the appropriate steps to prevent it from happening and the ball is in your court. Smile because you are now in control.

Choice:

You now have a choice to choose a mindful action. So what's it going to be?

There is no shame in calling for reinforcements, so if you decide your anxiety is getting the worst of you or your addiction has popped one too many corks, you are now in the perfect position to mindfully make this decision for yourself. See how far you've come – you've just sensed something was about to happen and prevented it from going any further, through your strength, so it can only get better from now on in; with the added help of a professional or a loved one.

Or,

you've come this far by yourself so you're happy to persevere and go all the way. In which case:

The next time you briefly lay to rest whatever personal transgression is bothering you, exercise it out. The benefits of mindful movement are a mere 'tip of the iceberg' for what endorphins and exercise can do to your state of mind. And why not try to exercise mindfully and kill two birds with one stone. If you need any advice with mindful exercise contact me at www.timinology.com

Do something for yourself and work on kindfully relaxing and caring for your mindful self. Make yourself happy.

Use mindfulness as a benchmark for your next activity. Go for a mindful walk or cook for yourself as kindfully as possible and then mindfully eat it. Try mindful swimming or mindful singing. So many options, just get mindful.

Shamash Alidina who wrote Mindfulness for Dummies[6] lists a selection of beneficial effects that the breathing space can have on anyone who gives it a go, which is more conclusive evidence that this is not something to sniff your nose at.

They include:

- You move into a restful 'being' mode of mind

- Your self-awareness increases

- Your self-compassion increases

- You create more opportunities to make choices

- You switch off autopilot mode

- You become an observer of your experience rather than feeling trapped by it

- You see things from a different perspective

- You walk the bridge between formal and informal practice

- You create a space for new ideas to arise

In terms of locations, once you've mastered the basics of mindfulness and begin to find it less of an effort to accomplish, know that you can do it almost anywhere and anytime, within reason (you can't meditate with your eyes closed when you're driving, for example, that's just silly – but you can, as I've explained, put some of the techniques to good use to keep yourself calm behind the wheel). Meditate on your way to work if you're on the train, or even as you're walking. Perhaps you just want to take some time out from the busy streets and meditate in the park.

Prayer and meditation can be effectively the same thing (as will be discussed in the next chapter) so, if it appeals to you, go to a church or a mosque or whatever religious building you align with and draw on the peace and serenity within to help you meditate.

Once you can free your mind from distractions and concentrate solely on the present moment, you can go anywhere. Find something that prevents your mind from wandering and you'll be there. If you can focus your mind appropriately when you're out running, use that time to meditate as well as keeping fit. A friend of mine takes so much care over chopping onions that when he is busy cooking his dinner, he is in fact also freeing his mind and meditating, in his own way. Just choose anything that you find frees your mind and you will be opening it up to positive change.

Timmy's Tips

- Expect nothing (other than alone time)

- Post notes in unexpected places (like your running shoes or your fridge door?) to remind yourself to meditate and be mindful

- Start with short amounts of time, then expand

- Brush your teeth with the opposite hand you normally use, or change the normal process of any activity you habitually do, in order to become mindfully aware of it

- Learn to observe all your thoughts, feelings, emotions and bodily sensations without ever criticising them, merely acknowledging and accepting them for what they are; whether seemingly positive or negative

- Try every technique until you find the one that works

- Combine techniques if you like them

- Experience peace, love, and compassion through meditation

- Try to only allow positive thoughts into your mindful space but don't get cross with yourself if you can't, or if you lose focus; just observe, acknowledge, accept and then smile

- Make your meditative and mindful methods suit you, not the other way around

Religion vs Spirituality

Although spirituality stems from the ideologies of many religions (Buddhism being a dominant influence) its presence within us supersedes any of the dogmatic, rule-driven or scripture based teachings affiliated with the theological doctrines of the establishment. Spirituality is the fundamental basis for using our minds in the most systematic and life-enhancing ways possible. Learning to lead a happy life from our hearts rather than a fearful one informed by suffering. Our suffering resonates through our thoughts, which can only be rectified by accessing our spiritual selves and turning all of the fear, which controls our lives, into love.

This isn't just another namby-pamby self-help book, written by someone who wants to put across his obscure views of the world. I am iterating this point because I mentioned the word 'love', alongside life. There is a later chapter dedicated solely to Loving oneself but before you reach it, you need to understand the impact it has on your life, and your spiritual growth. All religions know this but they substitute you, the most important thing you need to love, with whichever provident deity they choose.

I'm going to throw something controversial out there now. When the magnificent religious figures of the past, say, Moses or Jesus or Mohammed, reflected upon their life plans through deep, heartfelt prayer (what I might call meditation), the God they heard and responded to is the same God, or quiet voice, that we all hear. We hear it when our minds are cleared from all the frustrations and distractions of everyday life and open to the beauty, love and serenity of an undistracted, clear head. The quiet voice is that of your own thoughts and, just as we can have good and bad thoughts, we can mistakenly understand the sinister thoughts we may be experiencing, as 'voices' in our heads, which is when things can begin to feel out of control. I have explained to you the importance of quietening your mind, through mindful meditation, allowing the loving, innocent thoughts to permeate your psyche as Godly apparitions.

I am not here to tell you to believe in a God but I do know that the human race does not exist to wage war against itself. We, as a species, are a naturally loving and empathetic race. Whether or not the good thoughts and feelings we have manifest themselves as a God to worship, or merely an insightful way to lead your life, however you choose to label the practise that helps you achieve it we are all in it together.

Throughout this chapter, I will chronicle my own spiritual upbringing, the paths that I took, turned from, and am now taking, to reach my own enlightenment. When I mention 'Religion' I am talking about a rule-driven, scripture-based belief in a higher power that requires unadulterated commitment to staying truly faithful. When I talk about 'Spirituality' I am talking about a mindset that allows you to see the good in everything, and something that uses meditation to help connect the instigator with their higher, loving, happy selves, which is, if you like, God.

I am not going to berate any religious doctrine. Each and every one of them has influenced and moulded the lives of many millions of people on this planet and to chastise something so close to people's hearts is nonsensical and unnecessary. Surely the very existence of so many different religions must be cause for questioning whether or not you're practising the right one, or if there even is a God. I will come back to this presumption later.

Most religions base their teachings on the fundamental morals of how to lead a good life but those morals don't derive from the religion itself. They are often the basic principles of humanity. My friend George, who fancies himself as a bit of a theologian, devized his own concept for this, stating that 'morals are just an evolutionary extension of [reciprocal] altruism'. He is a scientist and a veterinary surgeon, a background from which he has derived this viewpoint, but in defining his statement he remarks that morals have nothing to do with any religion. Instead, they have evolved through natural selection. Take animals that live in their own structured societies, for example, like monkeys or meerkats or lions. As a species, it helps that they all get on with one another. If Dave the monkey keeps stealing food from his family, he may benefit from a short term gain (chewing away on his coconut chunks) but if all monkeys did this, the likelihood of the species surviving would diminish considerably as fewer young would survive. It boils down to common sense, or moral sense.

(It's Fun to Stay at the) YMCA ♫

When I was about thirteen – an impressionable age – my God-mother, for whom I have an unending amount of admiration and love (and who also happens to be Hannah's mother), gave me the gift of a week long camping holiday. The predetermined location was a Christian retreat centre. My Godmother is an incredibly devout Catholic and probably one of the most sincere and mindful people I know. I took her up on the offer gracefully and persuaded one of my greatest childhood friends, Tom, to join me on this adventure.

My memories of attending this camp bring back fond recollections of deep, though brief, friendships. The first few holidays were before the dawn of the internet or mobile phones, so keeping in contact with my new friends was hard, especially as I lived with my parents on the other side of the country. We did write letters to each other, which I still look over now and again, but as is the case with most long distance relationships, we eventually all lost touch, especially if they didn't come back to the camp the following year. I think Tom and I managed about seven years in a row at the camp and my experiences there had a phenomenal effect on my state of mind during these years, as you'll see in a bit.

When I started going to the camp I was young and very open to what the world had to offer. I don't regret going to them; I had some of the best moments of my childhood there. My only objection was to the way in which they drummed their views to a captive audience of incredibly impressionable teenagers.

Of course I was going to take on board their teachings; I was only thirteen and hadn't really been out of the country, bar a few family holidays, let alone had any life experiences to otherwise influence my burgeoning psyche.

The activities during the day were standard youth camp frivolities, from playing various team sports, shopping in the local town to swimming, eating and socialising. In the evenings, the whole ethos of the camp took on a much more hands-on approach to Godliness, where the camp organisers tried to subtly prompt us into committing our lives to their God, remonstrating stories of how our lives would end up if we failed to adhere to the apparent truth. Accompanying the stories they also played us very downbeat, rather sombre songs in a bid to influence our way of thinking. Only they could apparently offer us salvation from the shitty lives we had been led to believe we now faced.

I know now how I want to lead my life and I won't be swayed by some artful musical interlude. Between the ages of thirteen and twenty, however, I had no idea of the direction in which I needed to go and was very open to suggestions. For seven years my whole view on life was altered dramatically. I believe it was this that instigated a lot of my self-loathing, as will be described in the self-love chapter.

So there I was. I already had a general moral compass for leading a 'good' life, thanks to my parents, but I'm being taught again because it sounds better coming from a course leader with a pious stance. I remember being told that God would not be happy if I kept listening to Guns N' Roses, because apparently they worshipped the devil. What? I was no longer allowed to listen to this music because the course leaders heard something that 1) was probably not true and 2) even if it was, had no bearing on how awesome they sounded. I think they said that we could listen to Genesis if we wanted to.

I didn't do yoga then but I strongly support it now, especially as Katie, my younger sister, is a trained instructor. I have vivid memories of being told that yoga was the work of the devil because it was all about concentrating and devoting time to yourself, not thinking about anyone else or trying to save the world. In reality, it's an activity that effectively grants the participant physical and mental wellbeing, which can then easily be used to benefit countless other people as an unequivocal payback.

Yoga originates from meditation, which, as you already know, has the power to completely readjust and invigorate a previously mindless life. It was the mid-nineties when I attended these camps, long before the worldwide acceptance of meditation as a common practise, so I know that the course leaders would have savagely renounced it, because of its primary objective of self-focus and self-love. When it boils down to it, though, prayer and meditation are in many ways exactly the same thing. More on that later, though.

Back to the Christian camp. Despite the difficulties, for me to have attended it for seven years in a row there must have been something that kept me asking to go back. Hannah's presence at a few of them was definitely where our initial attraction arose. She didn't go every year, though, which I knew in advance, and it wasn't until I had stopped attending the camps that we started going out, so she was not the fundamental reason.

I genuinely considered what I experienced at the very first camp to be a spiritual awakening. It was that initial experience that inspired both Tom and I to attend it for a further six years. You may have seen films or programmes where charismatic Christian brethren sing joyously, laying hands on their followers who consequently fall to the ground in jubilation, with tears in their eyes, whilst chanting some unintelligible drivel (speaking in tongues). Well, that kind of peculiarity happened at the camps. Remember, I'm thirteen, I haven't experienced much of life, I don't understand the power of the mind and I have never seen anything quite like this before. I was absolutely mesmerized when Emily, a girl who was being prayed over on the straw bale in front of me (I forgot to mention this was all conducted in a barn, in the countryside, hence the straw), started wailing in some kind of ecstasy before effectively passing out and then chanting 'carla rash ma langda whitsdangley crang a dang my lang' or something very similar, whilst crying her eyes out. This to me was conclusive proof that there was indeed a loving God (who got his kicks out of watching us make fools of ourselves).

I didn't care about the crap we did during the day. I wanted to watch the spirit of God move around the room each evening and entangle itself within all of us. This was captivating wonder. I made it my mission to be 'filled with the holy spirit' and to replicate the incredible experience that I had witnessed.

I found myself standing at the front of the barn with a straw bale at my feet. A course leader came over to me, extended his arm and gently laid his hand on my forehead. Oh my goodness (not God, blasphemy was a massive no), I thought to myself, it's about to happen. The course leader started murmuring some kind of mumbo jumbo. That's okay, he's speaking in tongues, it's not meant to be understood. It's coming, it's coming, I whisper in my mind.

'Hummmmmmmmm' Maybe humming will help, I think to myself. 'Hummmmmmmmmmm'. Keep at it. I persevere, 'hummmmmmmmmm'. Shit, nothing is happening, maybe I shouldn't have sworn, damn, is that better? Fuck, no, shit, no, be calm. 'Hummmmmmmmmmmm'.

A few minutes went by until the course leader moved to my side to invoke the holy spirit through someone else. Why didn't it want to come to me? I thought to myself, just as Matthew, the kid on the straw bale next to me toppled to the ground and started laughing his head off (another way in which the spirit moves, apparently, unless he was laughing at himself for falling over).

I was a bit down at this point. Why didn't it happen to me? I wondered. I looked around the barn to see an array of completely different scenarios all happening at the same time. Some kids were sitting silently, some were crying, some were lying motionless on the floor, some were laughing hysterically but I had nothing, absolutely nothing. I noticed Hannah in the corner of my eye who was sitting very quietly, as if she had been crying. Although I'm sure she wasn't, she looked very sad and I didn't like that, which made me sad. I thought about it for a while, well, more about her, and I then thought about why I had not been chosen. These two things together brought a tear to my eye and I suddenly started crying.

Wow, maybe it has happened? I convinced myself. I didn't want to wail, so I moved my hands to my head in a bid to maybe show Hannah that I, too, had been visited by the holy spirit. It worked, she somehow noticed me crying and leant over to give me a tissue to dry my eyes. Yes, I thought to myself, this holy spirit truly works in mysterious ways.

The annual Christian camp trip to maintain my ethereal mindset meant that I needed to somehow top it up in the intervening months. This saw me establishing a youth club at my local church, with another young Christian, Stefan. We tried to go on trips similar to the summer camps I attended, and we met up each week to pray and talk about the wonders of God. Looking back on it now, I can't see what, if anything, we achieved from any of it but I guess it was a good way to pass the time and in good company. I don't remember how the youth club ended, when or why, it just slowly phased out to become a small blip in my memory.

I know that religious experiences are different for absolutely everyone but mine was so overwhelming that until I took the time to understand my own existence and question the need to seek solace in such a fantastical interpretation of Why We Are Here, my life was never going to develop past this sophomoric state of obscurity. If you point-blank refuse to question a belief you have maintained your entire life and if yet still your questions and prayers are not being answered, perhaps, just perhaps, you don't really believe what you are trying to practise.

As I mentioned at the start of this chapter, in no way am I trying to ridicule or belittle any religious doctrine, that is not why I am here. With the correct mental attitude, it doesn't matter who or what you worship, because you can still get the same results from whichever God you pray to, or whichever system you adhere to. Ultimately, for me, the problem was the way in which I had been taught at such a young, impressionable age.

I don't doubt that I wasn't the only kid to have been affected in such a negative way by the camp's teachings. I also know that the positive messages that they tried to convey did resonate with plenty of the other kids, who have consequently gone on to lead devout and happy lives. My course-attendee friend, Tom, is one of them and now has a dream job in the foothills of the Scottish Highlands. He is an Elder at his local church, met and married a delightful woman with the same faith and now has three wonderful children. We have spoken about this chapter and he doesn't agree with everything I have written. He found different, and many more positive, lessons at the camps. What we have both learned, somewhere along the way, is to have enough respect and love for each other to know that whatever disagreements we may have between our faiths, these have no impact on our long-standing friendship.

The Spirit in the Sky ♫

Prayer and meditation are intrinsically linked. Let's put William, a devout Christian, and Oliver, a mindful meditator, in the same room for a while to conduct their daily rituals. William kneels on the floor, positions himself in as comfortable a position as possible, closes his eyes and then peacefully petitions his dear Lord for a placid and loving existence. He concentrates on the love he believes he is receiving from his God and correspondingly encompasses loving grace in return.

Oliver, likewise, places himself cross legged comfortably on the floor, fixes his gaze on a small mark on the wall in front of him and slowly takes a deep breath in, whist envisaging an abundance of love, in all shapes, sizes and colours, entering into his body and circulating itself throughout it. On his out breath, with his gaze still fixed on the small mark directly in front of him, he populates the room with peace, love and tranquillity, at the same time freeing his mind of any obtrusive thoughts and observing and accepting the present moment he finds himself in. He continues the same routine with each in and out breath, numbering them from one to ten and then back to the start again.

At the end of the session, both William and Oliver recall similar transcendental experiences and leave feeling fulfilled with love and peace.

Although the intended focus of rituals were completely different, they mindfully managed to nurture and nourish a fond love for themselves through their individualized regimes. You may believe your meditative mind has the power to cultivate the wonderment of love and peace in your life. You may believe the God to which you have devoted your life has the power to reciprocate the same thing. Either way, if you entrust enough faith and assurance of it happening, it will.

I Need a Miracle ♫

Deepak Chopra has written an insightful book called *Is God an Illusion?*[1] questioning the plausibility and existence of spirituality vs science. In the book, he says that 'spirituality provides a way to know yourself beyond the personal, which is enlightenment'. His adversary and co-author of the book, Leonard Mlodinow, the scientist and staunch atheist of the argument, holds a very black and white viewpoint on the whole debate, steadfastly refusing to believe in the existence of anything that can't be scientifically substantiated. Yet, miracles that can't be explained by any scientific means happen all the time. I might not be a God squad adversary any more, and I may well have stepped away from organized religion, but spirituality is a completely different kettle of fish.

When it comes to miracles, every religion has a selection of unquantifiable stories that depict scientifically unprovable circumstances that have actually taken place. You just need to Google them to read a few of the fascinating stories. I'm sure some may have been fabricated, but the by and large of them are trusted by the reputable clergy. But how do we define a miracle? In physical health, for example, the Miracle

Commission of the Catholic Church will only acknowledge a cure for an illness as miraculous if it is 'spontaneous, instantaneous and completely healed' [2]. There also has to be absolutely no natural explanation for its occurrence and the patient needs to have been told beforehand that there is absolutely no way they will survive.

Sticking with the Catholic Church, before an individual can be canonized after their death, their life must first be thoroughly investigated and deemed virtuous enough. There then has to be conclusive proof of two miracles attributed to them before they can be given a sainthood. Pope John Paul II, who died in 2005, has recently been canonized after two individuals prayed to him and were miraculously completely healed of an illness that was expected to kill them.

I read an incredible story a few years ago about a man who lived up in some mountains and had to drive exactly the same route to work every single day, along very windy and precarious roads. On one occasion, although he had never done so before, he suddenly felt the urge to stop in a lay-by. Upon bringing his car to a standstill, after questioning why he had just done something so unnecessary, just before he decided to set off again he noticed a lorry on the opposite side of the road, swerve erratically. It ploughed into the corner of the junction, exactly where the man would have been had he not suddenly decided to stop the car for a few seconds.

I'm not saying this was a miracle and I'm not saying it had anything to do with any particular God, because as far as I recall he was an atheist. But why did he randomly feel the urge stop on a route along which he travelled every single day? What prompted him to make such an unusual decision – and one that potentially saved his life? Strange occurrences, although maybe without such potentially dramatic outcomes, happen all the time. How many times have you been thinking about someone you haven't spoken to for a while and then they suddenly call you? Maybe you're thinking about your favourite old song, when you turn on the radio and find it playing. Even though you're not looking, why is it you somehow know when someone else is looking at you? These coincidences and apparently inexplicable situations occur all the time, yet we have all become so accustomed to them, we shrug them off as just something that happens, without giving it a second thought.

The fact that some people have such devout faith and belief in a cure for whatever their plight, and to then go on and receive it, must set a few alarm bells ringing for the non-believers. It happens within every religion. But everybody has the power to perform unprecedented acts of wonder within themselves, if they truly believe that whoever or whatever they believe in has the power to incite it. Just because the results of a miracle cure are unquantifiable and unexplainable, that doesn't mean they didn't happen, but it does mean that the individual in question had enough faith and belief in whoever or whatever they prayed to, to make it happen.

However you look at it, religion as we know it is a man-made institution. Some may have been around for many thousands of years but the first and last word of all scripture was written by a human being. Science, capable of explaining many of the worldly mysteries of years gone by, is a relatively recent introduction, compared with the postulations of respected scholars back in the time of Jesus.

Take a solar eclipse, for example. As such an irregular occurrence, you can only imagine the anxiety and fear that would have consumed witnesses in the year dot, when the sun momentarily stopped shining and our ancestors had no idea why it happened. If you'd been brought up to believe that there is a God and a devil at war with each other, it's highly likely you'd see the eclipse as a manifestation of their battle. In fact, even today, some cultures still see these events as a bad omen, Hindu mythology being one of them, equating the blackout with Rahu swallowing the sun. Consider the depth of understanding today's doctors now have. If somebody suffered an epileptic fit back in 10AD, it wouldn't surprise me if they'd been snubbed or worse by society, even though there was a plausible medical reason, which nobody understood. That said, there is so much happening even today that can't be justified by science (but may well be in the future) and yet fanatics claim it as a religious feat.

Until we are old enough to think and choose for ourselves, religion is often thrust upon us. With each religion comes a set of honourable morals to adhere to, providing justification for instilling a given religion in the minds of the young, to be continued into adulthood. I was brought up a Christian by my parents and I think that overall it probably made me into a much more grounded person.

Perhaps it was only the manner and my impressionable age, when I was subjected to the teachings at the Christian camps, that led my life down a slightly more bumpy road. The point is, perhaps, that it's not what is taught but how we teach it that is the problem, and at what age. As you're probably beginning to see, there are many ways of explaining miracles and it is not what happens but how we learn from it, pass it on, and respond to it that is important.

I am not trying to tell you what to do, I'll leave that up to whichever religion is (or is not) summoning your faith. I will, however, having researched the fundamental differences between a spiritual lifestyle and a religious one, note down the significant discrepancies between the two, a section of which can be found at
www.bibliotecapleyades.net/mistic/mistic_10.htm

Spirituality is more or less always chosen, whereas religion is often, but not always, forced upon the passive.

There is a plethora of different religions to choose from, whereas spirituality has only one doctrine.

Every religion has ritualistic and formal characteristics, whereas spirituality offers spiritual ascent without dogmas.

Religious text is set in stone and, although the wording can often be interpreted differently, whether you agree with it or not it requires guidance for a follower to fully conform. Spirituality, conversely, is led by your inner voice and is freely open for anyone to discover.

Religion is highly structured and rule-driven, in contrast with the reasonableness and openness of spirituality.

As I found out myself, religious teaching can depend on threatening tactics to scare you into a particular way of thinking, whereas all spirituality offers is inner peace. It is the difference between fear-driven belief versus confidence-driven belief. It is important, however, to note that this is due to the manner in which the belief system is taught.

Christian religion speaks of repentance for sin and fault whereas spirituality encourages you to live in the present moment and to not feel remorse for that which has already passed.

Religion itself is not actually God, it is a set of principles that requires the believer to fully conform with and obey, in order to please their God; spirituality, however, is infinite consciousness and all that 'is' (which, in effect, includes God).

Religion requires an unadulterated belief, in order to realise its potentially misleading messages. Spirituality merely discovers.

Religion does not encourage questioning; spirituality questions everything in order to find a plausible answer.

All religions have rules; spirituality itself is divine and has none.

Religion is divisive, prompting war; spirituality is united, prompting peace.

Religion lives in your thoughts, is dialectical and is in charge of 'to do', spirituality lives in your conscience, is logical and is in charge of 'to be'.

Religion feeds your ego while spirituality allows you to transcend your thoughts.

Religion is adoration; spirituality is meditation.

Religion dreams of glory and paradise, spirituality lives in the present moment, the here and now.

Religion lives in the confined memory and believes in eternal life, spirituality finds liberty in awareness and is conscious of all that is.

Just imagine if all the religions of the world took on a spiritual approach. Minus land and politics, most of the wars in the past have been fought over imaginary forefathers and Gods, who exist only within our faiths. How peaceful the world would be if we no longer needed to fight over and die for them. Some of the bloodiest and most grotesque wars have been fought over religious ideals for which people have laid down their lives. It's preposterous and yet it keeps on happening.

Because our minds are so incredibly complex, they are easy to manipulate and control, often without our say so. Further to the stories I shared earlier, at the Christian camp, I did eventually succumb to the 'holy spirit' one evening. I have vivid memories of finally collapsing during a prayer session with a course leader, shortly before fluently reciting some mumbo jumbo that came to me. Although it was a very enlightening experience for me and something that prolonged my rhapsodic affair with my adopted lifestyle, I also vividly recollect that I willed myself to collapse on the floor and I purposefully and knowingly mumbled what was coming out of my mouth. I just chose to subconsciously, temporarily erase those thoughts from my head every time I tried to convince people to join the club.

I have no contempt, whatsoever, for anyone who chooses to worship a God or higher being with whom I have no affiliation; that is their choice. For me, the problem arises when they decide to force their beliefs upon unsuspecting individuals. All religions stem from a moral basis, so if a sect decides to embark on warfare, mayhem and harm in a bid to somehow promote their cause, they are not only going against the doctrine they apparently represent, they are destroying the fundamental peace of life to which everyone should be entitled. People get so brainwashed with these ideas and before long they are causing the destruction of the lives of bystanders. But how do we stop it?

F.E.A.R. ♫

I became completely focused on the religion I had been taught at the camps, although I didn't benefit from the good bits. There was one, single, underlying reason why I became transfixed and dependent on God, and that was fear. Fear of what might happen to me if I didn't believe what I was being told to believe. I was taught to be afraid and because my mind was so supple and open, I foolishly let my inner self believe everything I was being told by the course leaders. My life was dictated by fear.

As I saw it, there was no better system for keeping control, back then, than Obsessive Compulsive Disorder (OCD). The habits and behaviours this entailed became my way of trying to remedy a bad thought – by compulsively carrying out another activity to take my mind off it (this is covered in more detail in the Happiness chapter). By leading my life in this way I could ensure I didn't upset God, thereby not partnering up with Beelzebub. It was easy. It made sense.

I was petrified of upsetting this God who apparently loved me so much, or more prominently, of siding with the devil who was always out to get me and lead me astray. Yet, obeying what I was taught at the Christian camp was going to set a lot of limitations on my life. I couldn't listen to all the music I used to frequently play. I couldn't read certain books or watch certain television programmes. If a friend of mine said anything that opposed the leaders' views, I ended up telling them how they were upsetting God. I'm sure you can all recall from school, when someone says something hare-brained to a popular kid, you side with the cool one and renounce the idiot – this fear and the things it compelled me to believe and say was the very reason I struggled with popularity at school. By the time I left school, I was old enough to understand the implications of such preposterous talk but it took me until I was prompted to leave to realise this, shortly after propelling a firework into a dormitory, which I guess could have been my way of trying to show the world that I was no longer a deadhead.

The Bible and the course leaders told me that the number 666 was evil, which added yet another angle of despair to my already pretty hectic thought-processing. It saw me trying to avoid any situation which might be linked to a solitary six, because that was only a couple of sixes away from the apocalyptic 666. How I managed to lead a vaguely normal existence, I do not know. With the evil sixes and the 'sordid' activities in which I was no longer allowed to participate, I tried to create ways of living an easier existence in order to manipulate my life around these constraints. Things naturally evolve and as the OCD got its hold on me, I began to develop it further. I completed tasks in cycles of numbers, so if the sequence ended anywhere near a six I would have to do the task again in order to steer clear of the devil. I then started having to do things in even numbers, to make sure I got back to the same position I started at; but six being an even number threw a real spanner in the works because I also needed to keep away from that dreaded number in order to complete the task successfully. So, it took a lot to keep me satisfied.

It is worth mentioning at this point that as messed up as I once appeared to be, I was still pretty content with my life, I just didn't know anything different. Only through acceptance and self-love have I managed to successfully rise above everything that was bringing me down. It's also not that hard to achieve when you know the path, which will all be discussed in the Self-Love chapter.

Ghosts were my childhood nightmare. I was absolutely petrified of anything to do with death and evil spirits. My fear was almost certainly instigated by my time at the Christian camp and didn't right itself until after I stopped attending. I don't think I ever saw one but I certainly convinced myself that every obscure noise I heard in the night, when I was sleeping at my parents old farmhouse in the deep, dark countryside, was a chilling ghost. Of course it wasn't, but I thought it was, and so nights weren't quite as relaxing for me as they are now. I remember always wanting my friends to stay over because I figured I was much safer if somebody else was in the room. Why is it that some people do see ghosts though, yet there is no conclusive evidence that they exist?

Fear has incredible potential for completely altering your sense of reality. It was my fear of God and the devil that prompted me to seek refuge in the Christian camp's teachings, which induced the all-encompassing OCD that prevented me from living a normal existence. The worst of it is that I don't think anyone close to me noticed the awkward, methodically instigated rituals that I used to perform, because I was acutely aware of how strange they were. Even my familiarity with the confusing, arcane roots of the problem didn't have the power to convince me to put an end to it, because I was so afraid that something horrific might happen if I was to stop. If my fear of a God I was told about when I was thirteen dictated the remainder of my childhood and made me collapse on the floor chanting obscure words, laugh and cry my eyes out without so much as a single drop of alcohol involved, it seems highly conceivable that other people's lives can also be completely transformed for the worse through whatever they may have been taught to fear.

In just the same way as an utmost belief in a positive outcome will make success far more likely than if you doubted it ever happening, if you are that afraid of ghosts and you have that much belief in them, chances are you most probably will see one when you are shivering under your duvet and peeking out to watch it lighting up your room. The brain is a masterfully powerful instrument, and thoroughly dependent on your belief system but there are indeed two sides to every coin. Don't get me wrong, there are some things you should be afraid of, like killer sharks or violent psychopaths. Realistically though, they are tangible things you can hopefully try to avoid. Fear helps you to achieve that; fight or flight is a naturally occurring response. So I'm not telling you to not be afraid of those things. It's the fear of illusive, mythological teachings of which you need to be wary.

Whatever your fear, it effectively incites a strong belief of its own. Bearing in mind the power that fear can have, think now of the power the same feelings could have on a positive scenario. Transfer the strong belief, minus the fear, to a

97

warm, loving and enlightening situation and you will have developed a connection with your inner, higher self, that can only enhance your life. Believe, with the same fervency that you fear failure, that you really can study excruciatingly hard and learn enough to pass the exams that will help you achieve your life's ambition. Believe, instead of feeling helpless, that you have the ability and drive to set up a homeless shelter this coming winter, in order to give the less fortunate people in your local area a step up to help themselves. Whatever you put your mind to, with enough belief, you can achieve it. I am not talking about a strong desire, either, I am talking about a categorical, implicit, forthright, head-over-heels belief that you will be able to achieve something. The slightest doubt will not make it an easy path to follow, so research the criteria and the challenges you need to confront, know that you can do it and push. Absolute and final. You do obviously have to be vaguely realistic with your goals, if you are currently clinically obese and the next Olympics are in a couple of months, it's pretty unrealistic that you'll achieve your life goal of winning a gold medal in the cycling. Within reason, anyone can do anything. Belief becomes knowledge that can be trusted and on that basis, you can finally admire yourself.

Mind Games ♫

After revisiting my youthful years, the religious indoctrination to which I was subjected at the Christian camps, and looking at how open to new ideas my evolving mind was, it became apparent to me that it is much harder to change a grown man's mind than it is to develop it from a young age. Everyone within the teaching world knows this, which can explain why most children who are brought up within a certain religious doctrine generally stick with it until they reach an age to think logically, for themselves. That's how mindfulness and meditation are so different, there is nothing illogical about it, the proof of the pudding is in the eating.

I've shared with you the benefits of meditation, which will have hopefully brought home to you the impact it can have on absolutely anyone. The Dalai Lama knows this full well, stating that 'if every eight year old in the world is taught meditation, we will eliminate violence from the world within one generation.' So what then about teaching it to the young and seeing the effect it can have on flourishing minds?

I wholeheartedly want mindfulness meditation to be taught to the young for its positive benefits; I don't, however, advocate any prompt that potentially scaremongers the young into believing in it. Neither can I, for one second, support any whimsical discipline that will implant and ignite 'God-given' superiority over anyone else on this planet – a notion which, in itself, creates war.

A school board in San Francisco, was looking for ways to help the troubled teens that attended classes within the area. After much deliberation, they decided to implement a programme called 'quiet time', whereby the children were given two fifteen-minute slots a day in which to quietly practise transcendental meditation. After four years of running 'quiet time' the results speak for themselves. Within the whole school, there was a 79% decrease in suspensions, a 93.8% increase in attendance, and an increase of four in the grade point average. [3]

Obviously it's good to know about religious beginnings but maybe slide that across to the history class and swap religious education for meditation? I'd love to think that this book will change the lives of everyone on this planet and before long the world will be free from war and I will have won the Nobel Peace Prize. I'm not holding my breath. If enough open-minded people do read this, though, and understand the importance of self-love, then maybe they will be able to recommend the addition of meditation classes to all schools. If that happens, just imagine the possibilities.

In the *Is God an Illusion?* book that I mentioned earlier, Leonard Mlodinow, the stubborn atheist, remarks that scientists employ 'precise objective measurements and precise objective concepts for good reason' [4] and that they seek to ensure that their 'measurements and concepts are not influenced by love, trust, faith, beauty, awe, compassion etc.' What he fails to ever recognise, however, is that those exact feelings are what humanity depends on to evolve into a more enlightened species.

He's right to highlight the necessary absence of these feelings and traits during experiments, because explanations must be guided by truth, which cannot be what we inwardly want to hear with peace and love as our benchmark. We don't want the results of an experiment to be influenced by the invisible thought processes of the scientist but we equally shouldn't want some of the essential elements of what we need in life to be swept under the carpet in favour of hard science. I'm not trying to prove to anyone that there is a God. I am, however, providing conclusive evidence that spirituality, or maybe just mindfulness, is here with us, it works, it's evident through its effects and there are no scientific experiments that can falsify its presence.

I haven't made up the stories that have put me where I am today, they're not fantastically mystical like a large proportion of religious texts, so I have written them down in the hope that more people will take note of my progress, adopt a similar attitude and then slowly make the world a better place. It's not a magic pill by any means, it takes dedication, hard work and most importantly, belief. Science has proved a lot of things that have not only helped to advance the human race phenomenally but have also helped develop our understanding of how we first arrived on this planet. Science shouldn't, however, try to brush under the carpet the presence of a tenet that has helped and continues to help hundreds of thousands of people every single day – and nor should we do this to religions.

Losing My Religion ♩

Literally a couple of weeks before sending this book to be published, I went to visit some friends in Worcestershire. They drove us to a delightful setting from where we took their dogs for a walk in the hills. Upon arrival, I suddenly realized that we were in the exact place I used to go to on summer walks with the Christian camp, suddenly transporting me back almost twenty years to my previously fearful mindset. I realized that I needed to revisit the community to finally lay to rest the silent thoughts that had troubled me for years.

With a little help from Google Maps we eventually found the commune. I nervously stepped out of the car and approached the entrance, my heart thudding. I noticed a slight, middle-aged woman wearing a blue overall and walked towards her.

'Hello, can I help you?'

'Hi, yes...ummmmm....' I paused for a moment to regain my composure. 'I used to come here many years ago for the camping holidays that you used to host'. I noticed the penny dropping in her eyes, leading to a much more friendly connection between us.

'Oh yes – what is your name?'

After telling her who I was, she said that she remembered my name, gave me hers, and then told me about the group leaders who were still living there and all the ones who had left. A few that I remembered still remained and she managed to call them over to come and say hello. I didn't recognise any of them, not that I expected myself to (owing to the head injury) but we all got chatting about the people and times we had shared and a true sense of genuine love and enthusiasm encompassed us all.

We chatted for about half an hour before I asked if I could walk around the property and go back to the barn where all the events used to take place. The camps had all finished many years ago but despite the barn no longer being full of bustling teenagers, and despite there being no tents in the field, it all seemed pretty identical, which brought about a massive sense of nostalgia; no remorse and no fear.

The group leaders were still just as approachable. Although I no longer practise the same religious doctrine as they do, the love that we all still managed to disseminate amongst ourselves in that short meeting, after so many years, was testament to the mindful approach that they, and almost all religions, undertake in order to distribute a common good to which everyone on this planet has access.

During my chat with the group leaders, I mentioned this book to the woman who had originally welcomed me and told her how I had written about some of the negative effects the camp had on me (even though I continued to attend for seven years running). I didn't tell her this to make her feel guilty; I just wanted her to know that my mindset was not in the right place to fully appreciate the results that they were experiencing from their Christianity. To my amazement, she apologized profusely to me for all the hurt I had unintentionally received and I noticed tears in her eyes. At that moment, I properly understood that regardless of your extended beliefs, mindfulness encompasses absolutely everybody if your heart is in the right place. The love that she still shared after all those years was testament to her belief and resounding faith.

Like Humans Do ♫

We, as a species, have evolved extraordinarily since the dawn of time, so maybe, even though there are currently no scientific ways to measure it, our consciousness is ever so slowly developing. I'm not talking about the man-made third dimension of consciousness that is rapidly encapsulating the human race into a computer-driven society, I'm talking about a sixth sense that animals far more evidently have (perhaps in part because they haven't lost their minds to the internet) allowing them to instinctively sense danger from around the corner, and act accordingly. Yes, the internet is the epitome of the technological revolution, which I have no doubt will continue to help and advance the human race for ever more. Nevertheless it has become a common tool yet is preventing us from advancing, developing and evolving our innate consciousness into a power far greater than any app or programme will ever be able to accomplish. But what exactly is consciousness?

Scientists and spiritualists alike have for many years fought over the understanding of consciousness. It is, to all intents and purposes, a condition of your brain, but no one involved in the ongoing exploration of it has ever been able to comprehend, fathom or pinpoint the anatomical location from which it stems. Its main purpose is survival – the awareness of danger and then the ability to act accordingly; but the genius of mankind has way overshot our innate ability to simply envision risk, and has consequently developed a formidable understanding of a lot of what this world has to offer us; except, of course, the reasoning behind why we have evolved our consciousness in the first place. Although scientists can't prove it, they insist that it is a biological function within the brain which cannot be separated from it. 'The hard problem of consciousness (Chalmers 1995) is the problem of explaining the relationship between physical phenomena, such as brain processes, and experience (i.e., phenomenal consciousness, or mental states/events with phenomenal qualities or qualia). 21 May 2009'.[5] Spiritualists, however, firmly believe that the mind and body are in actual fact detached from one another and that our consciousness has the ability to transcend time and space. Consciousness is a spirit, or a soul, if you will.

Like spirituality, the essence of every religion denotes a separation of body and soul. As we are all destined to die at some point, we as a species have developed an intelligence that far outreaches every other living organism on the planet, an intelligence which can't settle for the concept of a definitive end in death. It is this that has led to the idea of a soul leaving our bodies when we die. But how realistic is this belief?

As a spiritualist, I should be gunning for the separate mind and body side of the argument but I can definitely understand the scepticism held by a large proportion of the human race. I still think that the mind is incredibly powerful, with the ability to achieve far more than we can ever imagine. That doesn't mean, however, that it has to be an entity separate from the brain. The two distinctions have no definitive bearing on what our minds can achieve.

It would make perfect sense for consciousness to be evolving, as speculated, because, after all, our bodies have have been doing just that for the last few millennia.

Derren Brown is one of the UK's most successful psychological illusionists. He presented a fascinating show for Channel 4, in 2016, entitled Miracle. He is a professed atheist and, following on from another show he aired in 2010 (in which he managed to train a complete novice to perform as an evangelical missionary healing the sick), he posed as a faith healer, to show that it is not so much a God that performs miracles but our minds that allow them to happen (if only temporarily). Through using an array of mystical lighting and sounds, he transformed the theatre into a holy shrine-like chasm, from which he instilled in the majority of the audience the belief that he had the power to heal them from their troubling woes. As the lighting flashed and the speakers reverberated, his words and the visual effects set forth a massive release of dopamine into their brains, which consequently, if only for a short while, expunged the problems they were experiencing.

By the release of certain chemicals into our brains, as explained by Derren Brown after the act, our bodies can overcome and diminish a variety of different conditions in an instant. Other things take time though, so what about them? Since the dawn of scientific medicinal testing, scientists have given a selection of test subjects placebo pills, to check the reliability of the results for the drug being tested. It just so happens that in many cases, a few of the patients who have been given the placebo pill end up making a full recovery from whatever they were being treated for.[6]

A maintenance of the utmost belief is the answer, regardless of whether or not a specific God to which you're praying exists, or the pills you are taking are merely tablets made of sugar. The next step in developing this is to work out exactly how to knowingly instigate it. Many cases exist of individuals who have gone down the solely holistic route, only to be completely overcome by whatever it is they had been trying to eliminate from their body; proving to the staunch scientists of the world that there are no cures available other than through scientifically tested medicine, consequently drawing a veil of confusion and doubt over spiritualist beliefs.

Pure Shores ♩

I've talked about reaching your inner, higher self, but what is this? Although there may be conflicting arguments relating to the specific dwelling place of our consciousness it is still, no matter which side ends up taking the higher ground, a permanent, paramount and ever-present part of the human condition. Owing to its importance, it also holds the key to the deepest most revered state we can all reach, in order to fully transcend, which is that of pure consciousness.

Pure consciousness is about not caring. This doesn't mean not caring about people and happiness and love but rather not caring about the everyday things that bring you down for no plausible reason, like needless arguments, football results, how your hair looks, your next door neighbour having a better car than you, the way someone spoke to you or how they looked at you, flatulence (if anybody is in the room with me for too long).

Up until we reach a specific age, normally about three, we all experience pure consciousness. Pure consciousness and happiness are not too dissimilar from each other, which coincides with the point I made previously about children having to start searching for happiness after a certain age because they are no longer happy with themselves. I'll be going back to this in the self-love chapter.

Pure consciousness and happiness run hand-in-hand, so to reach it you need to be fully aware of how to assess it for yourself. I recently came across a fantastic analogy to describe this concept, written by a spiritual teacher called Rupert Spira. He likens our minds to the Earth and the Sun and the way in which when the earth turns away from the sun, consequently experiencing darkness, it is similar to the way in which our minds are turned towards objects and away from pure consciousness. This is when darkness and unhappiness is experienced. Like the sun, happiness is ever present and always shining with the same intensity. He goes on to explain that the brightness of the sun is only diminished by the angle of the earth, which coincides with how there are only degrees of happiness for our mind-made selves, or egos, dependent on the extent to which we are facing away from the source. He then likens the way in which the mind derives temporary and partial happiness from objects, relationships and situations, to the dim light reflected by the moon, in reality emitted from the sun. In the same way as the light from the moon is filtered light from the sun, our happiness and pure consciousness is filtered through temporary objects and relationships, through our minds. To falsely mistake objects, relationships and states as the source of pure happiness, is like mistaking the moon as the source of light. They are real but they are not the source and they are not pure: 'To experience happiness the mind need only face its source'.[7]

Having researched this concept of pure consciousness at great length, other than the previous interpretation that I just mentioned, I have found very few sources that convey it in a simple way. Yes, it is an incredibly significant and vital process for reaching your inner self, but if the spiritual gurus and teachers of the world deem it such a necessary step for transformation, the least they can do is document it for us in as transparent and straightforward a way as possible. Inner peace and higher being should not be a practise only reserved for the spiritual elite, it should be simplified in such a way that it can be reached and understood by every single willing person on this planet. For that very reason I will try to explain to you the fundamental techniques required in order to gain an understanding of spiritual enlightenment, without the plethora of jargon that is usually associated with it.

Pure consciousness, known as a central psycho-spiritual state of consciousness, has received adequate evidence to show that it is a healthy, life enhancing, self development technique. In a book called The Wise Heart by Jack Kornfield,[8] he mentions that 'When we rest in consciousness we become unafraid of the changing conditions of life'. But what is it, and how can it be reached? It boils down to transcendence. I've mentioned this term many times before but I now want to take it apart for you. Trans comes from the Latin 'across, beyond, through' and scandare means 'to climb'. When you achieve transcendence you effectively traverse all limitations, or move beyond physical needs and realties. Beyond our everyday engagement, meditation is a trusted technique for reaching inner silence, a retreat from all the hustle and bustle that life throws at us.

Although you may not have known it at the time, the starting point to accessing pure consciousness has been described in the Kindfulness chapter. By following the later chapters on the subjects of love and then happiness, you will be well on your way to accessing it. To reach this state of pure joy is not hard, you just have to understand and want it, which absolutely anyone can do. Pure consciousness is about maintaining the state for longer than a few seconds, to receive the benefits associated with it. The qualities, although subtle at first, will accumulate the further down the line you go and are as follows (derived from Deepak Chopra's account, in Is God an Illusion?)[9]:

Pure consciousness is:

- Silent and peaceful. You are free of inner conflict, anger and fear.

- Self sufficient. You are comfortable simply being here. The mind is not restless in its quest for stimulation.

- Fully awake. Mental alertness and freshness. The mind is no longer dull or fatigued.

- Infinite potential. You are no longer bound by fixed habits and beliefs. The greater your experience of pure potential, the more creative you become.

- Self-organized. You are experiencing this quality when things fall into place of their own accord. There is less struggle to force different parts of life to harmonise, because you are more in tune with the natural harmony that runs through everything.

- Spontaneous. Breaking free of old constraints, whatever they may be, makes you feel safer about expressing who you are and what you want without constraints. This is the state of absolute freedom, which you experience whenever you feel liberated.

- Dynamic. You experience this quality when you feel you can fully embrace life. You have the energy and the will to do great things.

- Blissful. This is the route of happiness and its highest expression. Any surge of happiness, whatever the cause, is a taste of bliss. An orgasm is blissful, but so is compassion. Every experience of love can also be traced back to its origins in bliss.

- Knowing. It contains the answers to all questions and, more crucially, the practical knowledge needed for unfolding the universe, the human body, and the mind. Any experience of intuition, insight or truth taps into this quality.

- Whole. You experience this quality when your life makes sense and you feel a part of nature; you are at home simply by being alive.

Nutrition

I cannot remember the books I've read any more than the meals I have eaten; even so, they have made me

– *Ralph Waldo Emerson*

An important step on the way to attaining your desired state of self-love and sustained happiness is learning to develop, control and transmit that developing happiness through eating the right things. This is not merely about losing weight, it's about eating the things you need to maintain a healthy lifestyle. If you do want to lose weight, this chapter will put you well on your way to your coveted physical state.

Nutrition and healthy eating have not always been a subject close to my heart. In fact, before learning to love myself, I happily ate anything and everything that came into my path. They say the body is a temple, which most certainly was not the case for me, unless, of course there are temples dedicated to kebabs, chips and copious amounts of cheap alcohol.

I didn't like being tubby but the allure of a pasty and a pint of cider far outweighed my drive to stay in shape. When I tell people now that I used to be fairly overweight, it is often met with sheer disbelief, now that I have an entirely godlike physique...well, okay, it might not be quite that good, but then that's never been what I was aiming for. I am now fit and healthy and no longer feel ashamed of my body. I'm 6'2" and I now weigh 13–13.5 stone, depending on my mood. Back at university, however, in my chunky days, I remember hitting 17.5 stone, which gave me a BMI around the 31 mark, up in the obese range. I was fat and I hated myself. I thought I hated myself because I was fat but I now know that the eating and drinking were just ways for me to forget about deeper underlying problems. I'll tell you more about these later and how they had elevated my weight to catastrophic (in my eyes) proportions. I was living in a vicious circle of self-hate and eating.

As we'll explore further in the Self-Control chapter (focusing on addictions), certain 'enjoyable' activities release the naturally occurring neurotransmitter, dopamine, into your brain, which in turn makes you feel calm and good about yourself. I certainly wasn't addicted, but I came to trust in the feel-good sensations I received from eating too much food, to cover up my awareness of all the other things I felt were wrong with my life. The simple result was that I put on an unnecessary amount of weight, which only made me more unhappy.

I did find a way to temporarily lose the flab every so often, by taking part in endurance races like marathons and quadrathlons (swimming, running, cycling and kayaking). I would get myself into a routine of hardcore training, which had the bonus effect of suppressing my appetite for kebabs and burgers, allowing me to slim down to a normal weight. As soon as whichever event had passed, though, I always regained my former weight and reverted back to my slovenly ways.

If there wasn't an impending endurance race to take part in, I occasionally fought the bulge with a variety of fad diets. The majority worked in the short term; I lost weight fast but as soon as I got bored of eating paper and feeling pretty shit about myself due to lack of nutrition, I always found my way back to the greasy kebabs.

Running used to be my get out of jail free card when my favourite pair of jeans no longer fitted me. Skiing off the cliff and shattering my ankle put an end to that past time, owing to the lack of cartilage I now have around the joint. Instead, I got heavily into cycling, which saw me riding twenty to thirty mile circuits around the countryside, six days a week, when I was living with my parents. This increased my fitness no end. The problem with being in the country, however, was that I was struggling to develop Tier One and socialise with my friends. If I moved to London, though, I knew that I couldn't cycle like I did in the countryside, for fear of being mown down by a lorry. If I couldn't cycle to keep fit, I would eventually retrace my slovenly lifestyle and become lazy and fat again. This confused and self-punishing mindset held me back from independence for some time.

Keep Young and Beautiful ♫

The media likes to stress that you can only achieve your desired weight through healthy eating and exercise. It's true that staying fit is a way of not only keeping your body healthy but your mind, as well. Exercise is another generator of dopamine and serotonin, the latter of which reduces depressive tendencies. But I could write a whole other book on exercise and its positive effects. What I am interested in here is this. Delve into that media proclamation a little more closely and you will find that your weight is controlled by what you put into your mouth, and when. Exercise helps to speed things up when it comes to weight loss but only if you're eating the correct foods. What I didn't know back in my heavy eating and heavy exercise days (and what I have discovered through researching for this book), is that the food you decide to eat is of fundamental importance to your general wellbeing. So I urge you to emphatically take control of what you eat.

As will be discussed in the chapter on self love, if you wouldn't treat a child the way you treat yourself, then you're doing something wrong. I am fairly certain that I would be had up for child cruelty if I fed my kids kebabs, chips, pizzas and beer every night, so I needed to stop doing it to myself.

A couple of years before my eventual move to London, my older sister, Bex, married a charming Australian chap called Greg. I don't want to praise him too much (he is an Aussie, after all) but he is an incredible asset to our family and much loved. Although he is fanatical about watching inane sports on the television, he is also an incredible cook and passionate about nutrition and the scientific evidence that promotes wellness through food. I can remember one particular evening many years ago, having supper at

Bex and Greg's, cooked by his own fair hand. It was only something very simple, chicken thighs with sweet potato, carrots and spinach, but it was lovely. I did what I always did and removed the delicious crunchy, brown, crackled chicken skin from the flesh, placing it at the side of my plate. Nothing wrong with that. Lots of people do it. Greg, however, after devouring his, questioned why I had done such an absurd thing. I instantly told him that I didn't actually want to be fat and that he should be careful of what he eats. The ensuing conversation was the impetus for my now very, and rightfully so, strong views on nutrition and wellness. I developed a massive interest in this topic. Coupled with my burgeoning desire to love myself, I discovered that the two – what you eat and how you feel about yourself – run hand in hand with each other.

The year I moved to London, as you will know, was the same year that I was introduced to meditation, mindfulness and everything that accompanies it. I may not have been willing to risk cycling the streets of London for fitness but I had another trick up my sleeve: my newly found desire to cultivate, nurture, love and care for myself. I could have joined a gym and carried on my cycling on a static bike but I was cash-strapped and I have never been able to get any enjoyment from sitting in a gym with lots of other sweaty, groaning, panting people. I was learning to love myself, not spectate and compete against a bunch of fitness fanatics. I was doing it for me and I was actually starting to enjoy being around myself, all alone, for the first time in many years.

To keep fit, I walked everywhere – and I mean everywhere. Not only was it a good way to fight the bulge, it also saved a lot of money and cultivated my geographical awareness of my new city. I may have turned up to the odd dinner party in a muck sweat (I walk hard and fast) but that was a small price to pay for being lean and clear-headed.

Bootylicious ♫

Although I could (and they can offer temporary results for some people), I'm not going to suggest a fad diet for you to follow, because they don't work. None of them do. I tried many in my fatty days and although some of them shed the excess weight in short spaces of time, they were quite frankly unhealthy things to frequent and impossible to continue for more than a few months. Every single fad diet I have come across either limits certain foods or prompts you to ingest unhealthy amounts of one particular fruit or vegetable or grain or whatever substance over which the media is going berserk at the time. But none of them work for life; they're not designed for that. Have you ever met anybody who used to be fat but has managed to keep the weight off by following the same fad diet they started twenty-odd years ago? I know you haven't, because no one ever has. If they had, it would have made the headline in every country and there would no longer be any fat people in the world. Sadly, there are hundreds of millions of overweight people and they, like the population, keep growing. The current inhabitants of the planet (minus a few tribes and countries that are at war or fighting famine) are the unhealthiest and fattest we have ever been and if we continue to grow at this current rate, who knows – the Earth might implode under our weight.

There are many people who have, at some point, been clinically obese but have since managed to lose the excess weight and live long, happy lives. They didn't do this through following some fad diet. They did it through perseverance, will power and, most importantly, observing the right things to eat at the right times. The remainder of this chapter will be devoted to teaching you the most fundamental approach to a healthy lifestyle, wellness and exceptional nutrition.

First of all, it is only right to point out that every one of us is completely different. Obviously we all look and behave differently but how we portion, digest and metabolise whatever substances that pass our lips every day is also completely different for everyone. Some diets work for some people and not for others – and vice versa. So to claim that one particular product, or food item, or technique, can change your life immeasurably is utter trite. Unless, of course, you are talking about ingesting something like cyanide before you go to bed tonight, which will definitely do something to you but then you won't be able to read the rest of this book tomorrow, so don't.

The food you consume is not solely for energy. It is meant to provide you with all the essential vitamins and minerals your body needs to function effectively. It is also meant to taste good and most importantly, it is meant to be enjoyed. If you go on a fad diet to lose weight, it'll be a bit of a pyrrhic victory if you achieve your desired goal after consuming only cabbage for 2 months solidly. You'll stink, your house will stink, you'll have terrible wind and you'll be sick of the sight of the stuff. This is an excellent example of a dreadful fad diet. I hope none of you have tried it. There are far better approaches to losing the belly, which will not only provide you with all the necessary, essential nutrients; they will taste good and you will enjoy them. In the same way as misery can feed misery (as described in the context of my own self-punishment/eating cycle), happiness can feed happiness; if your food makes you feel better about your body, your body, in turn will make you feel more positive about your food. You'll be well on your way to becoming that well-balanced, Timinological hero.

Heal the World ♫

So, if none of these diets work, what am I suggesting you do about it?

I, like anyone else, cannot claim that my wise words and techniques in this area are the answer to your problems but there is a considerable amount of scientific evidence to support what I have brought together here, coupled with first hand personal case studies conducted by yours truly. What I can confirm is that none of what I propose will induce any negative side effects (assuming you're not allergic to anything, in which case, be prudent).

It is through this chapter that every topic I cover within Timinology can be utilized specifically to help you achieve your desired weight and or nutrition plan. You can't expect to have the perfect body if you're not happy with your life, if you don't love yourself and if you don't even believe that you can achieve it. As you'll have learned by now, perseverance, dedication, mindfulness and belief are the foundation blocks to Timinology and to leading an optimal life. All I am trying to do is to make you and everyone who reads this realise that you have the ability to do anything if you are happy, you love yourself and you believe. Come back to this chapter once you have finished the book, in order to access the information again, through the eyes of a self-loving, gloriously happy, future You. At this point I will again stress the importance of mindfulness; it brings everything into perspective.

Whether you need to reconstruct your daily eating habits to lose weight, or simply in order to lead a healthier life, the following information that I am about to share is all scientifically justified to do just that and will hopefully inspire you to modify your culinary regimes, assuming you're not already doing it.

This is only one chapter and forms part of a holistic whole so I am not going to label and categorise every different detail of every type of diet. What I will do, however, is note down the basic, fundamental points for making a start to your new eating regime. You can then feel gloriously inspired to research the next level yourself and, in the same way as with your mindfulness, create a system that fits you, not the other way around.

As discussed, fad diets don't work in the long run and aren't intended to, they're merely a quick fix that won't last. It may sound rather drastic at first but along with everything else I have mentioned in this book, you need to alter your train of thought to properly adjust to a brand new lifestyle. It's not a diet, it's a lifestyle approach and the longer you do it, the more natural and easy it will be to follow. There is NO quick fix. You have to work at getting your body back to how it should be. When trying to adopt a new lifestyle, the majority of people get bored and are happy to just slip back into their old ways of living before giving it a chance. If that happens to you, you have to question your commitment and drive for becoming fit and healthy in the first place. If you don't want it, you won't achieve it. If you do, you will. That is a really negative way to look at it but hopefully it will spur you on to categorically commit yourself to your new lifestyle and to re-establish the fond love and affection for yourself that you deserve. I should just emphasise here that this is not about being 'thin'. It is about being healthy, in body as well as mind, to the point that is appropriate for you to feel good about yourself.

Let's deal with the common sense of dieting, first. The more you put in to your body, the more you need to burn off. There are established guidelines for the amount of energy required to fuel your body, relating to age, weight, sex, build and height. It's pretty simple. If you over-indulge on any particular day, you either need to eat less the following day, or partake in an exercise regime of sorts to burn it off. If you fail to do either of those two things, unless your body is incredible at metabolising, you are destined to gain a little bit of weight.

I read an excerpt from a book entitled *Changing Habits, Changing Lives*, by Cyndi O'Meara[1], an acclaimed Australian dietician. She puts forward the notion that practically everybody would change their lifestyle and diet if a doctor told them that they were going to die very soon unless they changed their eating habits. That's just it, many of us will die considerably sooner than you might think if we don't make a concerted effort to make sure the way we eat is healthy. Your diet is connected so intrinsically to your health, which impacts your every living moment.

The 'five a day' recommended fruit and vegetable consumption isn't a fabricated statistic to follow as and when you feel inclined. The vast amount of trusted scientific data from almost every health board in the world is geared towards making people realise the importance of the nutrients, vitamins and minerals that we can obtain from consuming said foodstuffs. It should actually be seven a day (it is in Australia), to comprehensively cater for as much of the goodness we should be receiving on a daily basis. Some recent studies have suggested as many as ten a day but five a day is more workable for the entire population (a bit like setting yourself a meditation target you can meet). Despite this, even that is very rarely met by the vast majority of people you talk to.

We, as a human race, should be shying away from foods created by technology and processing, instead welcoming and cherishing everything that nature provides, because therein lies the key to health and wellbeing. There is a plethora of different food groups that have a whole host of contrasting effects on our bodies, so it is imperative that you learn and understand how your body reacts to certain food types, before giving up on the chance to allow it to fulfil its potential.

Although, as we keep being told, cases of obesity have multiplied significantly in the last decade or so, we have also experienced a very positive and necessary food revolution by seeing the availability and inclusion, in the majority of our supermarkets, of almost every naturally-grown foodstuff from around the globe. There is so much readily available choice in fruit and vegetables – far more than in meat and processed foods – that you could probably eat different varieties for every day of the year and still not have tried everything. The stepping-stone to fulfilling the needs of your body is quite literally at your fingertips, so take heed of the glorious gifts on offer to you, which have never been so easily accessible as they are today, and start loving your body. If, in addition, you choose to eat seasonally, you're doing something good for local food suppliers and for the planet, too.

Health doesn't need to cost you more money than you already spend. If anything, you may find eating healthily reduces your outgoings on food. It costs nothing to learn about the extraordinary benefits natural produce can offer, yet many people are so stuck in their ways that they don't want to even contemplate a routine change that could significantly enhance their wellbeing, let alone actually do it.

I know that when I was overweight I still seemed pretty happy on the outside – but that was just a front to cover up my inner demons. I will get into trouble with a lot of my friends for saying this but our bodies aren't meant to be fat. You may very well seem to be the happiest and 'bubbliest' person your friends know but for those of you who are inwardly struggling with your weight, until you can confront your inner turmoil (as I'll explain in the Happiness chapter) you will never be able to develop a fond love for yourself and put an end to the over-eating and plus-sized jeans.

The biggest division between fat people and thin people hasn't got anything to do with money, even though that seems like a plausible excuse, it boils down solely to education and mindful awareness. There just needs to be some sort of collective nutrition hub that brings everyone together and explains the benefits and ease of eating well. But where? Maybe at a Timinology mindfulness retreat that brings everyone together?

Magic Beans ♫

As good as the media and supermarkets have been for igniting the much needed shake-up in the nutrition world, they are also very good at 'unintentionally' excluding the poorest of us, by proclaiming the boundless benefits of superfoods and organic crops, while merrily hiking up their prices to such preposterous heights that it only leaves the wealthier half of the population able to benefit from them. Superfoods are, frequently, foods that have received super PR. There are categorically no proven health benefits to choosing a cheaper alternative to whichever gem of a produce you have been told will offer the elixir of life.

I watched an incredible programme on the BBC called The Truth About Healthy Eating [2], which put 5 'superfoods' up against their cheaper alternatives. The results are fascinating and prove that with enough positive PR you can raise the price of anything. The documentary contrasted the claimed health benefits of goji berries, chia seeds, coconut oil, kale and quinoa, against their 'budget' counterparts.

Goji Berries: Although high in vitamin C, which is their selling point, there was no noticeable difference between their levels and those of a strawberry or even a bag of frozen summer fruits, which falls under one of your five a day and costs a fraction of the price.

Chia Seeds: Apparently are a good source of Omega-3, yet no difference was found between the amount released by sesame seeds, pumpkin seeds, sunflower seeds and linseeds, which are all much cheaper.

Coconut Oil: Claimed to be a 'good source of saturated fat'. I must admit, I have fallen for this particular 'superfood' but I do quite like the coconut flavour I get when using it for cooking a stir fry. When contrasted with its oily counterparts, though, it scored no better than some of its rivals. Interestingly, rapeseed oil, which already has a good name for itself, is quite often what you get if you look on the back of most supermarket own-brand vegetable oils; so be investigative when purchasing your oils. Many people swear by olive oil – to the point of dosing up on an eggcup a day of the golden elixir, even if they're not cooking with it. It's great for your hair, skin and nails amongst other things too.

Kale: Low in calories, high in fibre and low in fat. Having said that, so is cabbage or spring greens, to look to its most similar counterparts. When it comes to flavour, however, I much prefer kale, so on that front, it wins every time for me; it's also not terribly expensive and in some cases can actually be cheaper than its peers.

Quinoa: Releases carbs slowly and has lots of proteins but then so do pearl barley and spinach. Depending on whether or not you know about the plight of the Bolivian farmers [3] and how the global distribution of Quinoa is affecting their economy, it might alter your opinion on this 'superfood'.

The survey was conducted for the BBC by Reading University's Dr. Gunter Kuhnle and the programme was presented by Fiona Philips. They spent £36 on the superfoods but only £6 on the cheaper alternatives. Conclusive proof that you do not need loads of money to eat healthily.

Dear Doctor ♫

A lot of dieticians and nutritionists tend to over-complicate the whole issue of weight loss/gain and fat, making it a minefield of perplexing facts that only qualified professionals are able to navigate. Thankfully, however, there are a selection of these professionals – one being a friend of mine called Rosie – who help to tear away the confusingly detailed limitations attached to this gargantuan life issue. Rosie organises presentations, normally conducted with a set number of highly qualified experts, with the intention of dispelling a lot of the rumours surrounding nutrition and to bring about a much broader and more scientific general understanding of one of the most prevalent topics of our lives.

Organic vs non-organic

The last presentation of Rosie's that I attended had a Q&A session at the end, during which the question arose of whether organic vegetables are actually any better than generic vegetables. According to a research study published in the Journal of Science, Food and Agriculture [4], there is in fact no clear evidence that organic food has higher nutritional value than food grown by non-organic methods – much like the scenario of the superfoods. The question of pesticides and preservatives and all of the other things that go with large-scale modern farming is a different matter but this does not affect the nutritional value of the produce. Organic farmers are doing great things for sustainability and the environment, which are good things to support but if you're worried about nutrition and you don't have enough money to spend on the organic variety, you're not missing out on vitamins.

Detoxify

Another of the presentation's hot topics, needing the trusted opinion of a professional to dispel the myths surrounding it, was that of detox dieting. Another fad that has received enough consummate PR to elevate it to a dietary must, it is in actual fact an exercise that provides the consumer with minimal benefits. The previously mentioned BBC documentary assembled two different groups of people to test the effectiveness of detox dieting over one week. The first group were prescribed a traditional balanced diet, consisting of meat, fish, pasta, rice, fruit, veg, eggs, dairy and wholemeal bread, with the odd glass of wine and cup of coffee (just to represent a normal diet). The other group (the not-so-lucky ones) were effectively banned from the majority of the first group's diet and asked to eat raw and steamed veg (not so bad), with one daily portion of rice or quinoa, and steamed fish (their only meat) every other day. They were given detox tea or coconut water to drink twice a day in an apparent bid to boost the liver, which is our bodies own detoxifier. They also got a daily boost of hot water, lemon, maple syrup and cayenne pepper, which supposedly cleanses the digestive system.

For a full week, the participants stuck to their prescribed diets and underwent an array of tests comparing their liver function, heart rate, skin health, appetite and general well being, to see if the detox diet had any evident benefits.

The results favoured the traditional healthy diet group, showing far more positive functioning in their liver and heart and healthier weight and appetite. The detox dieters only benefited slightly – from healthier skin. The conclusion was that healthy, balanced dieting is the optimum way of living your life.

Pills

When it comes to getting the correct amount and balance of vitamins and minerals for your body to function as healthily as possible, is it really necessary to prescribe yourself a plethora of supplements? We, as a nation, now spend in excess of £300million a year on vitamins and fish oils, the biggest money spinners being multivitamins. Surely if we are spending that amount of money on such necessary nutriments, we can't be wrong...can we?

Naveed Sataar, Professor of Metabolic Medicine at the University of Glasgow, has studied this topic. He has found that, assuming you're not eating chronically unhealthily, taking multivitamins has no added benefit to your overall health and consuming extra doses to try to increase the storage of anything will not boost what you already have. Multivitamin trials have also found that they are conclusively ineffective at preventing heart disease, cancer or any other form of chronic disease[5] – where, by contrast, the food

121

sources in which they can be found are effective. Other research has also indicated, in extreme circumstances, that the unnecessary consumption of some vitamin pills, in a bid to stay as healthy as possible, can actually put you at risk of developing lung or skin cancer.

When it comes down to it, if you know you're not eating a healthy balanced diet, no amount of supplements will be able to boost your health and fend off illnesses due to your inability to look after yourself. So the best way to protect and look after your body is to eat a healthy diet.

Meat

Meat has been receiving a lot of bad press recently, with the World Health Organisation (WHO) revealing that some meats have the ability to cause cancer and are linked to heart disease.[6] 98% of people in the UK eat meat, with the average annual consumption equating to around 54kg. With such an abundance of it being consumed, surely it can't be as bad as its made out to be?[7]

Lets take a steak, for example. Nutritionally, 100g provides us with: 1% Calcium, 1% Vitamin D, 5% Magnesium, 13% Iron, 25% Vitamin B-6 and 36% Vitamin B-12, which, apart from the Calcium, Vitamin D and Magnesium, provide us with sufficiently high levels of the required vitamins needed for a healthy lifestyle.

Processed meats, however, have received the worst press of late, with the WHO professing that they are a definite cause of bowel cancer.[8] What exactly is processed meat, though?

Meat is classed as processed when something has been added to it prior to consumer purchase (that something could be flavouring, salt, sugar or preservatives); or it has been modified in some way to make it last longer or to change its taste. Most types of meat are available in a processed form but the main provider of it is the pig. From the humble pig we get our most common forms of processed meats – ham, sausages, salami and the one thing that can turn even the most fervent of vegetarians: bacon.

To process a bit of shop-bought bacon, the joint needs to be cured by adding a mixture of preservatives to it, to extend its shelf life. Salt, sugar and sodium nitrite are added to the curing brine of the joint before leaving it to infuse for a number of weeks. Sodium nitrite is the only known preventative of the bacterium Clostridium botulinum, which can be extremely toxic to human beings, leading to a disease known as botulism, a deadly form of food poisoning. Sodium nitrite is the main ingredient at the centre of the health warnings about processed meat, although its presence has no detrimental effects to the nutrients contained within the meat prior to processing.

Sodium nitrite is used to protect us from the bacteria that forms with the food going off. Despite this, it is also a potentially harmful substance when it reacts with our stomach acids and merges with the meat, forming compounds that are cancer causing. The WHO suggests that there is an 18% chance of cultivating a cancerous reaction to this. [9] There is extensive research being carried out to replace sodium nitrite with a harmless substitute.

Risk analysts have suggested that eating two rashers of bacon is likely to shorten your life expectancy by the same amount as smoking three cigarettes. A sobering thought. You have to ask yourself, is processed meat worth the risk?[10]

What about the health risks of unprocessed red meat? No processing and therefore no nitrite. Easy? No, although the WHO doesn't put it in the same category as processed meat, it still believes it is 'probably' cancer causing. It is currently recommend that we eat no more than 70g (somewhere equivalent to the weight of two decks of playing cards) per day of either processed meat or fresh red meat, in order to give us the maximum nutritional benefit while limiting the risk of cancer. It doesn't, however, limit our intake of white meat. So you can eat as much chicken as you like.

So there's cancer but what about heart disease? The link between red meat and heart disease is well known, so in order to find out how much meat is actually safe to eat, a three-month experiment was conducted at Nottingham

University, by Professor Andy Salter[11], to test whether cutting down the consumption of meat has the power to slow down or prevent heart disease. Forty volunteers who took part in the experiment were restricted to eating only half of their normal consumption of processed and red meats, which, for some of them, was quite a considerable amount. The other half continued eating as normal. They were all given blood tests throughout the experiment to measure any changes in cholesterol levels. The results found that by halving the consumption of red meat in your diet, levels of saturated fat in their blood significantly lowered, thereby reducing the Low-density Lipoprotein (LDL – bad cholesterol) and reducing your risk of heart disease.

The quantity of red meat consumed has actually dropped quite remarkably over the last fifty years, with lamb going down 60% and beef by 25%.[12] We are, however, eating substantially more chicken; in fact, a whopping 335% more now than we did forty years ago,[13] owing to the introduction of battery farms and the like. There is a deluge of different chickens available to buy, from the cheap and cheerful supermarket value range, all the way up to the organic, free range or corn-fed chicks. The way they are reared obviously has a massive impact on the welfare of the bird but if we sideline that (fundamental) aspect and concentrate on the nutritional state of the meat, is there a significant difference?

Nutritionist Dr. Laura Wireless conducted an experiment to uncover the health benefits and risks, if any, of eating five different types of chicken. The fat content was measured between a cheap supermarket chicken, a corn-fed bird, a free range supermarket chicken, a top end organic chicken and a forage diet farm bird.

Surprisingly, even though there is a shockingly huge price difference between the cheapest and most expensive, there was very little fat content difference between all of the birds; the corn fed one having ever so slightly the highest and the free range one having ever so slightly the lowest. When it came to assessing the fatty acids, with Omega-3 being beneficial and Omega-6 being detrimental, the corn-fed chicken's ratio of the two was slightly less beneficial compared with the free range and the cheapest of the bunch, making the corn fed chicken the one you should avoid if you're looking for a low-fat meat. Which is great if you want to save some money. Overall, though, chicken is a lean meat and low in saturated fat.

If you find chicken a bit boring and don't want to risk the potential dangers of red meat, offal (the organs of the animal you normally devour), is not only substantially more nutritious than the rest of the body (over 50% in some cases), it is also very cheap. It used to be the staple of the British diet, in the form of pies and the like, but since the introduction of cheap fast food it has all but vanished from our everyday menus, declining in consumption by an incredible 88% in the last 20 years. Some offal is available from supermarkets but the best option is to try nipping into your local butcher to pick up a bag of offal for next to nothing – good butchers will be willing to share cooking advice and recipes, too, if you're feeling nervous about the idea.

Fat Bottomed Girls ♫

Back to fat. As recently as only a few years ago, the media, government and any ill-informed well wisher (myself included), would have told you that consumption of fat is the reason people are overweight, period. It's in the name. People were fat because they ate too much of it. Thankfully, it's not quite that simple, which means that we can indeed eat the fatty skin from a roast chicken or devour a glass of full fat milk, without having to worry about adding an extra tyre to your midriff or keeling over before your time. Not only this, we need healthy fats in our diet.

For millennia humans have been eating fat without any weight gain issues at all (do you recall any fat people in cave paintings?). It is only today that obesity is a full scale epidemic but it is the mainstream, large-scale food producers that are to blame. We, as a society, have been trained to fear the very mention of such an essential dietary requirement and, as such, buy low-fat alternatives in a bid to steer clear of the apparent evil. It's not evil, though, and until the whole world can finally understand the intrinsic importance of fat, we will continue to do the opposite of what our bodies need when it comes to fats.

It is slowly becoming evident that since the advent of the false assumption that fat is evil, manufacturers have cleverly managed to disguise the taste of fat with sugar, thereby eliminating its apparent malevolence with a sweet poison that we are only now beginning to understand. Before I confront the stronghold that sugar has over us, let me first categorise fats. Yes, some are bad, so you will do well to avoid them, but the bad fats are all manufactured fats, hence the lack of obesity in former generations.

For as long as I can remember, fat has always been the supposed driving force behind the weight problems of the world. The fact that it bears the same name as the end result of eating too much of it, doesn't really give it a good one. If it received the same kind of PR that some high-ranking fad diets (Atkins, Dukan) have been fortuitously given, we would be able to turn around, gradually, the weight issues of the world. Here's an idea. Let's call fat, 'mirth'. It's not a particularly pretty word, much like fat, but it means 'laughter', which is what people might experience if they stop seeing it as the driving force behind their weight troubles. It won't bring joy to all the weight-loss food manufacturers, though, and as they have the money and the power to control the world's views on fat, don't expect to be given a stocking full of 'mirth' for Christmas, quite yet.

Big Fat Lie ♫

There are two main types of fat. Unsaturated fats, predominantly found in foods from plants and vegetables (almonds, avocados, vegetable oil, olive oil, walnuts, sardines, seeds, flax seeds, salmon, macadamia nuts and the like) and saturated fats, mainly found in animal products (meat, and dairy, as well as nuts, coconut, chocolate) have both played a pivotal role in nurturing and evolving our bodies, brains and nervous systems into the fantastically structured beings we are today. These fats contribute to a healthy liver, enhanced immune system, depression of tumour growth, hormone production, successful blood clotting, satiety (when we feel appropriately full) and the transport around the body of essential fatty acids. None of these things would be possible without these fats.

Have you ever wondered why you don't feel full on a fat free diet? The satiety your body reaches after eating enough isn't an accident. Your body knows when it has replenished the stocks needed to function correctly and naturally tells you so. If you're on some fad juice diet, of course you're not going to feel full, because without fat, your body can't distribute the essential compounds you're ingesting. You'll find your body will continue to insist on more food until it gets it. In the short term, it will use up its fat reserves, which is why fad diets sometimes appear to work in the first instance. Your body, however, cannot continue to function without input of more good fats, which is why it's tiring, miserable and ultimately unsustainable remaining on those diets.

Cholesterol

Cholesterol is a waxy substance, made in the body by the liver but also found in some foods such as egg yolks. It plays a pivotal role in the function of every cell and is also needed to make vitamin D, bile for digestion and some hormones. Too much cholesterol, however, can increase your risk of getting heart and circulatory diseases. Cholesterol is distinguished between 'good' HDL (High Density Lipoprotein) and 'bad' LDL (Low Density Lipoprotein), depending on the density of the protein used to carry it around the blood. The good stuff is protective, whereas the bad stuff compiles to form a gloopy substance in your blood.

Although I am telling you both saturated and unsaturated fats are fine, health boards have consistently favoured unsaturated fats over saturated fats. But why? Unsaturated fats, both polyunsaturated (omega-3 fatty acids, fish, sunflower oil, corn oil, soybean oil) and monounsaturated (avocado, olive oil, canola oil, peanut oil and sesame oil) are categorized by the number of bonds between the carbon atoms present in the fat, accentuated by the solidity the fat exhibits upon refrigeration (monounsaturated fats tend to be rigid at lower temperatures). These unsaturated fats have been linked to reducing LDL cholesterol levels in the blood, helping to lower the risk of coronary heart disease and strokes.

Monounsaturated fats also have the added benefit of being high in vitamin E and helping the body to maintain or develop cells. Omega-3s and Omega 6s both contribute to brain function, Omega 3s being able to lower your risk of cardiovascular disease and reduce inflammation.

An over-indulgence in saturated fats is commonly thought to provoke bad cholesterol, which in turn will increase your chances of cardiovascular disease. There is actually very little evidence, however, to fully support the presumption that this bad cholesterol is linked to saturated fats and a few studies have proven that the links are very tenuous, if present at all.[14]

Trans fats

Trans fats are the real evil of which you should be wary. Although originating from a naturally unsaturated fat, these are fats that have been hydrogenated (where a liquid fat is turned into solid fat through the addition of hydrogen) in order to increase shelf life. This is what stops shop-bought biscuits going soggy and makes margarine and spreadable butter, spreadable. Manufacturers created this product in part to provide a food that was not associated with saturated fat (because of the bad press that type was receiving) but that still supposedly tasted and behaved the same way. Numerous studies have since been published to show how trans fats can clog your arteries and are far worse for your body than saturated fats. Your body is designed to be able to break down and make use of natural fats such as those found in real butter but when confronted with this altered, effectively manufactured fat, things can go wrong.

So why the perpetual fat-bashing?

As soon as a health board announces its reasoning behind a world problem, teams of people club together to come up with ways to ameliorate it and rightly so. When the rationale for the initial conclusion changes its path, though, the teams of people (who have by now invested a lot of money into fixing the first problem) are not so keen to re-evaluate. They would have to change their business model to address the scientifically proven, updated formula, and are understandably reluctant to do this, for fear of losing out on lots of money and looking foolish for acting so hard and fast on the first hypothesis.

I'm talking about the companies that produce the low-fat, fat free and weight loss products. You can't go into a super-market now without seeing an abundance of items that have been processed in such a way as to cut out or diminish the naturally occurring fat that was always meant to be there. I think one of the first things to be altered was milk. It's even cleverly colour-coded so that you know how much or how little you are going to enjoy it.

Semi-skimmed I can just about understand, although you don't get the thick creamy layer at the top of the bottle (actually, due to homogenisation, you don't even with full fat now unless you buy that special gold-top stuff – see above re my colour-coding/enjoyment analysis. Might be showing the 'ish' part of my youngish age here) but skimmed milk? WTF. It's the most rancid, tasteless gruel I have ever had, yet people buy it on a daily basis because they believe the lack of fat in it will stop them from getting fat. No! The only thing it will stop for you is your enjoyment of milk the way it should be – and some of the processes your body should and would be able to conduct if you drank the proper stuff instead. Having said this, professional athletes and long distance runners do actually imbibe skimmed milk to hydrate, owing to the water, electrolytes and protein content; so I mustn't vilify it too much. It might be more useful, though, for the purposes of an everyday healthy diet, to think of it as protein-rich water, rather than actual milk.

One of my biggest bugbears of the low-fat upheaval is crème fraîche. Its deliciousness is all to do with the high amount of fat it contains – and high it is, at up to 45%. When some well-intentioned food activists decided to introduce a low-fat version, it completely destroyed the very essence of crème fraîche, altering its consistency to such a degree it's no longer possible to cook with it in the same ways, because it curdles under high heat. 'Don't buy it then' I hear you cry, which would be the obvious answer. Unfortunately, due to the populist supermarkets' approach, those around me only stock a limited amount of the full-fat version; so limited, in fact, that it is rarely possible to purchase this nectar of the cream world as the other savvy high fat consumers got there before me, because they're so healthy and nimble. The erroneous common belief that fat is the devil's friend is actually preventing us from accessing and eating what we should. Don't even get me started on yoghurt.

Dairy products were the starting point for the negative food revolution (maybe because they are in the dreaded saturated fat bracket) but, as is the way, nothing was safe from its steely grip. I was a 'fat is evil' believer many years ago, when I carried the paunch, and remember buying a low-fat oil to spray onto my food before frying it. It a) cost significantly more than a bottle of olive oil; b) tasted pretty gruesome; and c) took away all of the beneficial nutrients that I should have received from a high fat oil.

Not only are these products going to give you far fewer essential nutrients, they are also priced considerably higher than any of the foods they are trying to emulate. The manufacturers of all of these low-fat products have profited so much from this revolution that it will take years before fat is no longer seen as the enemy, because they control the market and they don't want to stop cashing in on it. When it comes to fat, there is no 'wonder product' you need to buy; just eat and cook the naturally-sourced foods that our ancestors did, who didn't get fat and who didn't have chronic heart disease. The low-fat food manufacturers can't make any money out of this, so they're not going to advertise it. Take it from me – I'm only interested in spreading the happiness (and the butter).

Pour Some Sugar on Me ♫

In a bid to disguise the blandness of a diet that results from detracting the fat from all the food we love, as I mentioned earlier, the manufacturers devized a way to substitute the great taste of fat, with sugar. Sugar, as the majority of you know, is a granular substance that you sprinkle over whatever food you like to make it sweeter, which plays an important role in certain cooking and baking processes. It is also a substance that the body breaks down and converts into energy. We need it to survive but you can have too much of a good thing.

Food manufacturers, again, seem to have taken fat substitution to extremes and used their wonder compound, 'sugar', to mask over and unnecessarily augment fat's former domain. Nearly every food product that you can buy now has a low-fat alternative and the ones that use sugar as a flavour replacement are by far the worst. A selection of products you need to be wary of include: any form of cereal, low-fat or not, low-fat yoghurts, low-fat coffee, low-fat bread, low-fat peanut butter, low-fat salad dressing, low-fat cereal bars, low-fat cookies, low-fat sandwich spreads and low-fat muffins, to name but a few.

So what happens to all this sugar that we are now ingesting in place of naturally occurring fats? Our bodies break down sugars and then convert them into energy. In between the conversion and consignment stages of the sugar, it is stored in the liver, before dispatch. If we have ingested too much sugar and there is no room available to store it or appropriate activity to burn it, although it is not actually a fat, the liver doesn't really care and so converts it into a fatty acid. It then sends that fatty acid into the bloodstream, where it is taken throughout the body and stored as – you guessed it – fat. If that isn't enough, the fat then finds its way into our organs, if it's not welcomed on the way by your belly or hips. It consequently reduces organ ability, raises blood pressure, decreases metabolism (which doesn't help with the weight loss) and weakens the immune system. All of this because you apparently shouldn't eat fat.

Newly released documents[15] show that in the 1960s the sugar industry paid scientists to play down the link between sugar and heart disease, placing the blame on saturated fat, instead. It has also been strongly suggested that five decades of research into the role that sugar plays within the field of nutrition, dietary recommendation and heart disease has been not only influenced but shaped by the sugar industry. Stanton Glantz[16], a professor of medicine at University of San Francisco and an author of the JAMA Internal Medicine paper, says that 'they were able to derail the discussion about sugar for decades'.

In my research I have also found accusations that Harvard professors were paid the equivalent of $50,000 USD in today's money, by the Sugar Association, to publish a 1967 review in the prestigious New England Journal of Medicine, reportedly minimising the link between sugar and heart health and casting aspersions on the role of saturated fat.

It might interest you to hear that some of the biggest players in the sugar enveloping market hail from the States, the largest of them all being Coca Cola. The New York Times posted an article on the 8th August 2015,[17] revealing that Coco Cola, the word's largest producer of sugary beverages, had provided millions of dollars in funding to displacing the link between sugar and obesity and to place the blame on lack of exercise.

With many low-fat foods using sugar to displace the apparent harm of fat and with the fizzy and still (orange juice, for instance) drinks industry playing such an enormous role in leeching the poisonous effects of too much sugar into almost everybody in the western world, we (and this is a serious first world problem) are on the cusp of an epidemic of huge proportions and need to act now to prevent the premature death of millions of people.

Just to help you to visualise the amount of sugar in any particular food or drink you might be compelled to devour, look at the ingredients, find the sugar value in grams and divide it by 4. The value you reach is the number of teaspoons of sugar you will be about to imbibe. A can of coke has 35g of added sugar. You do the math(s). Admittedly, I am only talking about the amount of 'added' sugar, because a lot of food labels only mention the sugar as a total mass, regardless of whether or not it has actually been added or not to the natural sugar. The best way to decipher a label is to look at the amount of total sugar on it and then look on the ingredients list and see if added sugar is within the first three ingredients, as this implies this ingredient is in the product in the largest quantity.

Protein

It is essential to eat protein, which can be found in a number of different foods including beef, poultry, fish, eggs, dairy products, nuts, seeds and legumes (things like black seeds and lentils). Our bodies are constantly manufacturing protein to repair, build and maintain our muscles, organs and immune system. Proteins are broken down into amino acids, which can then be connected in a variety of different ways to create a different protein for a different job. Twenty-two of the approximately 500 known amino acids are vital for our health, of which our bodies can create thirteen. The remaining nine essential amino acids must all be obtained from eating protein-rich foods and are the very reason we need protein in our diets.

Fibre

Fibre, like protein, is another essential part of the human diet, with the power to prevent heart disease, weight gain, diabetes and some forms of cancer. It is also an intrinsic element in improving digestive health. Most people don't get enough fibre, which is a confounding reason for ill health due to a poor diet. Fibre, however, can be found in most foods that come from plants and is broken down into two categories, soluble and insoluble.

Soluble fibre, as the description suggests, dissolves in the fluids of your digestive system. Although it is not a fat, it has the capacity to reduce the amount of cholesterol in your blood, much like HDL. Foods that contain soluble fibre, include oats, barley, rye, fruit such as bananas and apples, root vegetables such as carrots and potatoes, and golden linseeds.

Insoluble fibre (you guessed it) doesn't dissolve in your bodily fluids. It keeps your bowels healthy and helps prevent digestive problems. It passes through your gut without being broken down, helping other foods move through your digestive system smoothly. Good sources of insoluble fibre include nuts, seeds, cereals, bran and wholemeal bread.

Carbohydrates

This is where my research and personal case studies come to flight. A few years after my 'cut out all fat' stage, I became an avid All Carbs Make You Fat supporter. I never consciously committed myself to the Atkins diet but I most certainly independently made sense of what it was trying to convey and more or less stopped eating carbs. I mean, it is the perfect diet for men, loads of meat and not so many vegetables. Splendid. I did lose weight but, as I mentioned at the start of this chapter, fad diets are impossible to maintain, especially if you want to be healthy. I did, however, notice a link between weight gain and certain types of carbs, and consequently developed parts of the diet into an eating plan that can be worked into a lifestyle including all the good things that I have mentioned throughout this chapter.

As the Atkins diet implies, mixing fats with carbs will promote a bit of weight gain. But why? I researched this topic a little further in preparation for work on this chapter and started to find a connection between this and everything else I had been investigating. As carbs are broken down and enter into the bloodstream, they increase the amount of sugar, because they are, after all, sugar molecules. Carbs can be broken down into three categories, depending on the amount of sugar molecules they contain. Monosaccharide and disaccharide are simple carbs, containing one or two molecules accordingly, consisting of glucose, galactose (milk), fructose (fruit), sucrose (table sugar), lactose (milk) and maltose (beer!). Meanwhile polysaccharides are complex carbs, consisting of starchy foods such as pasta or potatoes, or fibre, which helps with digestion.

When a carbohydrate is simple it is easily absorbed into the bloodstream because of its simple molecule structure. Complex carbs take longer to break down into sugar and are not so quickly absorbed.

As carbs are broken down into sugar and enter the bloodstream as glucose, they are then transported to the liver, organs and muscles. Any excess glucose that is not used by the body for energy will be stored as fat. If you happen to be consuming a carb that causes your blood sugar level to rise rapidly, your body will not have enough resources to apportion it appropriately and will therefore store it as fat. These are known as bad carbs. Good carbs, on the other hand, are absorbed slowly into the bloodstream and have little effect on the blood sugar levels. Combining a bad carb with an excessive amount of fat will cause you to gain weight.

So what are good and bad carbs?

Almost every vegetable is a good carb, except for potatoes because the starch in them raises their glycemic rating to a level above and beyond the desired amount to distribute the sugars evenly. As soon as you fry them up as chips, you are effectively asking your body to store both sugar and oil, as fat. Like with skimmed milk, I'm not trying to vilify the humble potato, it is, after all, one of the world's most prominent vegetables and an excellent source of fibre in forms such as the baked potato. Instead of banishing them from your diet, control the amount you eat and with what you eat them, because that is what will affect your blood sugar levels (so don't eat loads of crisps and chips).

Every fruit is considered a good carbohydrate, until you tamper with them by adding extra sugar, or turn them into a juice.

Grains are good carbs, like quinoa and brown rice or any wholegrain product. As soon as a product is played around with and 'refined', it makes it into a bad carb, because a lot of its nutritious values have been extracted. White rice, white bread, breakfast cereal, couscous, white pasta, baked goods like donuts, cakes and muffins, and corn.

All nuts are amazing. They may be high in fat but its a good fat that will help to strengthen and develop your body. As soon as you sweeten the nuts, though, you will straightaway plough them into bad carb territory. Unless you get natural, unsweetened and unsalted peanut butter, you will be doing a disservice to the nut world.

All dairy products are good carbs, from butter and cheese to cream and milk. Ice cream, however, and any product that has been sweetened, like yoghurt, is bad, so maybe only have it as a treat. Skimmed milk is not only revolting, it is also a bad carb because it is missing vital vitamins like A and E. Unless you're a long distance runner who doesn't like water, ditch it.

Believe it or not, mayonnaise is a good carb, as is mustard, vinegar, soy sauce, Worcestershire sauce, pickle, relish and oils. Add sugar to them, though, and they become bad, like tomato ketchup (I ignore this one because I love it so much), honey mustard, bbq dressing and any low-fat salad dressing.

Just like with meat, as soon as you process something to either lengthen its shelf life or to play around with the flavours, you'll normally find that it will turn a good carb into a bad carb. Take oranges, for example. As soon as you extract the juice from a bunch of oranges, play around with the compounds and then bottle it for consumption, you're effectively consuming maybe five or six oranges in one glass, which isn't a natural amount to be eating. This, coupled with the obscene amount of fructose oranges contain and the fact that the fibre has been effectively removed (even in juice 'with bits'), your body will have no other option than to store the converted sugars into fat, because it will have received an overload of it, leaving you with three options: exercise it off, consume less the next day, or do nothing and increase your belly. Eating one orange for a snack is not a problem, drinking lots of orange juice is. As a teenager I remember thinking that I was so healthy by drinking loads of orange juice, no wonder I was a tubby kid.

As you can see, it is only when you introduce sugar to a product that it turns it into a bad one. Carbs are not bad. Add sugar to them, or mess around with their construction, and they are. Simple. It's a shame Dr. Atkins didn't know this.

Bamboléo ♫

One diet or lifestyle regime which has transfixed the nutritionists of the world for many years is the Mediterranean diet. It is quite simply a way of eating, rather than a dietary plan to follow, featuring foods eaten in Greece, Spain, Southern Italy and France. It is not so much about recreating dishes derived from these countries but rather emphasising the consumption of fruit, vegetables, oily fish, high fibre grains, wholemeal pasta, multi grain bread, cereals, beans, nuts and seeds. It uses olive oil as its key monounsaturated fat source, suggests a moderate/low daily consumption of dairy products and poultry, permits a minimum amount of red meat and allows for the moderate consumption of wine.

This diet gives the body access to a wide range of fruits and vegetables, maximising the sources of vitamins, minerals and other trace nutrients, which, over time, contribute to a healthier life.

Investigations into this diet found that inhabitants of places such as Greece and southern Italy had considerably lower levels of heart disease than other people in Europe. Combined with moderate exercise and not smoking, this diet can almost guarantee health benefits.

The total levels of fat consumed in this diet are practically identical to those of other parts of the world, yet cases of chronic heart disease in these regions are significantly lower, suggesting an emphasis on the types of fat that we ought to consume, rather than the quantity. The Mediterranean diet is high in monounsaturated fats found in foods such as avocados, olive oil and nuts, compared with other diets high in saturated fats, found in red meat, processed meats, animal products and full fat dairy products.

Instead of red meat, the diet recommends the consumption of fish at least three times a week, especially oily fish, such as salmon and mackerel, which has a high concentration of the Omega-3 fatty acid that I have mentioned throughout this chapter.

Although the Mediterranean diet regulates the consumption of saturated fats and dairy products, it doesn't mean to say they're intrinsically bad for us. I have not once suggested you should consume a lot of it but I have told you that the benefits of eating moderate amounts of it are far greater than cutting it out completely. As with everything you eat, the single rule you should stick to hard and fast is: to moderate.

***

I've explained to you the distorted truths about fat and the deceit that has got us hooked on sugar. I've also briefly mentioned the importance of proteins, fibre and good carbs, so I'm now going to tell you what to do about it.

If you're unlucky enough to have lost them, there is no quick and easy way to recapture your former worry-free, belly-free days. Do not be fooled by some fad diet, because they are merely ways for other people to make lots of money out of you. It's a cliché I hear everyday but: eat a healthy, balanced diet. By following the scientifically proven facts and techniques I've discussed in this chapter, you will be well on your way to slimming down, or if that's not your focus, eating a nutritionally balanced diet that allows your body to function like it should.

The Downward Spiral[izing] ♪

I remember going on a date with a girl, many years ago, and waxing lyrical about the unbelievable invention of the spiralizer. Needless to say, the date didn't go so well but I think I got my point across because at the end of last year I got a random text from the same girl, telling me that she had just bought herself a spiralizer (or she secretly wanted me to ask her on another date...who knows). Anyway, if you've never had one, get one. They are the most incredible devices you will come across, which shred whatever vegetable you are using into long spirals that you can then fry, steam (wait for it, I'll be championing this momentarily), boil or just eat raw. I remember one of my staple dishes at university being the classic spaghetti bolognese (hence the gut, in part because I ate copious amounts of white spaghetti with the meat). Fast forward to now and I will either spiralize a few humble carrots or a sumptuous courgette in place of pasta, to create the perfect, healthy, tasty base for the bolognese. And that is only the beginning, you can do so much more with them, so get one and start experimenting.

Steamy Windows ♪

This isn't new, it's been around for a long, long time, but start steaming your vegetables. You can buy awesome tiered steamers that let you steam up to 5 different items at the same time, or you can just place a colander filled with a particular vegetable or vegetables, covered with a lid, over a pan of boiling water, to create an economical version. Don't, however, use a plastic colander over a gas flame, like my soon to be ex-(just kidding) housemate did last night, because that won't end well for the colander, your veg, or your relationships with the people whose kitchen you share. Steaming vegetables ensures that vitamins such as vitamin B, riboflavin, thiamine, niacin, biotin, B12, pantothenic acid and vitamin C, as well as minerals such as calcium, phosphorous, potassium, and zinc are all retained. When you boil or fry your vegetables, you lose a lot of the goodness into the water or oil.

<u>Timmy's Tips</u>

- If you find yourself over-indulging on one particular day, enjoy yourself because that is what life is all about. Don't, however, punish yourself for having fun. Instead, know that you have to refrain from beer for the next few days, and treat yourself to a massage or a cinema trip instead, or whatever makes you happy.

- Use the 80/20 rule. Eat normally and healthily 80% of the time, let yourself go a little bit, 20% of the time. You will still stay a healthy weight if you keep to this ratio.

- Try to exceed your five-a-day fruit and vegetable intake. The more colour you have in your fruits and vegetables, the wider the range of nutrients. Spiralize your vegetables to create healthy alternatives to white spaghetti. Steam your vegetables in order to retain all the goodness.

- Try to include as many nutrient-rich foods as possible, such as eggs, liver, sardines etc. Eat more fish to boost your Omega-3 supplies. Get as much of it as you can. These are a great means of adding depth of flavour to a largely vegetarian dish, too.

- Serve yourself smaller portions if you're trying to lose weight and don't go for seconds. Instead, add another course to your meal in the form of a herbal tea or similar, that gives you something to focus on after the main event.

- Eat slowly. The longer you take to consume a meal, the more likely you are to feel full before you finish it. It takes longer for your body to know it is full than it does for it to digest everything. Chew your food for longer, which will help with slowing down. It will also help to stimulate the release of digestive juices in your gut.

- Eat mindfully. This will help slow you, too. Appreciate it and think about what it has gone through to get onto your plate. What does it look like, first? Did you think it would taste like that? Do you like the texture of it? Do you like the taste?

- Drink a glass of water before you eat as it will help to lessen your appetite. Drink water anyway because it is so important. Love it. Love yourself. Be happy. Smile. Laugh. Have fun. Be joyful.

- If you're a bacon and red meat eater, don't restrict yourself from eating it completely, rather, save it for special occasions and maybe don't consume it everyday. If you're not eating bacon or steak, eat chicken, and eat as much of it as you want. Not only does it taste great, it is also incredibly lean and a great source of that all-important protein.

- Develop a way of making offal taste amazing and then eat it yourself before launching a brand new restaurant that changes the health of the country.

- Moderate the amounts and types of food you consume.

- Balance your diet to include a healthy amount of fibre, protein, fat and good carbs.

- Look at labels - If you don't understand the word on the back, don't buy it.

- Go to your local green grocer to bulk buy vegetables.

Self-Control

A battle is going on inside us all, it is a terrible fight between wolves.

One is evil; anger, envy, sorrow, shame, regret, greed, arrogance, self-pity, guilt, resentment, inferiority, lies, false pride, superiority and ego.

The other is good; joy, peace, love, hope, serenity, humility, kindness, benevolence, empathy, generosity, truth, compassion and faith.

So which wolf wins? That's easy, the one you feed.

– Adaptation from an old Cherokee teaching

You've reached the chapter that is perhaps the most controversial. But the unconventional is often uncomfortable until it becomes familiar. As ever, there is method in my madness.

When it comes to self-control, there is a selection of mental conditions that have the power to overrule virtuous intentions, causing the individual in question to wage a ferocious battle between conflicting arguments in their mind. One of the hardest battles to fight is that of overcoming an addiction. After experiencing the devastating effects that addiction can have on an individual, through obtaining some invaluable first-hand evidence from several willing subjects, I have written this chapter to help anyone gain back the self-control needed in order to successfully fight an addiction.

At the start of this book I mentioned the power of thought and how by managing and retraining our thinking through the Thought Theory model, we have the ability to bring about a distinctive change in how our lives evolve. Gaining control over conflict between intention and desire is never an easy thing to achieve, especially if your mind has succumbed to an addiction, but by following the approaches outlined in this chapter, you will be in a much better position to retrain your mind, or help to retrain that of a loved one. Everyone experiences a weakness in self-control at certain points in their life, so regardless of whether or not addiction is a problem in your life, I hope this chapter will be able to help you tackle whatever personal transgression you feel is compromising your poise.

During my research for this chapter, a friend asked me how addiction and obsession differ from each other, because without looking too closely they are similar kinds of afflictions. Although they appear fairly connected, they are very different. Let me explain. Obsessive behaviour often involves repetitively enacting the same routine, over and over again, with the belief it will prevent or invoke a certain circumstance from occurring, (as briefly mentioned in the context of my own OCD, in the religion vs spirituality chapter). It is also widely associated with individuals who become transfixed on an object, or a person (for instance, the dreaded ex), or a thought. The individual becomes perpetually preoccupied with the focus of their obsession and repetitively (and sometimes scarily) dwells on the imaginings of impossibly attainable situations involving whoever or whatever they might be pursuing.

Addiction, on the other hand, does involve repetition, but this time through either consuming something or performing a ritual of sorts, for instant gratification. The need for that gratification becomes so ingrained in the everyday needs of the individual that it turns into a physical and mental dependence. The sufferer has to compulsively repeat the act to gain the satisfaction to keep them at peace.

Whether the addiction is to drugs, alcohol, smoking, gambling, sex, eating or even shopping, to name but a few, the scientific process behind the 'high' that results, sees the addict's brain producing increased levels of the naturally-occurring neurotransmitter dopamine, which, among other things, modulates the brain's ability to perceive reward re-inforcement.

Addiction used to be considered a trait that afflicted the morally-flawed or weak-willed individuals of the world. Scientific consensus has changed over time, however, and addiction is now often considered to be a chronic disease, which changes both the structure and function of the brain. In a similar way to how cardiovascular disease damages the heart, and respiratory disease damages the lungs, addiction hijacks the brain.

The Problem with Starving an Addiction

Because there are no pharmacological cures for this plight, there is a lot of scepticism and conjecture about the actual possibility of a cure. Moreover, divisions of the medical world don't even believe an addiction can ever be removed from a person's psyche, only covered up and controlled. Starving the addiction is the accepted management approach. Just as for many other diseases, however, there is an attainable cure for addiction, which is what this chapter is all about, regaining self-control. With 100% devotion to crushing your addiction, there is a strong chance that you can be freed from its grip, gaining back your self-control, and freeing yourself of the fear of its return.

Unlike the approach of Alcoholics Anonymous (AA) and other similar groups, which aim to terminate not only the addiction but also the activity itself, the model that I am going to introduce to you is designed to stop the addiction but not the continuation of the actual activity (assuming it's not illegal – if it is, this needs to be stopped for reasons beyond your well-being). If you are currently addicted to a class A drug, then obviously there are exceptions and that needs to be halted. If, however, you drink too much and want to still have a social drink every so often without the fear of reprising your addiction, as someone who is not an addict can, then this is the direction for you. It is, in many cases, the addiction that brings people down, not whatever it is that you are addicted to.

Just to quickly emphasise a point here. If you have been sober for the last five years and you are happy with your life, DO NOT nip down to your local bar for a stiff whisky. If you've managed to control your addiction by abstaining from it, I applaud you and in no way do I want to encourage you to reignite it again by falling back into old habits. You have found the method that works for you and that in itself is a key tenet of Timinology. If you are new to curbing addictions, however, then read on.

We've all seen the films where some character has to stand up in front of a big group of people at an AA meeting, introduce himself to everyone as an alcoholic and then affirm that he will never touch another drop for the rest of his life.

Imagine you've been on the wagon for the last three years and then one day you lose your job, your spouse leaves you and your dog dies. I would say that nine times out of ten, the initial response would be to go and drown your sorrows in a bottle of whisky. Almost anyone would but you can't, because apparently you're an alcoholic, even though you've been sober for the last three years. You reach your favourite old bar and contemplate entering it for a few seconds. Marriage, job, dead dog....whisky. That's all there is to it and you enter the bar and recommence your hazy past.

If you've been following the dogma of AA, you've now failed yourself and the last three years of commitment that you've put in. You now see yourself as a failure, so continue drinking.

The next morning you wake up with a splitting headache and try to piece together the evening's events. Shit, you think to yourself, I really am an alcoholic and this is always going to keep happening; fuck it, I'm going to drink the pain away.

And that's what happens. By setting yourself up for such a devastating blow in the form of total failure as the alternative to total success, you are eternally at risk of eventually hitting rock bottom and reviving the addiction. I'm not saying that will definitely happen and as I said, if abstinence is already working for you, that is great. But if you are yet to find your answer, the chances of success are far greater if you implement the approach I am about to teach you.

Imagine if our jobless, spouseless, dogless friend allowed himself a small drink every so often. His mental reaction to getting mindlessly drunk after such a bad day would be significantly different than if he had been completely abstinent to the bottle for the previous three years. Enabling the mind to justify the activity can be an important step towards dealing with the mistake appropriately. An understanding of context and perspective is the first step towards this.

Although our friend is addicted to alcohol, it wasn't the alcohol that put him on that path, it was an invisible thought that prompted him to take it up in the first place. I can't tell you what these thoughts are, everyone's are different, but I will help you to uncover them and then confront them in order to prevent the addiction from taking over your life.

There is a lot of conjecture about chemical vs psychological addiction (will power), and how the two differ. If your mind has become accustomed to and is dependent on the ravishing effects of whatever drug or substance you may be consuming, is it harder to free yourself from these substances than to free yourself from gambling, which involves the introduction of no additives into your body? I've had the opportunity to question people on both sides of the fence and their answers were quite enlightening. Addiction to alcohol is a substance addiction, and your body will need to be weaned. However, you will also be psychologically addicted to it and need to engage your will power to tackle the addiction head-on. Chemically addicted individuals tended to claim that the battle to gain control was longer and harder for them, because they had to shake the physical effects before they could confront the mental effects. What it boils down to is that the hardest thing to confront is your will power, regardless of what you are addicted to. Once you have that under control, the physical effects, if you need to address those, can be dealt with accordingly.

In gaining control of your addiction, you are in the driving seat and you can take it wherever you want. Control only comes through understanding your addiction's existence; once achieved, it is at your whim. By using the disease model, as the AA does, they might very well be bringing an end to participation in an activity that causes a lot of heartache and pain – but that is all they do. They do not try to understand the underlying reasons for someone deciding to drink in the first place, meaning all they can do is cover up the problem instead of addressing it. 'Once an alcoholic, always an alcoholic' is a slogan that springs to mind. That is complete bullshit. They treat their members like senseless children, devoid of the baseline faculties required to control their own destiny. It is far easier for them to cut something out completely than to take the time to research the reasons for its existence.

It may last for a couple of months or maybe even a few years but you live in constant fear that the pain of the repression will eventually get too much for you, that you will one day crack under the pressure and revert back to your addiction. It's not the addiction that causes this pain, it is the repression. It is known as a repressive time bomb and until you understand how to completely free yourself from the addiction, it could unexpectedly explode at any given time. The fundamental ethos behind AA and all other 12 step programmes is to repress wholeheartedly the addictive state. No wonder they have such a low success rate.

If you carry on repressing your addiction, you may well find yourself partaking in other addictive activities to try to divert your mind away from what you're trying to forget; such as smoking, drinking, excessive exercise, overeating, drugs, workaholism, obsessive sexual activity etc.

If you don't take up anything else, you could find yourself in absolute agony trying to push the desire out of your mind; afraid to go outside, watch TV or do anything that might trigger another episode. Your fear of the addiction's reprisal actually makes you worse off than when you were knowingly partaking in the activity.

If you want to stop smoking or stop drinking and never touch another drink or cigarette for the rest of your life, then by all means get in contact with AA or another similar programme. Even if it does work (which only happens 33% of the time) you will be living your life in darkness, ignorant of the very reasons behind your enforced sobriety. Should you not be worried that without understanding its cause, it could manifest itself in another way? Getting to know your demons helps you to take charge: keep your friends close but your enemies closer.

So, What is an Addiction?

Before I delve into the basics of overcoming an addiction, I want to explain to you the variety of different occurrences of it and what defines whether or not you have one.

Have you found yourself partaking in a particular activity more often than ever before, leading to withdrawal symptoms when you no longer partake in it? Have you found yourself lying about your use of the substance or about how you have been behaving in relation to it? If you answer yes to either of these scenarios, there is a strong chance that you have developed an addiction, so I urge you to take note.

As soon as you find yourself craving intensely the activity, losing control of yourself over its use and then steadfastly continuing, despite adverse consequences, it has control of you. You have to decide whether you are going to beat it, or let it ruin you.

Addiction was once only associated with the use of drugs and alcohol, owing to the introduction of unwanted chemicals into your body. Scientific research has since concluded that even everyday pleasurable activities such as shopping and watching television, which introduce no toxins to the body, can also have the adverse effect of becoming addictive. The cultivation of an addiction can occur when, through whatever activity or substance you may be consuming, you manage to access on demand your brain's ability to discharge excess dopamine into a cluster of nerve cells underneath your cerebral cortex. The result is that you feel you need a constant supply of it. You don't and I will explain how you can regain control of your senses and achieve self-control.

Amid my research for this chapter, I came across an interesting book entitled The Truth About Addiction and Recovery, by Stanton Peele, Ph.D and Archie Brodsky.[1] It was written in the early nineties, so a lot of what it says is now very dated. Despite this drawback, apart from having no idea who any of the featured 'celebrities' were, (not that I would be any better with today's fame-hungry public), this book has helped to cultivate my premise for how to battle addiction and regain self-control.

Recovery techniques aside, the biggest point this book tries to convey is that addiction is NOT a disease. A large proportion of the book is centred around this very proposition, which led me to spend a lot of time researching the plausibility of that assumption.

It all depends how you perceive disease and more importantly whether or not you think it is curable. The writers of The Truth About Addiction and Recovery firmly believe that addiction can be cured from the very root of the problem, by eradicating it entirely from your mind. They refute the proposition that addiction is genetic (a dominant factor in the disease theory model). Looking at it this way, life experience has to be the catalyst for addiction (even the staunchest disease advocate has to agree that if the genetic link is lost, then life experience has to play a greater role).

The disease model claims that because you are so addicted to something, you cannot make reasonable choices, especially when it comes to how far into the addiction you lose yourself. You are effectively at its mercy and not just for a few weeks, for life. You will never be free of it, which means you can never come into contact with it again (a real shocker if you're addicted to food). The addiction will then grow and grow over the coming years, completely taking over your life, devouring you like AIDS or cancer. There is nothing else you can do to prevent this from happening unless you comprehensively sever all ties to the substance or activity. (I'm seeing lots of naked clothes-shopping addicts).

Under the disease model, if you think that you can overcome your addiction through will-power, changes in your life circumstances or following the awesome teachings of Timinology, then you're deluded and in denial. Addiction is seen as a disease of the body, only controllable by a plethora of medical treatments. It has also affected your spirit, so probably best to go and join a support group where you can all lament how bad your lives are.

The Oxford English dictionary defines a disease as 'A condition of the body, or of some part or organ of the body, in which its functions are disturbed or deranged', so you could probably be justified in deducing that an addiction is a disease of the brain. But is it?

Addiction is currently labelled as a disease, so on that premise we'll let sleeping dogs lie and refer to it as that. It is an illness of the mind but it can be rectified with the correct guidance. It is an illness that doesn't require you to seek external help and join dispirited support groups. If your mind is in the right place, you will achieve your addiction-free dream and regain self-control. Before addiction received medical recognition, it was frowned upon as an indication of weak judgement and lack of will power. Society today, in calling it a disease, can sometimes make addiction a condition to be merely sympathized with. This can sadly have an adverse affect on the sufferer, leading them to believe that because the addiction might not be present through any fault of their own, they can lie back and let it ruin their life because the addiction is now beyond their control.

The long and short of it, whichever way you choose to label addiction, is that it can be cured.

Everyone's at It ♫

Although everyone probably knows a smoking addict, there is another addiction that is fast becoming the worlds most common addiction, which is making a mockery of the human race, and that is eating. If you are fat and can't stop yourself from shovelling that extra burger into your mouth, or from drinking another bottle of fizzy soda, why do you think you are overweight? The very fact you can't moderate and control your eating clearly spells out that you are addicted. Similarly, on the opposite side of the coin, although sufferers of anorexia claim that by managing the amount of food they eat, they are the ones in control, they too have been manipulated by the dopamine fix they receive from not eating enough, and have become addicted to thinking that they are the ones in control. The reasoning behind addiction, therefore, has less to do with the chemicals we introduce into our bodies, and more to do with the invisible reasons that fuel it. We adapt to our environment.

There may be a few medical exceptions but the long and short of it is, if you're overweight, you have an unhealthy addiction to food. Similarly, if you are under-nourished and suffer from one of the major eating disorders such as anorexia or bulimia, you too will be addicted to the idea of not eating. If you are fixated by your weight enough to have drastically diverged from your healthy food intake, you are suffering from an addiction. It is maybe for this very reason that the labelling of addiction as a disease helps to categorise the plethora of disorders into an 'easy to understand' bracket, taking the blame away from the person afflicted by it, making it the fault of the disease, not the individual's will-power. My point is that the 'disease' is not the cause but the symptom. This chapter is about reinvigorating your will power. No-one is blaming you in the slightest for where you are at the moment. The invisible reasoning and thought processes you have are completely out of your control; but you, and only you, have the power to turn the tables now.

When it comes to self-control and composure, there is one addiction that hits sufferers much harder and can potentially last for much longer than others and that is addiction to grief. Most people naturally transgress beyond everyday misery when faced with the death of a loved one or the break up of a previously perfect relationship. As strange as it may sound, however, grief can subconsciously turn into an addiction. It's shit but we will all suffer loss at some point or another, that is just the way life is. The way we deal with it, however, differs immensely. The loss of a loved one is always going to be painful but the grieving process should not control your existence. Yes, it's very normal to be heartbroken and inconsolable in the immediate aftermath of the event but that should not last. Self-control is paramount in these circumstances.

Researchers at the University of California, Los Angeles [2] conducted a study between 'complicated' and 'un-complicated' grief-stricken individuals, finding that long-term grief activates neurons in the reward centre of the brain, potentially giving memories addictive-like qualities. Mary-Frances O'Connor, the assistant professor of psychiatry and lead author of the study stated, 'the idea is that when our loved ones are alive, we get a rewarding cue from seeing them or things that remind us of them. After the loved one dies, those who adapt to the loss stop getting this neural reward. But those who don't adapt continue to crave it, because each time they do see a cue, they still get that neural reward'. She then went on to state that all of this is outside conscious thought, which ties in perfectly with the invisible thought processes linked to addiction, which will be comprehensively explained in a bit.

If you have recently lost a loved one, or have broken up with the person you thought you were going to spend the rest of your life with and can't seem to get over your loss after what feels like a normal period of time, there is a strong possibility that you are addicted to your grief. It sounds like a very peculiar thing to be addicted to but by following the later mentioned approach to freeing yourself from its grip, you will be able to recommence a healthy existence and gain back your self-control.

My Friend the Addict ♫

A couple of years ago, I attended a weekend meditation retreat at a stately home in Oxfordshire. I learned several things over the weekend, which we'll come back to in The Happiness Chapter. In between the meditation sessions, we were all segregated into specific groups to discuss the issues affecting our lives. In one particular session, the group leader propositioned us to divulge any addictive states that had prevented us from accessing profoundly our inner selves. From a group of about eight people, the obvious inclusion of smoking addiction came up a couple of times, which didn't really move me. What did move me, however, were three other testimonies that left me completely mesmerized.

Mike, a short, slim and quite bronzed, twenty-something year old, confessed his addiction to his smart phone and social media. I think we all simultaneously giggled when he first brought it up, because I guess it is something we all jokingly think we are partially addicted to; it makes a noise, we immediately react to it. In acknowledgement of this, on the evening of our arrival at the house we were all instructed to turn our phones off and leave them in our rooms. I think it was this that properly drew Mike's attention to his addiction. This session was on the Sunday morning, so we had all been without our phones for a couple of days.

For my part, I missed not knowing if I'd been liked by any girls on Tinder (a dating app, for those that have never heard of it) but all in all it was actually quite refreshing to not be at the beck and call of my phone. Mike, however, took his phone out of his pocket in front of us (to the sound of a lot of tutting) and professed that he could not be away from it. He went on to explain how he played a multitude of games on it, had about fifteen apps that he constantly played with (Facebook being the main one) as well as texting and WhatsApping his friends non-stop. He said he watched TV on it, he listened to music on it and, sometimes, although very rarely, spoke to people on it. He said that when he was with his phone he genuinely felt a sense of security. He went to sleep watching it and in the morning is woken up by its alarm. He readily admitted that he used it while driving (at the risk of losing his license), while at the cinema, while eating out, while eating in with his family, and while walking to and from work. There was genuinely no alone time he spent away from it, unless he was in the shower. He couldn't even acquiesce in the simple request to leave phones in rooms during the retreat. The concept wasn't funny any more and I understood how Mike's phone was limiting his awareness from everyone and everything.

Emma was the next of the group to astound me. I'd say she was late thirties to early forties, average sort of height but most definitely severely above average kind of weight, for anyone. I was not surprized when she told us her addiction was to food. Because I used to be quite large (as you will have found out in the Nutrition chapter) I could partially understand how she had reached such a size. What I couldn't understand, though, was why. From the sound of it, she was from a very well-to-do family, she succeeded at school and university, she had a lot of very good friends and she had a very good, well-paid, job. Everything you wouldn't expect from a horizontally challenged person and it was her case that prompted me to research the invisible, rather than the surface, reasons behind addiction.

The final addict to confess his sins to the group was a tall chap, mid-forties, called James. I'd noticed him around the house over the course of the weekend because he came across as quite confident and he spoke with a degree of authority, which was kind of bemusing after hearing what he had to say. When he opened his mouth to speak in this context, his whole demeanour changed in an instant.

'I have a sexual addiction called Transvestic Fetishism, or TF, he awkwardly revealed. The rest of us looked at each other quizzically for a few moments before he carried on. 'I have a sexual fetish for wearing women's underwear, which has developed into an addiction, because it is taking over my life'.

'So you're gay?' a guy called Tom blurted out.

'No, I'm not, I'm married, thank you very much.' James responded. 'I also have two children and I love my family dearly'.

'So you're a transvestite, then', Tom came back.

'No, I'm not gay and I'm not a transvestite, Tom, I just get sexually aroused by wearing women's underwear, and then take it off when I climax.' That told Tom. 'The issue is, minutes after orgasm, I get the urge to do it again, and so begins a vicious circle. I don't want to be a girl and I also don't want to be addicted to this. My wife knows about it and often supports me with it, but she doesn't know how often I do it, which is why I want the addictive part of it to end'.

I was fascinated by the idea of an addiction that wasn't dependent on chemicals or drugs or something you ingest, like both Mike's phone addiction and James' TF addiction. I got talking to them after the session and asked if I could use them as case studies for this very book. James kindly agreed to help me out and so will be mentioned extensively throughout this chapter; Mike was not so keen.

I did a lot of research into James' addiction and found that apparently one in twenty men are affected in one way or another by this condition. I question how such presumptions can be made because after speaking to James, it is clear that what he suffered from gave him such shame that he kept it secret for most of his life, so I'd be very surprized if that many people admit to it. If such a statistic is correct, however, virtually everyone will know someone who regularly indulges in this activity. For all I know, some of my closest friends partake in much more enigmatic activities than wearing the underwear of the opposite sex, but I will never know because they keep it to themselves. There are no set rules for addictions including or excluding someone just because they come from a certain demographic or went to a specific school. Everybody has a secret they don't want to share with the rest of the world, which is fine, assuming you're not negatively affecting or hurting anyone or anything.

As with most addictions, people are very good at disguising TF, or denying it even exists. Addicts are renowned for doing that and, as I mentioned earlier in this chapter, as soon as you notice yourself deceiving friends and covering up your tracks, it's a pretty good indicator that you might need to address something.

TF is defined as 'a paraphilia marked by recurrent, intense sexually arousing fantasies, sexual urges, or behaviour involving cross-dressing, in a heterosexual male' [3].

Before I actually took the time to research and analyse this condition, I, like a lot of other people, assumed that it was a sordid, immoral, unscrupulous activity in which to be participating. I had no idea why some people get such satisfaction from doing it. James, like many other men in the world, got so much pleasure from it and yet he told me he saw so much evil in it, too. It was like a see-saw effect, loving it one day, hating it the next. He could go for months without doing it and then suddenly it would come from behind, grab him, and take control of him for however many days or weeks it wanted him for. He told me that he would get so entangled in it that it became something he came to depend on, and as a result of that, he consequently lost all self-control and became addicted to it.

As with all addictions, he was controlled by it. It started when it wanted to and it didn't finish until it was happy. Although it was coming from him, it had a separate identity and the only way for him to crush it was to learn how to gain control over it.

The Invisible Reasons Behind Addiction

To free yourself from addiction, you need to mindfully understand the reasons why you took it up in the first place. I say mindfully because it is not about uncovering the reasons and then lamenting, cursing, regretting and wishing you had never been subjected to it; I say it so that when you do uncover the very reason for your addiction, you learn to wholeheartedly accept it and then acknowledge and observe its existence in the present moment without ever dwelling on it. I'm not talking about the palpable reasons, I'm talking about the invisible ones that led you to where you are now.

The destructive invisible thoughts that you harbour are the cognitive reasons why people turn to addictions and they are completely different for absolutely everyone. It's not like you flick a switch to start an addiction, it's something that develops over a number of years. Take smoking, for example. Nine times out of ten, children start smoking around their peers in order to somehow impress them. Only once they've realized they don't need to smoke in order to impress anyone do they then blame the chemical nicotine for causing their addiction. Invisibly, however, there are much deeper reasons for why they are hooked, and nicotine has nothing to do with it, although the chemical addiction associated with it can often blur the lines.

James has four sisters and a pair of incredibly loving and supportive parents. What, therefore, could have caused him to seek refuge in TF? From a lot of soul searching and long, deep conversations he had with his therapist, it became clear that his desire stemmed from his overwhelming jealousy and need for his mother's love and attention.

He is the second youngest of five siblings. When he was born, his mother gave him the appropriate amount of attention for a newborn. Even as he grew older, during the period while he was the youngest he naturally needed to be looked after far more than his three older sisters. What he didn't realise, though, was that he came to depend solely on his mother's love and affection, leading him to demand and expect it non-stop.

When his younger sister was born, everything changed. No longer was he the metaphorical apple of his mother's eye, he felt like he had suddenly been pushed into fifth place. The arrival of his youngest sister put a halt to the exclusivity that he readily desired from his mother, culminating in a gradual mutation of his state of mind.

With the help of his therapist, James uncovered the uncomfortable truth. Once his status as youngest child had changed, James thought that he was being treated differently. Being the only male child, his developing mind sought to somehow put him in the place of each of his sisters. The only way that he thought this was possible, as ludicrous as it seems, was to try to erase the one, fundamental, major difference between all of them: their gender. His method of doing so was wearing their clothes.

He has a vivid memory from when he must have been about six, of being told off by his mother for wearing his sisters' knickers, and being told to take them off. From that moment on he realized that it was not a normal thing to do but because it was kind of helping him to deal with the rejection of love that he perceived to have occurred, he continued to sporadically partake in the activity of wearing his sisters' underwear until he grew old enough to buy his own.

As the years of engaging in this distinct pastime continued and as James grew old enough to realise that it no longer had anything to do with being loved any more or less, the reasoning for engaging in it slowly started to morph into a sexual desire rather than a cry for help. This subsequently incited the production of dopamine every time he did it, leaving him wanting more and more, again and again, culminating in an addictive state.

After discussing it with his therapist and with me, James began to understand the transgression of the disorder that he had attained. From recognising how it started and consequently developed, we were able to piece together a picture of its humble beginnings and he no longer felt guilty or ashamed for participating in it, as he had done for so many years. Through a newfound pride and acceptance in its existence, he was able to slowly manipulate and control the presence of his addiction until he eventually governed and regulated it 100% of the time. When he did it, he was in control and he therefore understood what he was doing and why. If he didn't feel the urge strongly enough, he merely let it go, rather than encouraging it to fester, like he had previously done on many occasions.

Stop! In the Name of Love ♫

Contrary to popular belief, most people who suffer from addictions, of any sort, actually recover by themselves without the need for any kind of treatment. The majority of these cases are situation related, where people learn to curb their drinking, for example, after leaving university and starting a new job, or having children, or just growing up. The small percentage of people who don't fall into this bracket, though, will benefit greatly from the rest of this chapter and from knowing that having a purpose and ambition in life is one of the fastest ways to stop an addiction.

Whatever you or someone close to you is addicted to, the remaining part of this chapter is designed to help you overcome the addictive state and gain self-control. Just think about it – whatever you have control of, you decide where to take it. You're driving a car, for example. If you want to take the next left, you do. If, however, you are on a bus and fancy taking the next left, if the bus is heading straight down the road, there is no way you will be taking the next left. So think of this chapter as a metaphorical driving lesson to grant you free rein on the road and give you the independence to take your life exactly where you want it to go, without the dreaded unpredictability of addiction.

I may well be stating the blindingly obvious but before you (or anyone you want to help) can overcome an addictive state and get the best out of this approach, you have to first accept that you are addicted. Acceptance, however, will not help you to modify your behaviour or situation until you have made a concerted realisation to WANT to change. This, as you by now know, is a ground rule of Timinology – you are the best person to help yourself and you can only achieve your aims if you WANT to. It is imperative that you have the values in place to oppose the addiction and create the ideal situation to move forwards. The more you fight and deny your addiction, the stronger it becomes. As soon as you accept responsibility for it and the state you find yourself in, the sooner you will be able to gain control of it.

If, like the vast majority of society, you see addiction as a disease and therefore take no responsibility for it, believing that the only way to free yourself from it is with medical treatment and professional counselling, because it's not your fault, then I'm afraid to say that you will always have this hanging over you.

Try instead accepting that you, and you alone, got into this state of mind, regardless of any events leading up to it. Observe your thoughts, actions and feelings and search for the solution to your problems within this chapter. Seek help or speak to your other half, they will play an important role in helping you through, but know that it is not up to them to overcome your addiction, it is up to you, alone.

Instead of berating yourself for the situation in which you have found yourself, be mindful about it; it's happened, there is no point in cursing whatever situation you find landed you in this spot, so try to meditate and clear your mind of all destructive thoughts every time you notice you are lamenting your plight. Try to meditate habitually.

What you are suffering from now is not a disease, it began with choices you made, it continued because of choices you made, but the wonderful thing about this is that it can be overcome through choices you make. You have the power to change everything. You can heal yourself truly, rather than simply suppressing your addiction.

With a Little Help From My Friends ♫

I watched an interesting TED talk by Johann Hari[4], who brings to light the concept that we are intrinsically designed to bond and connect with our surroundings, which normally sees us forming relationships with the people and things around us. If life deals a bad hand and you find yourself in uncharted territory with nobody or nothing to support you, we invariably end up bonding with something that grants us some form of relief, be that drinking, gambling, drugs, sex etc. It is in our nature, we invisibly find ways to make life easier. The majority of us don't become addicts because of the bonds and connections we have with work, family, colleagues, friends etc, for whom we want to be present. If you are an addict, rediscovering relationships, bonds and purposes will give you a much higher chance of making a full recovery.

I have used the sessions I had with James to cultivate and develop coping strategies that anyone will be able to read about and use. If you have someone who you trust implicitly, regardless of their profession, who can earnestly support you throughout the recovery process, I wholeheartedly recommend that you make full use of their comforting ear; because as the age old adage goes, a problem shared is most definitely a problem halved.

161

Before James met his wife and, after that, before he had the chance to discuss his TF with his therapist, although he always knew he didn't want to change sex, it sent his mind into overdrive and prevented him from living an ordinary existence. If you don't have another half, confide in someone close to you who has your best interests at heart. James's therapist aside, he also found that he received a lot of support from his wife, after confiding in her. Believe me, if you are honest about everything to the person you choose to approach, they will welcome you and your problems with open arms.

The earlier statistic that I mentioned about one in twenty men wearing women's clothes at some point or another includes the majority of men who have it under control – who never let it take over their lives. If you're married or settled with another half, the ones who have it under control are the ones who openly share and discuss the issue with each other and who set boundaries and limitations in place to allow it to exist but never flourish or take over. Fetishes are things for the bedroom and that is where they should stay; as a couple you work on keeping them there, together.

As incredible as many of us see the technological revolution of the past few years, it won't be your Facebook or Twitter followers that help you in your time of need, it will be your flesh and blood friends with whom you have deep, resounding, face to face relationships. On the surface, it may seem that this is one of the things that AA does provide to those who haven't been able to find it elsewhere. However, by joining support groups affiliated with programmes like that of AA, although it seems like you're all working together to combat an all consuming evil, you're actually lamenting ferociously about your problems as a whole and not taking care of the only person that needs it the most, you. So read on, take heed of the suggested addiction resolution techniques and then confide in your other half or someone close to you to help implement these strategies into your life.

I, sadly, didn't get the chance to work alongside Mike on his smartphone addiction, mentioned earlier in this chapter, but if he was to read this book, or if anyone who suffers from a similar affliction to his is reading this, then I can only emphasise the importance of forming connections and relationships with the close friends around you in real life, to conquer your addictive state and gain back self-control; step away from the Facebook.

In addition to the connections you make, an app had been developed to closely monitor and then inform you of the amount of screen time you are giving to your smartphone, which can be a very scary wake up call for a lot of people. If you wish to give this a go, 'moment' and 'quality time', for the iphone and android, respectively, will set the wheels in motion.

Invisible Thoughts and Where to Find Them

So what is an invisible thought and how can you establish what yours are? Let's take tying a shoelace, for example. When you were a child you probably spent many hours trying to figure out which lace went where, and which parts to tighten to create a bow. It was a very complicated exercise. Fast forward to today and you probably don't even remember tying your laces this morning, let alone the complicated threading and looping motions that made it happen. The act of tying a shoelace is now invisible to you and so you never consciously think about it. It is a skill you have acquired.

Invisible thoughts can formulate through any number of activities and the related manifestations that accompany them. For example, if I was to mention a banana, the immediate thoughts that might follow, along with that of a yellow piece of fruit, might include things like 'comical', or 'phallic'. You might have imagined peeling one, or the actual taste of it. The thought then sparks another, which will normally be linked to it in some way. Let's say you envisage a man slipping over on a banana skin. This can then activate another invisible thought that should be completely unrelated, diverting your next thought somewhere else. It's a bit like playing that game where you have to say the first thing that enters your head after hearing the last person's word. With absolutely everything comes a subjective invisible thought and it is the way we manage these thoughts that dictates how we react to them.

It is the invisible thoughts related to addictions that struggle to find a definitive ending or diversion. The continuous overload of these linked thoughts that keep refocusing on the addiction creates a massive dopamine imbalance in the brain, resulting in a futile quest to satisfy the brain's desire for the subject of the addiction.

Your brain doesn't need to use up conscious thought processes for everything that you do, so it puts a shortcut in place for you, making these thought routes invisible, or subconscious.

Within our minds, we are constantly developing new techniques to make life easier. The more we repeat something, the more ingrained it becomes and the less visible, or conscious. Not all invisible thoughts are as favourable as the next; some have the power to initiate and nurture an addiction. Not everyone's addictions are very clearly initiated and so the establishment of the invisible thought patterns relating to them is often easy to miss.

I watched another TED talk by a chap called Judson Brewer, called 'A Simple Way to Break a Bad Habit'[5]. Part of his talk focused on how, before the world became such a diverse and busy place, our ancestors had to search for food. They would have seen something that looked good and their brains, would have said 'calories...survival!'. The food then tasted good and they would have remembered where to find it in order to repeat the process. They therefore laid down a context dependent memory whereby they saw the food, ate the food, it felt good, and so they repeated it. As Judson Brewer puts it, 'trigger, behaviour, reward'. As our brains developed and we started to evolve, we realized that the 'feel good' sensation could override feelings of sadness and so we manipulated the same process to keep us happy, devouring a whole tub of ice cream even though we were not hungry. The trigger changed but the behaviour and reward stayed the same.

He goes on to say that likewise, as we grow up, if we want to be accepted by certain groups of people (trigger) we learn to fit into a certain scene, so start to smoke (behaviour) in order to be accepted (reward). From initially using this process to survive, we have morphed it into a technique that is destroying us. Addiction develops in exactly the same way and, before long, without being aware of its destructive force, we can become hooked.

Invisible thoughts don't have to stem from your childhood, they can precipitate at any given moment. So, when trying to establish yours, concentrate on every important event in your life.

If you do have an addiction and you really want to gain back self-control, I implore you to carry out this next task so that you can mindfully uncover the invisible thoughts behind your problem.

Meditation is Your Number One Weapon

Before completing the following exercise, it is of the utmost importance that you can empty your mind from all the noticeable, destructive thoughts that continue to feed your addiction. In order to do this, either revert back to whichever technique you found to be most beneficial in the Kindfulness chapter, or head on over to www.timinology.com and choose the body scan guided meditation. Once you have done that, dedicate as much time as possible, prior to completing the next task, in silent meditation; noticeably emptying your mind from all of the detritus that is preventing you from finding peace. It may take a long time but that doesn't matter, this time is for you, you are performing an act of precious self-love and you deserve everything that you are doing for yourself. When the time is right, you will simply know when your mind is clear and ready to continue with the next part.

Get a sheet of paper and draw a big circle on it. In the centre of the circle I want you to write whatever it is you're addicted to. Now around the circle, I want you to write as many reasons and below-the-surface, invisible thoughts as you can think of, which have developed alongside the addiction.

When James saw a bra, for example, some of the invisible thoughts that entered his mind included: security, innocence, support (emotionally, not for his man boobs), love, relief and importance.

Once you have uncovered the underlying reasons for your addiction, don't, whatever you do, reactivate them in such a way that they become stronger. Whatever the reasons are, they occurred and there is absolutely nothing you can do about it. Instead, use your newfound acceptance of your past to instil a different approach to life that does not allow for the introduction of any addictions to come into play, ensuring the discontinuation of some of the invisible thoughts.

I know I'm not a therapist but since developing and understanding the essence of spirituality and mindful meditation, I can see the biggest problem that James was deluding himself with was refusal to live in the present moment. Mindfulness, as I've already explained to you is all about appreciating and acknowledging the here and now, not, as he found himself doing, imagining himself as a member of the opposite sex, due to a situation that should have been left long ago in the past. Don't get me wrong, I don't think men wearing girls underwear is an intrinsically bad thing to do, so long as you do it knowing who you are, being honest with yourself and your desires, and don't imagine yourself to be someone else.

I Want to Break Free ♫

This chapter has taken a long time to write because there has been so much to research and then put into words. It has also been incredibly hard for James to be a willing case study, because he had to keep recapitulating something that he wanted to leave behind. He found the more I researched and questioned his addiction, the longer he seemed to spend contemplating his role in the whole affair. He told me that he's always been pretty good (or bad, depending how you see it) at procrastinating. When dressed in his own little world, though, procrastinating was just second nature, so there was often a lot of radio silence on his part.

Before I met James at the stately home, he had repressed his desire to dress in female underwear for nearly three years, after his second child was born. He genuinely thought that he had cured himself from its steely grip. Only now does he realise that he was sitting on a repression time bomb that eventually exploded in magnificent style, causing him to retrace his TF past. They do say that everything happens for a reason and if it wasn't for the explosion, he wouldn't have attended the meditation weekend, wouldn't have met me and wouldn't have helped me to piece together this successful addiction conquering strategy.

As you are now well aware, when you repress something, it will return in a frighteningly exaggerated form. Six months after the meditation course, when I started to write this chapter, I decided to contact James again to get some first hand documentation of how his addictive state had been manifesting. It turns out he had been repressing the TF again, only this time, he felt, because I had shown such an interest in its development. The more he thought about his addiction, the more he started piecing all the threads of his life together, until suddenly he realized that he was genuinely addicted to it and he needed to gain back his self-control. As you can imagine, the desires came flooding back and within a couple of days he had snuck off to a lingerie outlet and purchased himself some garments. He'd told his wife that it was all for research and so she compassionately agreed to support the activity.

It all came to a head one night when the children had been put to bed and he attempted to entice his dearest wife into bed. After getting a little frisky, he suggested that they bring a little TF into it. She point blank refused and told him that it was starting to get a hold of him again and take over their lives. Being the belligerent male, he told her that it was his way or the highway and sulkily turned on the TV. After about an hour of being a narcissistic child, he apologized for his mercenary attitude and made up with her. It was only later in the night that the answer to addiction dawned on him.

Because of the embarrassing and disreputable connotations associated with society's view of TF and because of the negative stance affiliated with addiction, James had unwittingly become profoundly ashamed of himself for partaking in it. Yes, he would easily be able to tell himself that it was a completely innocent past time that affected absolutely no one but deep down he was so humiliated and confused by his actions that the only way to console himself was to seek refuge within it. It was like a never-ending circle which kept repeating itself, getting stronger and stronger. The best way to make yourself feel better when you are down is to release dopamine, the easiest way for him to release dopamine was to indulge in TF and so the vicious circle continued.

So there he was lying awake after a sensual time with his wife and the penny suddenly dropped.

As the saying goes, the wolf you feed wins. Through the shame, guilt and dishonour that James harboured from indulging in TF, he was feeding the addiction that would take over his life. He might have needed his wife to point out the destructive force it was having on him but, once he recognized it, he learned how to put an end to it and then, with great generosity of spirit, shared it with me.

As completely preposterous as it seems, this is genuinely how he managed to end the addiction almost in an instant: by realising that he had to form an innocent affection for it. In doing so, you're not feeding it, you're just appreciating its presence within you. By cultivating an affection for it, you no longer need to devote 100% of your time to it, because you've already accepted it. He was mindfully observing, accepting and discovering its inner workings.The shame doesn't come from the addictive action or substance you may be abusing, the shame comes from the loss of all control that the addiction has over you. You are at its mercy. Developing an affection allows you to control the relationship.

I'm not saying form an affection for the addiction itself, I'm telling you to form an affection for elements of the activity, which means that you no longer feel ashamed of your actions. The shame was feeding James' addiction, not starving it. Mindfully cultivate a curiosity for your new friendship and then question its meaning. Because it is now your friend, you can delve deep into its workings and, by being curious, you can question its very existence.

James set his mind on a new train of thought and affection for TF, beginning to replace the time he spent indulging in it with his mindful meditation sessions. As soon as he did this, the addiction loosened its grip on him and granted him the mental space to think about women's underwear as just another generic piece of clothing and to no longer feel the need to use it in the way he had been doing. For the first time in many years he was able to think nonchalantly about a previously lascivious item of clothing. He was free from its addictive grip. He had gained back his self-control. He never repressed the thoughts and actions of dressing but every time they arose, he set himself specific times to indulge in them, mindful of why he was doing it and what effect it was having on him but always mindfully conducting himself with respect and pride. He lost the negative, shameful thoughts that were previously feeding the addiction. Over time, the desire and yearning for it lessened and lessened and, from what he has told me, I won't be surprised if it eventually leaves him for good.

What he will never do, however, is allow it to gain control over him again. He now owns his addiction. He is in the driving seat and is no longer ashamed. As long as you don't ban and repress your desires to indulge in an activity to which you were previously addicted, assuming you have learned to mindfully respect and approve of it, you will never lose control of it again.

This method of thought that helped James to control his TF can easily be shaped to remedy a multitude of other addictions.

Following on from the breathing space meditation discussed in the Kindfulness chapter, James' acceptance and awareness of the TF gave him the ability to notice exactly how his body felt just before the addictive state was about to take control of him, thereby effectively signalling the moment for him to take some time out for himself. He would conduct a mindful meditation, acknowledging and accepting the present moment, preventing his thoughts from progressing towards TF.

He told me that he would get this hollow feeling at the bottom of his stomach, which would invariably slowly move towards his genitals, indicating the start of a period of time before the feeling would eventually transform into a sexual desire. Anyone's bodily feelings towards whatever addiction they may have may well be completely different to this example but, by mindfully assessing your own state and understanding exactly how your body reacts to certain stimuli, you will be in a far better position to gain control over it. If you're addicted to eating and are constantly hungry, instead of giving in to it, try observing that feeling instead; spend the time you would be eating to just curiously appreciating and accepting your desire. Remind yourself to always observe yourself before eating. If you don't feel anything, though, however hard you explore, do not worry, that is absolutely fine and nothing to be alarmed by. Focus, instead, on the thoughts that are activated during the run up to and initiation of the activity, and then piece together a recognizable routine of thoughts that your mind regularly enacts before you get into an addictive state. Learn to use that as a mindful alert to trigger an appropriate response.

Free As a Bird ♫

During your next meditation session, instead of blocking and repressing any thoughts connected to your addiction, try this time to just allow them to brew for a short while. Look past the addictive state into which it used to put you and appreciate and love its presence. Notice how it affects your body, feel its presence within you. Is it warm, cold, light or heavy? What shape is it? What colour is it? You're meditating, you're being mindful, you're calm and you're happy, so allow the activity you used to be addicted to into the same peaceful place that you are now in and laugh with it. Know that it will never control you again because it is now your friend and you can decide where to take it.

Use your circle diagram to highlight all of the invisible thoughts that have led you to where you are now. Bring these thoughts to the table and visualize how they have led you astray. But also notice how you are feeling in this exact moment and know that you have the power to decide exactly where to take it. Think about the dopamine hit you are receiving from your addiction: can you feel it? Where is it in your body? Know that without the dopamine you wouldn't have any care in the world for your addiction, so try to divert your attention away from the hit and create some mental space between you and the activity.

I am not telling you to suddenly repress the desire for whatever it is you're addicted to, because that will not work. Don't, however, carry on partaking in the activity like you were before you realized you needed to confront it. Instead, set yourself limited access to it, say once a day to start off with, enable yourself to make a choice about it. Enable yourself to control it, rather than letting it control you. Choose it. Then, every time you indulge in it, take note of why you used to be addicted to it and the negative consequences it is having on you.

Slowly begin to replace the time spent on your addictive activities by mindfully meditating over your whole body. Take some time out to do a body scan meditation (advice on this can be found on the website and it was described in the Kindfulness chapter). If you can feel when it is about to rear its head, take note of how and where you notice it and then learn to devote that time to yourself. Breathe love, joy and happiness into that space. If you can't feel anything, that doesn't matter, just notice your thoughts and accept the present moment as it is. Use these sessions to help redevelop a strong love for yourself and to appreciate this new activity. Be proud of yourself for confronting your addiction because this is one of the best things you have ever done for yourself. The Love Chapter is approaching, which will explain to you how self-caring like this will help you to slowly develop an incredible relationship with your inner self, that will turn you into the happiest person you have ever been. Pride will curb the addiction appropriately; in the meantime, maintain the control and the ability to CHOOSE. It is still your friend, though, so be harsh with it but not vicious.

The main emphasis of this technique is to foster respect and pride for the activity, whilst accepting its presence within you, not repressing the innocent side of it when in a mindful state. Remember that shame is the catalyst for addiction, so that is what you need to banish – but by giving it no home within your mind, rather than by repressing it.

Straightaway I can almost hear people remonstrating their points of view about how you should never be affectionate and respectful of an activity that is potentially life-threatening like smoking, excessive eating, drinking or drug abuse. That's just it, though; people don't take up smoking because it is a foul habit, they do it because there is something enchanting about it. Know that you need to give up but instead of concentrating on the negative effects of the addiction, inciting shame and secrecy, create a fervent curiosity for it whilst partaking it it. Notice how it makes your body feel and learn to mindfully lay to rest early warning signs of the addiction as soon as you feel them. Get to know your addiction; know its weaknesses. Know how the dopamine hit is the cause of the addiction and envisage how the activity is affecting your life. Visualise the invisible thoughts that have led you to the addiction and know that you are now in control of them.

When you're affectionate with someone or something, honeymoon period aside, you have to work at it to keep the love flowing. This is the one exception that you no longer have to work at. The reminiscing affection you start off with will eventually taper off into a like, to an 'it's okay' to an 'I can't be bothered'. But as I said at beginning of this chapter, if you ever fall off the wagon and have a sly cigarette away from your designated time, DO NOT feel ashamed, because that will re-ignite the addiction. Laugh about it, be open with yourself about it, be mindful, meditate to clear your mind and then get back to your day's activities. What I am teaching you is how to end an addiction and gain back self-control of your life. You can still have a drink and not be addicted.

Let's Twist Again ♫

During my work on James' story, he mentioned to me another activity in which he frequently indulged which he found would often intensify the pleasurable feelings he received from TF. This activity was quite simply denying himself the achievement of sexual climax.

I was a little sceptical about including this until I realized the phenomenal power that abstaining from the activity had on his psyche. This particular technique is called 'edging', in that it sees the practitioner masturbating until he (or she) nearly reaches climax, only to purposely stop the stimulation seconds before, in order to delay the eventual orgasm. Although James was abstaining from climaxing, it didn't terminate the pleasure he was receiving from the TF – in fact, it intensified it – and so he was therefore fixed in a state of awe and wonder, often for days (when his wife and children were visiting her parents, who live abroad), without a care in the world for anything else. Because the practise generates a high dose of dopamine, it was enough to keep him transfixed by the state. By purposely abstaining from orgasm, he would never allow the dopamine levels to subsequently reduce, which prevented him from ever reaching a post-orgasmic state of composure (refractory period) and the shame that came with it. This practise alone was a founding block for the addiction.

I had never heard of 'edging' before, so I was genuinely fascinated by how such a seemingly innocuous distraction could near on (temporarily, at least) control his whole existence. After a lot of research, I found a website that recognized it as a sexual practise. This website, which is called www.nofap.com,[6] classes the act of masturbating as 'fapping' and urges people under the influence of a sexual addiction to 'reset' their sexual clock by abstaining from 'fapping' for ninety days. It mentions that although edging does not incite an orgasm, it is effectively the same as fapping, owing to the resulting mass production of dopamine. As a result, to reset your sexual clock, any form of genital stimulation is banned.

Although James had not heard of this website before, his attempts to keep the addiction under control were very similar – he just tried to stop masturbating. Coupled with the extensively trialled aforementioned techniques, he is now in full remission.

As much as I wanted to make this book as child-friendly as possible (oops) I thought long and hard about whether or not I should include the edging/fapping accounts in it. Yes, it may seem a bit crude to be discussing masturbation but, hearing how after only a couple of weeks of abstaining from it, James was transformed from an irritable, self-possessed, resentful and addicted man into quite literally the opposite, I decided to include it. I figured this section will help anyone who is having trouble conquering a sexual addiction.

It was at this point that my editor, upon reading the draft, left me a highlighted, capitalized comment, expressing in despair that I had just quashed my whole argument about abstaining from repression, by advocating it in the final few paragraphs. So, just as I had to explain to her, I will explain to you how not 'fapping' for ninety days does not have anything to do with repressing your addictive state.

If the genitalia is not aroused, the desire to conduct sexual activity of any kind will significantly diminish, until the sufferer becomes less and less inclined to participate in the addictive activity. It will eventually become a thing of the past. James explained to me that the two work hand in hand (chortle). He said that the beneficial feelings associated with TF were always enhanced by the act of fapping, and that in abstaining from one half of it, the other half ceased to have any real point. He said it lost any sort of meaning and he found himself feeling rather ridiculous sitting in his bedroom wearing ill fitting underwear. This gave him even more drive to end the addictive state.

This approach is not repressing the addiction, but taking away some of the fuel. Let's take a BBQ (your sex life). The BBQ is a good thing, it needs to be alight to cook your food. You can throw anything into it and it will burn but some things burn more ferociously and violently than others, ruining your food. Let's say that masturbation is petrol. You don't want to throw petrol onto a BBQ because it will not only burn your food to cinders, it will also make it taste repulsive. Instead, throw on a bit of charcoal (in this instance, the controlled sexual desire time you have set aside for yourself) and let it slowly take light, as the blaze softens. Masturbation isn't a bad thing but it needs to be controlled. If your sexual desires are morphing into an addiction, take note of this whole chapter but start with the most effective strategy of all and make a concerted effort to prevent yourself from masturbating for ninety days.

If masturbation is your addiction, learning to curb and control your impulses for ninety days is paramount for you to regain self-control. By all means, when the ninety days are up, pleasure yourself every now and again, but from reading the personal accounts of a lot of past sufferers, your desires to continue your previous path will have diminished considerably. Do check out the website to get some more inspiration to start your ninety day Nofap.

TF, as I mentioned earlier, is known as a paraphilia. Although a paraphilia is not an addiction until it takes over your life, the controlled abstention method, coupled with the addiction strategies I set out earlier, are a strong hold way to get it under control. Although TF is a completely innocuous past-time while you have it under control, not all paraphilias are as innocent.

I must reiterate that if you happen to be partaking in an addictive activity that is illegal, be that taking drugs or sexually dominating another person who is either underage or has not given you their express consent, then you have to put an end to it now and seek professional help. The strategies I have explained to help you conquer an addictive state have been devized in such a way to help you gain pride in yourself for facing up to it, and then taking control. The approaches I lay out in this chapter are designed for situations (within the law) that are yet to reach the stage where professional help is necessary and to help prevent sufferers from reaching that stage. Establishing an affection for your addictive activity is part of the Timinological path to gaining control of it, but it is impossible to be profoundly affectionate towards an illegal activity, because you are either endangering the wellbeing – or even life – of you or someone else in the process. This type of activity needs to be stopped immediately. You have to seek professional help, now.

The next time you find yourself smoking, drinking, trying on underwear of the opposite sex or eating far too much, pause for a moment and take the time to question and be curious about your motives, while you are indulging. You'll be amazed with how prudent you can be when facing your emotive desires, head on. Even if you simply prove to yourself you are not addicted, you will learn something about yourself. Gain back your self-control.

Timmy's Tips

- To gain control of an addiction you have to face up to it and never try to repress it.

- When you have achieved a state of acceptance within yourself for the addiction, mindfully observe how it makes you feel, how does it affect your body, where can you sense it? Work out the shape, size, colour, scent and position of it; and then actively respond to any warning signs it might be approaching, and lay it to rest with meditative love.

- Develop an affection for your addiction, because the friendlier you are with it, the friendlier it will be back to you

- Shame will reignite the addiction. The more open you are about your journey, the easier it will be for you

- Every time you partake in the activity, be curious with it. Know that you now control it, not the other way around

- Remind yourself of the list of invisible thoughts you compiled that led you to the addiction, and then methodically create ways to change them

- Do not try to replace one addiction with another

- Regardless of how hard it is, learn how to deal with any situation involving your addiction calmly and effectively.

- Set yourself achievable start and end times for partaking in the activity, lengthening the time between each episode and shortening its duration

- When you find yourself engaging in the addictive activity, make a point of ceasing it without anger, resentment, apathy or depression

- If you slip up and resume the activity out of your scheduled time, do not punish yourself. Maintain your dignity over the addiction. You are in control.

- Develop positive, effective motivation, and keep good relations with all your friends, family and colleagues. They are the ones who will be there for you when the addiction has abandoned you.

- Form bonds with your close friends and family to help you rise above it.

Self-Love

For as long as you fail to love and accept yourself, you will judge that you are not beautiful enough, successful enough, rich enough, loved enough, lucky enough, or anything-else enough.

– Robert Holden, PhD., Be Happy [1]

This type of love is often wildly misconstrued as a moral fault, affiliated with vanity, selfishness and greed. True self-love could not be further from this presumption. In 1956, psychologist and social philosopher Erich Fromm determined that 'loving oneself is different from being arrogant, conceited or egocentric, meaning instead caring about oneself, and taking responsibility for oneself' [2]. It simply boils down to a regard for one's own wellbeing and happiness. Only once you accept, love and respect yourself can you begin your journey of self-discovery.

The Man With the Child in His Eyes ♫

The need to learn how to love yourself arises as soon as we leave the innocence and tranquillity of childhood and enter into a world that is constantly judging, belittling and taunting us into unobtainable perfection.

I have two amazing, adorable little nephews, who are such a pleasure to be around. Yes, they whine and cry a little bit but that's only because that's the most effective way for them to express their needs. But when they're fed, have had a good sleep and don't need to go to the bathroom, watching how immeasurably happy and content they are with the simplest things is truly breathtaking. Give them a cardboard box and they will literally play with it for hours, expressing such grounded pleasure, wanting nothing more; until my sister puts them to bed and then all hell breaks loose.

Obviously, as you grow up your needs change and satisfaction isn't granted in quite such simple ways as playing with a cardboard box. Nevertheless, to be able to obtain such pure pleasure and joy from something so uncomplicated is sadly a trait that leaves us as soon as we are taught to believe that there are better things out there. In today's world, where we're surrounded by technology and the need to constantly communicate and acquire, it is only getting harder for parents to shield their children from undergoing this change earlier and earlier.

Technologic ♫

This world is a place in which we attempt to satisfy our every whim, a place that is filled with things to keep our minds active for every waking minute. I'm not a parent yet, so maybe my mindset will change when a mini-Timmy appears, but I am utterly shocked by the dependence that some young children have on iPads, televisions and laptops etc. If we take our children's attention away from the world in which they are living and absorb them into a technological, separate dimension there is little left but blank smiles and distraction in between. It is the opposite of mindfulness, ingrained into children by parents, from a regrettably young age. iPads weren't around when I was growing up and my parents did a pretty good job, so why should we rely on these things to divert the attention of our children now? Smile at them, laugh with them, play with them.

I get that the world is constantly changing and we need to evolve and include things like these in our lives. The Mental Health Foundation website (www.mentalhealth.org. uk) suggests that the cases of mental illness are rapidly rising as a direct consequence of dependence on this new technological age. I don't know about you but I can't see the diagnoses declining any time soon if we continue to teach our children to depend on these devices.

I was only really talking about infants there, too. The children actually growing up just want to play computer games or play on their smartphones instead of building dens and campfires – and now even adults only seem satisfied when they're fiddling with a phone. I'm as guilty as anyone else when it comes to this but I can definitely see how it is slowly dampening the excitement about anything else in life. How can we expect to develop self-love when there is so much else going on to take our attention away from ourselves and the moment in which we live.

Take Facebook and other forms of social media, for example. I can honestly say that in real life I see about thirty or so of my so-called 1000ish friends. Yet, I too can become obsessed with seeing what people (who I will probably never see again in my life) have to say (on something about which I couldn't really give a shit). Many of my close friends have actually left Facebook for this very reason. Perhaps it's time to follow suit.

And celebrities, oh my goodness – there's something I will never get. I think before the accident I used to be a little bit celebrity savvy but upon not being able to recognise a large proportion of my friends' faces after the fall, I gave up caring what people I really didn't care about looked like, or did. I almost feel a little smug when someone mentions a 'celebrity' name and I have no idea who they're talking about. Yes, if it's a big news story, I might know what is going on but on some level even following the news is a sure-fire way to bring you down.

You can obviously still learn to self-love and own a smart phone, a tablet, or whatever other tech wizardry there might be, but you mustn't let it take over your life. I very rarely go on the London underground, because I love walking or cycling everywhere but the last time I subjected myself to it, I properly focused my attention on everyone else on the carriage. I think the London underground is maybe a poor example, because everyone acts in a very 'get in, get out' fashion, but I noticed that well over half of the commuters were staring mindlessly into their phones. Nobody was talking to one another and there was not one smile. It was truly dispiriting. I know people aren't expected to socialise on a morning commute to work but imagine if we couldn't hide behind these devices. If people did socialise, think how much happier we all would be. And with happiness comes a true sense of self-worth, which consequently develops into self-love.

Going Underground ♫

As it happens, there is a delightfully cheesy urban anecdote about the London underground, which some of you may have heard before but I want to share it with you anyway. So, if you will indulge me in a little bit of story-telling... are you sitting comfortably? Then I shall begin...

It must have been during the day, because there were a few seats available. A young chap boarded the train and seated himself next to a beautiful girl, who was hunched over, scribbling notes in her diary.

As the train moved from the platform and into the tunnel, the window opposite them became mirrored with the dark background, allowing the boy to see who he was sitting next to, without breaking tube etiquette and actually looking around him. On seeing her reflection, he realized he was alongside the girl of his dreams.

He turned to make a move but noticed that she was wearing headphones, so didn't want to disturb her from listening. The train drew into the next station and she stayed seated, as did he. When it set off again, he was once again able to see her reflection.

He was genuinely smitten with this girl's looks and knew he couldn't risk her getting off the train before he had the chance to say something. She was still busy writing, though, and listening to her music.

He suddenly had an idea. He reached over and tapped her diary. She glanced up at him, whereupon he politely gestured to borrow her pen, moving his hand in a writing motion. She handed it over and leaned back in her seat, expecting him to turn away and make his own note. He didn't move away, though, instead motioning to jot something on her diary.

Just before he made a mark, he looked at her, as if to ask if it was okay to write something, to which she nodded in bemusement and then watched him write:

'Hi, I know this is a bit unusual but I noticed you are listening to music, so I don't want to disturb you from that.' He paused and then began again. 'You are the prettiest girl I've ever seen. I couldn't let you get off without telling you that.' Her face automatically lit up and she smiled the biggest smile she had ever smiled.

I have no idea how the conversation went after that but the story goes that they both missed their stops and ended up going on a date a few days later, eventually marrying.

You can be forgiven for questioning why I included such an unlikely story. The point is that tales like this would never happen if the protagonist didn't love and care for himself enough to a), put himself in her position, not disturbing her from the music; b), make such a romantic gesture by writing in her diary; and c), wait and not rush the first date. Loving yourself is about seeing the good you can get out of every situation and how to diligently go about it. So if you want the Richard Curtis ending, follow my lead and see where it can take you. Is it still raining? I hadn't noticed...

Don't Hold Me Back ♪

Splendid, I thought. Before I tell you the techniques I used to learn to love myself again, I just want to go over a few things that restricted my self-loving development. At the time I just presumed that these are the sorts of things that everybody believes but only since researching the detrimental effects of loathing oneself, which is what I probably did, have I come to realise the resounding benefits of self-love.

Every time I walked with a group of three or more friends, I would always be walking behind everyone and not contributing to the conversation. I noticed it every time it happened and yet always shrugged it off because I felt that they probably had more important things to talk about. They weren't deliberately excluding me from the conversations, I just wasn't sure enough of myself to bring anything to the table, so to speak. I could have talked about anything, because that's what friends do, but I had so little belief in my conversation that I just let them do all the talking. It seems fairly insignificant but I only noticed it because it became a recurring situation which slowly started to impact on me.

As you will remember, Tier One was not receiving the success it deserved based on the amount of time I was spending on it. Alongside this, virtually all of my friends were getting married and having children. As a result of these combined factors, I found myself constantly comparing myself to all them. It wasn't just about the money and relationship aspect, it was about their whole lives. I remember going to a wedding a few years ago and speaking to Lels, the wife of my friend, Freddie. I was a little drunk, so I said what I had been thinking.

'I'm so envious of your life', I stumbled. 'You guys have such amazing jobs, which you both love, you live in such an incredible house, and are always so happy'.

Lels was a little taken aback by my presumptions of such perfection.

'I promise you, Timmy, yes, we love each other dearly and, yes, we've got well-paid jobs, but that doesn't come without arguments and sleepless nights'. I was a little astounded. 'We're not perfect but we work at it; these are the parts you don't see'.

I think that was the first time my naïve little mind got a glimpse of real life. Lels could have easily just thanked me for being so complimentary, which would have left me to commend and applaud the next of my friend's lives, but she didn't, and her frank honesty was a stepping stone for me to stop comparing my life to others'. It was quite an eye opener for me to be told that even the most 'perfect' of my friend's lives wasn't all that I believed it was. There are so many variables that we don't see, in each and every life, and by comparing your life to that of anyone else, without knowing the full story, will lead to harsh self-judgement. Even if you do know the variables, comparing your life to that of anyone else is a blatant sign that you are not happy with yours and therefore not experiencing self-love.

The Dalai Lama says that, 'Love brings self-confidence, anger brings fear [3]'. How very true that statement is. If I had had enough affection and love for myself at the time of speaking to Lels, I would have never expressed my jealousy of her 'perfect life'. As it was, however, I was just angry at myself for not making Tier One a success and consequently fearful of how my life was, supposedly, compared to those of all my friends.

Another trait of 'self-loathing' that I regularly allowed to dominate was that of constantly seeking the approval of others. Although I was running my business and doing my own thing, making my career path hard to compare with all my other friends' jobs, I was in constant need of reassurance from my peers that I was doing well in life.

Work aside, I got massively into cycling, every day, and if it wasn't for their approval, I genuinely think I would have stopped doing it. Luckily for me, however, there was no criticism and I have only had to stop cycling so fanatically since moving to London – as I said before, for fear of getting mown down by a lorry.

I am regularly coming up with new business ideas. Not so long ago I came up with, in my opinion, a fantastic idea, to revolutionise the way students learn material for exams. I told all my friends who, or so I thought at the time, said it was a great idea. I started researching and scoping ways to get it started. It was only a few months later that one of them took me aside and basically told me to stop wasting my life because it was a crap idea and they were all just humouring me because they didn't think I'd take it any further. I was genuinely quite shocked by their brutal honesty but because I was after their approval and because I wasn't going to get it from setting up this new business, I put the idea to bed. I haven't given up on it, though, and I still believe it will be a great success but only now do I trust and love myself enough to make a go of it. Remember: love brings self-confidence.

There were also two other reasons why I didn't pursue the groundbreaking student learning project, and both are intrinsically linked to not loving myself. The first is that I constantly doubted myself. I didn't have the approval of my friends but I also didn't believe enough in my own ability, which boils down to not loving myself. Here's a scenario: let's imagine a couple who've been together for a long time. Now imagine that they are a team, trying to achieve a specific goal. If they know deep down that the goal is achievable, they will put in everything they have to make it work, and each half of the couple will do the same. If, however, one thinks that it's too much work and isn't realistically viable, they will encroach on the idea and put it to bed. That's not a great way to support a partner, and shows a distinct lack of love. Transfer the same situation onto doubting yourself and you can straightaway see how it illustrates your own lack of self-love. Again, love brings confidence.

The second reason for holding back on launching this idea is that I kept reliving my past failure with Tier One. In my mind, if I couldn't make that work, then there was no way that I would have been able to get any other business to work. What a negative and downward way to look at things. Since learning to love myself, I have actually begun to see the demise of Tier One as a positive and now think of it as a massive lesson that I needed to learn and understand, before moving forwards.

The final symptom of lacking compassion for myself was how overly critical I was about everything I did. Revert back to the couple situation that I just mentioned. Imagine how you would feel if your other half constantly criticized you for everything you did. It's easy, you wouldn't put up with it, you'd argue and fight back, so why on earth did I tolerate my own constant negative influence on everything that I did? Tier One failed, you're a loser, give up. You'll never get a girlfriend, you're too ugly. You flunked school, you didn't get a great grade for your degree, you're so stupid. Your friends laugh at you. You're a waste of space. I genuinely listened

186

to these thoughts in my head every single day and yet I did nothing about it. I just thought that that was my draw and I had to deal with it. Oh, how wrong I was. I am writing this book to let people know that anything is possible and you just need to open your eyes to the certainties in life that so many people miss.

Who Feels Love? ♫

As I mentioned at the beginning of this chapter, it is only once we grow apart from the innocence of childhood that we slowly start to disengage with truly loving ourselves. We undoubtedly used to love ourselves, in the peace and happiness of childhood, so this next section is all about learning how to rekindle and nurture the love that has been misplaced.

There are of course exceptions in circumstance but on the whole, most people will say they had a happy, carefree childhood. Part of the reason for this is that children are inherently mindful, until the world teaches them to change. Can you remember the intensity of feelings that you had as a child? The vividness of particular memories? In part, yes, it's because life was simpler. In part, however, it's because as a child you were mindful. As a child, you live in the moment, which is why the world seems so intense, why textures, tastes and feelings seemed so strong. This was only possible because as a small child, you unquestioningly loved yourself – a state away from which most of us drift, during our teens.

The first exercise in the Timinological approach to self-love is to try and reignite the warmth you felt for yourself as a child, before you went to school, and see how the current life you are leading would be interpreted through the eyes of your inner child. How do you think your inner child would react to the ways you have been treating yourself? I know for certain that mine would have been in absolute turmoil until fairly recently in my life. Imagine telling a child that he is an ugly waste of space who couldn't organise a piss up in a brewery (well, perhaps just a milk-drinking competition in a dairy). If I actually treated a child in the way I was treating myself, there is no doubt that I would have been imprisoned for cruelty.

As an important first step towards recapturing the love you once felt for yourself, you need to envisage your inner self reverted back to that of a child and treat yourself appropriately. Try this for two or three days at first. Obviously you can still perform your normal life as an adult but talk back to yourself when your mind produces negative thoughts. Look after your mind, like it is that of a child again. Imagine that you are taking responsibility for a child. You'll find that you no longer berate yourself for past failures, you'll sympathetically acknowledge the mistake and calmly find an effective way to put it right. As an example, let's pretend that you've just received a parking ticket. I know that in the past I would have irreconcilably chastized myself for being so stupid and parking in the wrong place, and basically beaten myself up about it. When I treat myself more compassionately, though, like I would a child in my care, I would calmly observe what the mistake was, realise it's not the end of the world and maybe even laugh about it, allowing me to evade the stress, see it for what it is and move on with a healthy mindset.

I came across an aspiring self-help guru on YouTube, called Teal Swan, who says you 'can't practise loving anything before loving yourself'[4]. She has devized a very simple strategy to put this premise into practise and advised her followers to conduct it every day for a full year. I don't like to submit myself to prolonged regimes but I have given this a go and it has had a miraculous impact on my state of mind. I therefore implore you to also give it a go. Here it is: Before you make any decisions, I want you to ask yourself, 'What would someone who loves themselves do?' Whether it's a critically important decision about your future, or even something as simple as whether you go to pub A or pub B for an evening drink. Have a go at using this incredibly simple technique to help you determine an outcome. Putting your decisions to this test and doing so consistently for a set period of time will effectively help you achieve everything you spiritually need to reach a state of confident self-love. I say spiritually because loving yourself has no physical bearings in life. It is all about reaching a definitive goal which can only be accessed through your mind and, moreover, your spirit.

Ask yourself this question before absolutely any decision and your higher, loving self will immediately give you an answer. It is then all about having the courage to act on your intuition. You will be asking yourself to come to a decision through the medium of love, so don't ever doubt the answer presented to you. When people choose to be guided by love, they choose the right outcome and the most important relationship in life is the one we have with ourselves.

Teal's suggested self-loving questioning highlights the simple fact that loving yourself is about consistently carrying out actions that feel aligned with your heart, gut or intuition. Loving yourself comes down to your actions, nothing more, nothing less. You have the ability and power to start loving right now.

In taking care of and cherishing yourself (your inner child) – and the more often you do it – you will start to experience new growth within yourself. You'll witness an abundance of energy, a feeling of safety and a zest for life – like taking a Berocca for your soul. By continuing to participate in a lifestyle that neglects and ignores your inner child, you will notice a downward spiral in your self-esteem and self-love, culminating in a lack of the drive and happiness needed to promote successful living. I will therefore give you a list of actionable tasks to help get your self-loving started. You don't have to take them all up straightaway but do try to gradually introduce them into your daily schedule. You'll notice that the more you do, the less of a struggle life will seem and loving yourself will become second nature.

Lets start with one of the most basic, yet fundamentally imperative, actions required to reignite your self-loving.

Twist and Shout ♫

You need to be active. I'm not saying you should run a marathon, though that is certainly a great goal you can set yourself. Setting any kind of goal in respect to this will not only increase your fitness but will motivate you to take part in life. Achieving it will give you a massive amount of self-respect. If you are chronically stagnant for too long, the energy which is meant to be burnt off through exercise finds itself dwelling within your body and then turning itself into anxiety, stress and sadness, the polar opposite of what you should be feeling. So instead of playing computer games, watching TV or sitting in your office chair all day, go for a walk or a run, or go to the gym. Do anything that raises your heart rate a little. Jog up and down the stairs. Go dancing. Why not walk to work, if it's not too far. Or if you get the tube, get off a couple of stops early and then walk from that stop. If you drive, park a mile away from work and then walk from your car. Just change whatever you normally do in order to start burning off the energy which needs to be let out. It will also make you a happier person, so it's win/win.

Honey Pie ♫

You will have hopefully already read the chapter dedicated to Nutrition, so I'm not going to go into too much detail. Just know that the food you put into your body is not simply for fuel. Humans are not combustion engines. We are very complex, dynamic, organic and infinitely sensitive systems, so learning about what to eat is imperative to getting the best out of your body and mind. Gorging yourself on fast food whilst sitting in front of the TV is most definitely not a self-loving practise. Neither is watching the news, reality television or following friends on social media who are constantly negative about everything; so delete the negative friends because there is no reason you should be brought down to their level. They are the junk food of your mind.

I'm Only Sleeping ♫

We spend roughly a third of our life asleep, so make it good and make it count. The bedroom should be for sleeping, or for incredible sex with your other half. It shouldn't be a place to play with your smartphone and post mindless sentiments about nonsensical drivel you recently discovered. So take all electronic items out of your bedroom and cultivate a fondness for yourself and your other half. There is plenty of time to look at your phone in the daytime.

Mailman, Bring Me No More Blues ♫

Be more decisive about how you spend your time and start to set goals for what you want to achieve. Learn to say no to all the things that wear you down; be they socialising with people who don't share the same values as you, or taking on unnecessary work commitments that serve you no favours at all. Dedicate time in your calendar for all the fun, light and playful scenarios you can possibly partake in. The more you honour, cherish and simply spend time with yourself, the more you will cultivate your inner child and develop self-love.

Alongside your fortified sleeping regime and new-found healthy eating, start to take time out for yourself. There is no way you will be able to function effectively and help anyone else if you are not in top shape. So take a nap in the day if you need one and do not let anyone make you feel guilty about this. Meditate whenever you feel pressured by any situation and you'll be amazed by how quickly you can relieve your mind from constricting thoughts. Go back to the Kindfulness chapter and re-read the section on re-igniting the feeling of a past love, for yourself. Free your mind. Take your mind off everything. Just lie down on the floor and breathe.

Imagine ♫

You don't have to be alone to meditate but it's not easy to make a social activity of it either, so relish the opportunity to be by yourself and take full advantage of this quiet time that you have acquired. You're freeing your mind from all the detritus that has gathered in it but at the same time you're stimulating a love story with your inner self.

Roll Over Beethoven ♫

So you're rested, your mind is at ease and you've just got back from a great little run. This time is all about you, have some fun. You've got to incorporate regular play into your schedule. Retrace your life back to before you were working every hour of the day and think about what you did to entertain yourself. You could even take up something new that you've never done before. I got into painting last year and I will now happily while away many an evening trying to create some Timmy art, instead of staring at the TV or the screen of my phone until I am ready to go to sleep. I'm not saying I'm any good but it is certainly very relaxing and liberating. I used to be a bit of a wannabe rock star and only very recently have I picked up my guitar again and started trying to recreate Jim Morrison's poetic masterpieces. It has brought back many fond memories and is just such a great way to unwind. So recapture your playful, creative side and dedicate time for yourself, because it's one of the fastest ways to re-awaken your inner child.

Eleanor Rigby ♫

This exercise is about self-recognition and is purely to help you recognise, appreciate and acknowledge your achievements because more often than not we overlook a lot of what we have done well, passing it off as just another mundane act.

As mentioned earlier in this chapter, instead of always criticizing yourself and seeing the flaws in everything, look at what you are actually doing really well. It doesn't have to be the sudden realisation of how to achieve world peace – although any ideas are welcome, so send them to me on a postcard. It merely needs to be something that has brought you an element of pride and joy and helped you to focus on your own inner beauty.

'At the end of each day, write down every single achievement, however small'. It can be anything. You may have opened the door for an old lady. You may have found someone's wallet and handed it in to be reclaimed. Perhaps you completed your daily run 30 seconds faster than yesterday's time, or remembered to nip to the post in time, rather than missing it for the third day running. Maybe you won £10 on a scratch card and then gave the winnings to a homeless person. Whatever you have accomplished today, write it down and know that whatever is on that bit of paper is only there because of your brilliance. Every so often read over your recognitions and love that they were only possible because of you. Don't be Eleanor Rigby. If only she'd done this.

Love Me Do ♪

When you're with your other half you need to spend time with each other to cultivate your love. It's a normal recreation. But you also need to do that for yourself, which many people overlook because they either don't feel that they achieve anything from being on their own, or feel that they should be dedicating their time to others. To fully re-energise your self-love, you have to be happy to spend time by yourself.

As discussed at the beginning of the chapter, children are naturally happy and love themselves; it is only when we grow up and have to manage in this scheming world that we become detached from our inner selves. Spending quality time on your own is an excellent way to reaffirm love for yourself. Next time you are in the presence of a child, notice how happy and content they are to be by themselves. They can play for hours in a world of their own creation because they love themselves, naturally. On top of this, they are often extraordinarily free and giving with their affection. Only once you are truly comfortable, happy and able to love yourself, can you truly start to pass your love on to others.

There are plenty of activities that you can do by yourself, which will help to foster your re-found self-love. Try going for a long walk alone. I became quite adept at this after the accident, owing to my desire to walk properly again and my hatred of public transport. When I came to London finally, as you've read, I continued this habit to the benefit of my waistband and my wallet. The enjoyment and self-love that I got from being alone was an unpredictable after effect, which I now wholeheartedly cherish. Try going to the cinema by yourself. Rise above the stigma of going alone – you can't actually talk to whoever you're with anyway. It's definitely the worst place to go on a first date, unless you have nothing to say. So embrace your inner love and go alone. Maybe take yourself to a restaurant afterwards and then go for a drink in a local bar. In fact, take yourself on a full-on date. The more you spend time with yourself, the more you will grow to love yourself and the easier it will be to share the love around.

Everybody's Got Something to Hide Except Me and My Monkey ♫

One of my deepest fears about getting older was that of losing my hair. I was petrified of going bald. My father lacks a large proportion of hair; in fact, I've actually never known him to really have much. His baldness basically ingrained in me a life long fear for myself. They say it skips a generation or is passed down through the maternal side but I somehow always knew it was my fate. Sure enough, shortly after the accident, I started to notice a steady decline in my hairline. I went to many a doctor in an attempt to prevent the inevitable and ended up paying out large sums of money for hair restoration creams, pills and lotions. I kept the medication up for quite a few years, everyday leeching a virile substance into my scalp, with the mistaken belief that having a full head of hair would make me more loveable. It was definitely making me poorer but was I gaining anything from it? I still didn't have a girlfriend, so it hadn't helped me there.

Three years into my hair therapy I met Luke and started my meditative lifestyle. Luke recommended that I see a close friend of his who uses methodology from an acting theory, called 'the science of acting'[5] to coach people into a new way of thinking. I decided to follow this up and he introduced me to Elizabeth, who I call my mindful mentor. I have been seeing her on and off ever since, as a kind of counsellor, and a selection of the Timinology theory in this book has derived from her teaching.

At my first session with Elizabeth, I told her about my issues with my hair and she quite succinctly told me to stop damaging my body with dangerous substances and learn to love myself for who I am. I genuinely, on that first meeting, decided that I would buy no more of the lotion and I would instead learn how to love myself without a full head of hair. Yeah, the coverage started to diminish gradually but I didn't look on in horror at my receding hairline, I just saw it as a natural part of life.

I was recently offered a heavily discounted, chemical-free hair restoration programme. It involved the healthy hairs at the back of the head being surgically removed and then grafted into the receding hairline at the front (a process that is normally very expensive). The promised result was that I would partially regain my once-full head of hair.

I instantly said no to this idea because I basically thought that it would make a mockery of my self-loving stance in trying to cover up the problem. I thought it would make the messages in the book seem shallow if I didn't stick to everything that I have put forth. I dwelled on the offer for a few days and eventually put it to Elizabeth, expecting her to congratulate me on my selfless act of balding gracefully. Her reaction was quite the opposite.

She applauded me again for loving myself enough to no longer take part in unsubstantiated restoration trials of potentially harmful chemicals. That, however, didn't mean I needed to turn down the opportunity to mindfully, safely and self-lovingly put myself through a procedure that would restore my hair to how I wanted it to be. Just because I had learned to love myself with a balding head of hair, making the choice to replenish it gracefully (rather than responding to an idea of pressure or requirement to do it) meant that I could do so, and with my head held high. Sure, it doesn't bother some people if they go bald and they might actually prefer it that way. I had accepted it to a certain extent, although following on from the head injury I had in 2007, with my hairline slowly receding over the unsightly point of impact, to be offered a procedure to retain coverage over that area and to subsequently install in me a revived sense of self-confidence, suddenly seemed like a very plausible idea. I still loved myself without much hair but given the opportunity to be able to mindfully and lovingly have one or the other, I chose to cover up my shiny scalp. Just as with loving another, in loving ourselves, we need to be willing to change our stance.

May I mindfully accept with serenity the things that cannot be changed. May I cultivate the courage to change the things that can be changed. May I discover the wisdom to distinguish one from the other.

Don't Look Back in Anger ♫

Before you can completely regain the childlike love for yourself, the table has to be clean, so to speak. If you are harbouring misgivings about any past mistakes or unfinished business, let it all go and forgive yourself. You may regret having angrily broken up with an ex you've never seen since. They will have moved on, so you should, too. If it really is something you need to talk about, find their number, call them and then let it go – I've got my own tale for you on this, a little later.

I've already mentioned how you should never put yourself down and criticise your every action but a trait with which many people feed their self loathing is looking at every situation as if it were black or white and never subjectively assessing it. Yes, people make mistakes, we all do, but that doesn't make you a bad person who should be hated, especially not by yourself. Say for example you accidentally dented your car. Does that make you a bad driver? No, of course not. It doesn't mean you're a bad person, either. Instead simply see it as a small mistake which can easily be fixed and then smile because it wasn't any worse. The Thought Theory Model comes into play here. What would a person who truly loved themselves think?

Okay – I know that there are many worse things that could happen and some things aren't quite as easily righted by subjectively assessing the situation, claiming it was an accident and telling yourself you're still a good person. But that's just it, the worse the situation, the more important it is to dedicate time to forgive yourself, because if you don't you will ruin your life. Let's say – and God forbid it ever happens – you're at a party in a high rise building when you accidentally knock a bottle of wine off the balcony, which falls to the ground below, hitting and knocking out a passer by. What do you do? Straightaway you will feel remorse and regret for your actions, but you didn't intentionally knock it off, you were just being clumsy, so you're still a good person, aren't you? How can you go back to how you were before the accident took place? Situations like this cannot and are not meant to be easy to reconcile but it is totally possible to come to terms with it, as will be discussed in more detail a little bit later.

Until you forgive a friend or a family member for a past grievance that caused you an emotional pain, you're never going to intimately love them again; you can't, because it will always be hanging over you. On exactly the same premise, until you learn to forgive yourself for past wrongs, you will never regain the fond love that you should have for yourself. There are situations far more serious than a drunken argument with your spouse, ending in you calling her a worthless shit-stick, but however severe the incident, you will never regain a devout self-love again until you have learned to forgive yourself.

Whether it was meant to happen or not, when I started writing on this topic I couldn't really think of an occasion where I've had tremendous trouble forgiving myself for a negative outcome. A few days into writing this chapter, however, I went to a friend's thirtieth in central London and decided to hire a Boris bike on the way home, to ease my travelling woes. It was quite late so my usual concerns about lorry mowing were less severe; there was very little traffic about. I left the party and headed back home after enjoying a splendid evening of frivolity.

I was cycling at a medium pace along the embankment when I reached a narrow straight run and noticed a young woman walking by herself heading in the same direction as me. As I approached her to pass from behind, she appeared to open up a space for me to pass on her left hand side, so instead of slowing I decided to plough on through. At the moment I was about to pass her, I suddenly got this terrible feeling that she was going to unintentionally walk into my cycle path and sure enough, at that exact moment, she stepped to her left and then crumpled to the ground as the bike and I hit her from behind, at a fairly rapid pace. She let out a pitiful yelp before falling head first onto the path.

She lay motionless for a few seconds before regaining consciousness and then, in clear confusion, started checking herself over. I took one look at her, noticed a massive gash on the side of her head, which was bleeding quite profusely and told her that I was taking her to hospital.

'No', she said determinedly, 'I need to catch the last train back home and it's leaving in a bit'. I didn't want to argue with her, seeing as it was her decision and seeing as I was the guy who had just completely ruined her evening.

'Well, let me give you some money for a cab', I said, reluctant to leave her like this.

'No, that's fine...I'm getting the train...I guess I could have some for the other end'.

'OK.' I replied. 'Let me walk you to the station'. I helped her up, picked up the bike and we began slowly making our way to the station, which was only five minutes away.

'I am so sorry', I repetitively announced to her over and over again. 'I'm such a prick, I'm so sorry'.

I don't know why but it suddenly dawned on me that I needed to deliver my bike back to one of its designated bays, so I told her to stay where she was while I quickly dropped it off. She told me that she was going to wait in the central reservation.

'Great', I said, 'don't go away'. I knew where one of the return racks was, which would have taken me only a minute to get to, but I had to turn around because there were construction works in the road. I swiftly made my way to another one, only to find that it was completely full. It was only at this point that I thought how insignificant an overdue bike charge was, compared with this poor girl I had just mown down. I hurriedly made my way back to the central reservation, intending to give her whatever money I had in my wallet and to apologise yet again for my foolish cycling.

She was nowhere to be seen; she had completely vanished. I had no idea in which direction she could have gone. I then remembered that she needed to catch the last train home, so realized that was what she must have done.

The guilt and shame that swept across me in that instant, and continuously for the bike ride home, convinced me how careless I had been. I arrived back at my house and all I could think about was how she was and if she'd got home safely. I looked down at my arms and shirt and saw they were splattered in blood, which made me feel even worse. I showered before getting into bed and then lay awake lamenting the night's events.

Why didn't I get her number? I asked myself. I hope she's okay. I didn't even get her name. She must hate the thought of me. Why didn't I ring the bell so that she knew I was behind her? All her friends must think that I'm evil. Why didn't I just pass her slowly? All of these thoughts and many, many more kept resounding in my head when I realized that there was absolutely nothing that I could do. I couldn't contact her to tell her how sorry I was and how bad I felt. I also had absolutely no way of finding out how she was. I was lying in bed and I suddenly realized that I was completely helpless in the matter.

It was at this point that I understood how much I needed to somehow put it all to rest. If she knew how bad I felt, would that have made me feel better? If I had seen her again and given her the money for her taxi at the other end, would that have paid off my guilt slightly? If she had vocally forgiven me, would that have made me feel any better? And the answer to all those questions was no. The only way that I have managed to accept the events of that night is by forgiving myself for being such an arse. How was I going to do that?

To begin with, I was in a bit of a dilemma. I knew it wouldn't have been possible but I wondered, if I could have erased the accident from my mind so that I stopped thinking about it constantly, would that have been the right thing to do? It would have relieved my severely troubled mind but it would have been one of the most callous ways to go about it. That's not what the Thought Theory Model is all about. I was not meant to forget that the accident took place, I was meant to mindfully assess the malevolent, unnecessary thoughts that were hijacking my mind and systematically replace them with positive ones that accepted the errors of my ways. In a bid to somehow make this possible, I got researching.

Psychologist Dr. Frederic Luskin, director of the Stanford University Forgiveness Projects, has been conducting research into forgiveness for many years, and has worked alongside a whole host of 'wrong doers' ranging from unfaithful spouses to parents excommunicating their children. He found that the biggest obstacle to self-forgiveness is people's tendency to wallow in their own guilt. Straightaway I can relate to this, given how I felt after knocking that poor girl to the ground. The guilt was immeasurable and wallow in it I certainly did. There was nothing else I could do. I couldn't contact her or progress the situation in any practical way; the only thing left for me to do was feel irreconcilably guilty. It's like I had to, at least mentally, bear an element of the pain she was experiencing. I almost felt like I deserved it.

Dr. Luskin points out that instead of taking responsibility for whatever wrong has been committed and trying to repair the damage or make things right, people unconsciously instead bury their heads in the sand and feel guilty for the rest of their lives. When I read his findings, I made the decision to never cycle like a lunatic again and have consequently found a small positive in what happened that night: the fact that I will never again let it happen to anyone else. It's not an instantaneous feeling of ease, nor should it be, as explained in this excerpt, written by Dr Luskin:

Forgiveness is a tool with which we face what we've done in the past, acknowledge our mistakes, and move on, it does not mean that you condone or excuse what happened. It does not mean that you forget. Remember the saying, 'For everything there is a season'? Well, there's a season for our suffering and regret. We have to have that. But the season ends; the world moves on. And we need to move on with it.[6]

Stop Crying Your Heart Out ♫

Having researched the plethora of suggested ways to learn how to forgive yourself, I have compiled a list of the most beneficial techniques that have enabled me to find compassion for myself after cycling into the poor girl. These have all proved to be significantly advantageous, so instead of just regurgitating some researched tripe, I have tried and tested these very methods and can honestly tell you that they do work. Having followed this structure, I've now come to terms with what happened that night.

Recognise your misdemeanours: By acknowledging exactly what it is you have done wrong, you can break down what you did, get a little perspective and distance on the whole thing and begin the healing process.

I mindlessly rode my bike into the back of a girl, causing her harm and a lot of pain. I found the sooner I just admitted fault, instead of looking for excuses, the easier it was to move on (I didn't want to be blaming her for not looking before she stepped into my path).

Talk to someone: Define and give reality to the wrong you committed and the harm it caused, by telling a few close friends or confidants. Sharing reminds us that everyone makes mistakes. Confessing what you've done also prevents you from slipping into denial, suppression, repression and forgetting.

I told a close friend, who said even though the accident had happened and there was nothing that I could do to change it, I had done everything right after the incident and I should not wallow in guilt for not doing enough.

Understand what you want: Although the incident has occurred and you may never see the injured person again, what do you want to happen?

I want her to make a full recovery and I want to be free from the guilt and shame.

Identify the hurt: Realise that the hurt feelings, guilty thoughts and tummy-clenching stress you feel whenever you think of your offence is what's actually making you feel bad – not the incident itself. It's your reaction to it today that's causing a problem. It's a habit that has to go.

I simply have to understand that it happened and there is nothing I can do about it. I need to stop reliving the crash. The thoughts that I have are generated entirely by me. Knowing that I had the power to change my thoughts – and only I could do so – empowered me to gradually put an end to those thoughts. The power of the Thought Theory Model was truly showing itself.

Hit the stop button: *Reliving the crash over and over again in my head was not helping me in the slightest, nor was it helping the girl. It simply made me feel worse. Every time I caught myself ruminating the accident, I mindfully observed how I was feeling and how my body was reacting. The very act of focusing on and exploring the exact feelings that were preventing me from putting it to bed, allowed me to reach a position of clarity and understanding that softened and dulled the feelings immeasurably.*

Write about it: *As I have found with all of my problems, not just this, writing them down and putting them into meaningful words has a way of helping me come to terms with them and put everything into perspective. It is one of the most cathartic ways to help yourself. You don't need to write a book (although maybe you'll want to, because it really helps!), but if you need to forgive yourself for a particular negative situation, write it down and let it all out.*

Meditate on positive affirmations: *Go back to the Kindfulness chapter and meditate on positive affirmations to bring about forgiveness.*

I find myself often worrying about the girl and if she got home safely. I remind myself that if she was strong enough to go to the train by herself and compos mentis enough to know she had a train to catch, she was well enough to get back safely to her home, where she would have been looked after and taken to hospital if needed.

Go Let it Out ♫

Forgiving yourself and forgiving others are intrinsically linked, in that by reaching forgiveness in either scenario, you are granting yourself peace and harmony over the situation. I have very recently faced another situation that required me to truly forgive the perpetrators in order to re-find the love.

In order to pay the mortgage on my house, I need to rent out two of the rooms. One of my lodgers recently left, so I decided to try letting the room through Airbnb. I had my first guests, a lovely French couple, who came and went as they pleased during the booking period. We took it in turns to cook for one another every so often, sharing the different foods and wines that we loved, forming a good relationship during their stay.

After the French couple left, I had a booking almost immediately from an Australian couple, Clarissa and Paulo, who were house-hunting nearby. On their arrival, I greeted them with open arms, helped take their extensive luggage to the room, told them that they should treat my house like their home and that I would happily cook for them that night. They said they were busy the first evening, so politely refused the offer. Nothing wrong with that. They were only staying a week, so I didn't really get a chance to see much of them. I hosted a dinner party on one of the evenings, to which I again invited them but they were eating out, so they again refused the offer. As it happened, they arrived back early and subsequently joined in the frivolities of the party. All in all, it seemed to have been a pleasant week.

Clarissa and Paulo had originally told me they would be leaving at a particular time, so I rearranged my plans around this in order to show them out. Ten minutes before their scheduled departure, I was messaged by Clarissa to say that they wouldn't be back on time, which meant that I couldn't be there to see them off. I told them to post the key through the door and wished them luck with their house-hunting.

Now, as you may or may not know, Airbnb is an incredibly well-marketed online resource that helps people to privately rent a room for considerably cheaper rates than those of a hotel, or for the owners of a property to rent out however much of it they see fit, for extra income. Generating a successful account with Airbnb depends solely on the feedback delivered by both parties at the end of the stay.

The day after Clarissa and Paulo left, Airbnb asked me to review the stay. Looking back on it, the couple weren't particularly sociable but each to their own; I wasn't going to mark them down on that. They were both, dare I say it, obese, which I obviously didn't mind but it did explain the entire consumption of an extra large, brand new tub of chocolate spread that the French couple had kindly given me. It wasn't their appetite with which I had a problem, it was the fact that they never once asked if they could have any, let alone devour it. So I did have a minor issue with that but not enough to impinge on their other good reviews, so I wrote a warm evaluation of their stay.

Later that evening I received their review of me. They had posted a thoroughly negative account of their stay, stating that the place was a mess (even though they had no worries about dropping chocolate spread around the kitchen – and the French couple had given top marks for cleanliness). They said that my invitations to eat and drink with me and my friends were highly inappropriate and made them feel uncomfortable. This was after I had shown nothing but kindness and attention to their every need, after they had actually joined in with the party and after I had reviewed them positively.

I was enraged that people I had gone out of my way to please could intentionally ruin my chances of ever renting the room through Airbnb again. As only my second visitors, they now accounted for 50% of my feedback. I had made it my mission to create a perfect stay for them and they had kicked a pile of shit in my face. I was irritated and infuriated and felt helpless.

Once again, it suddenly dawned on me that I could do nothing to change what they had done but I could do everything to change the way I felt about it. I realized that I needed to put the Thought Theory Model into action and so had to rearrange my thinking in order to forgive them. But how?

After clearing my mind by meditating for a while, I re-instigated the compassion I had shown from the start. Instead of remonstrating, I sent them a text message apologising to them for the apparently poor state of the house and my obscure social attitude and invited them over for a drinks party, to show that there were no bad feelings. The moment I sent it, I suddenly felt a heavy weight lift from my mind, replaced with a massive smile. I felt amazing. I knew I had responded with generosity of heart, in the face of what seemed like calculated injustice.

Sadly, I never did hear back from them but I learned an incredible lesson from the whole episode and don't regret one thing about it.

It occurred to me after the event that perhaps Clarissa and Paulo were not as straightforward as I had initially thought. More often than not (as was explained properly in the self-control chapter), people become overweight through addiction to food. If this was the case for my guests, their ongoing quest for the elusive dopamine hit, fuelled by repetitively gorging on food, would have left them angry and uncompromising. This is perhaps a reason why they would have felt uneasy with unfamiliar social situations and overly irritable to maybe a dirty window, or whatever it was that had caused them to complain about the state of the house. The fact that the both of them appeared to be suffering from the same addiction maybe meant that they would have both felt the same unnecessary rage, without having an independent loving nudge away from their anger. In turn, this is perhaps why I got the brunt of it. Instead of bitterly chastising them, I now think about them with compassion and hope they will someday rid themselves of the afflictions holding them back.

Following on from the notion of the Thought Theory Model, I used this principle to help settle the mind of a great friend of mine, Amber. She had just found out that four of her close friends had failed to invite her to an annual gathering that they had all attended for the previous five years or so. Amber was beside herself with the idea that they no longer liked her and she felt a burden on them and everyone else. The more she thought about it, the more convinced she became of her presumptions. After confirming she hadn't recently done anything out of character to upset any of them, I worked on putting her woes to rest.

I suggested that she needed to detach herself from the negative assumptions and to instead mindfully assess the situation. For example, they were all married and some of them had recently had their first children; Amber hadn't yet entered into either of those situations. A couple of the other girls worked together, which would have straightaway made communicating about the event far easier.

If Amber could treat every single day as a different adventure, in which anything can happen, countless new benefits would manifest themselves in front of her, which would then give rise to not only making new friends but old friends wanting to spend more time with her, too. The instigation of this new thought-processing mindset is a sure fire way to cultivate even more love for yourself, which in turn will bring about love from others.

Wonderwall ♫

I have never been angry about my break up from Hannah but there has always been something that was preventing me from properly moving forwards, which you might have guessed from the way I write about her. Having written so much about Hannah, I messaged her a while back and asked if we could chat about what I was writing and if she would consent to me using her name. She said that she was pretty busy with one of her kid's parties but she'd call me in a few days. A few days came and I hadn't really thought about the enormousness of speaking to her for the first time in over seven years. As promised, she dutifully called me and so began an extraordinarily powerful catch up with my first ever real love.

She still sounded exactly the same and she was still just as sweet. I told her about what I was writing and the reasons behind it all and asked whether or not I could have her consent. She was so incredibly understanding and compassionate about the whole thing. It felt like we had been speaking for about ten minutes before she had to dash to attend to one of her kids but I realized we had been speaking for over an hour and a half. Hannah very kindly gave her consent for me to write about her and we ended the call.

I was left completely awestruck by the intensity of the conversation we had just had (although it might not have been quite so intense for her). I told her absolutely everything that I had been harbouring for all these years and she listened patiently and brought back some friendly memories of the good times we had shared.

The next morning, after this epic conversation, I thought back over the phone call, expectant of some sort of regret for not being with her still, or for not having said enough. To my surprise, there wasn't any, absolutely nothing. For the very first time in over thirteen years I was completely and utterly over her. I had been freed from this underlying regret that had stopped me from moving forwards. It's not like I'd wanted to get back with her. Despite that, I'd not only compared every relationship I'd had ever since with the one we had but I had also measured my current happiness against how I thought it was when we were together. That was suddenly and outstandingly no longer the case, leaving a massive opening for me to perfectly and intimately learn to love myself again, which is what I slowly started to do.

Love to Love You Baby ♫

Although it is important to spend time alone in order to love yourself, it is also paramount to invest time in your most fulfilling relationships. When I talk about generating and receiving love from others, I'm not talking about romantic love, I'm talking about unconditional love for your close friends and family. Yes, being infatuated with a sexual partner is incredible but the energy and strength you receive from platonic love – which can be for that person who is your sexual partner too – is quite remarkable. Whether these are with a sibling, a parent, a friend or a lover, cultivating the ability to love others as much as yourself, will have the bonus effect of making you feel good about yourself, which can only instil more self-love upon you. Once you have got the wheels of love in motion, starting with yourself, you'll gradually circulate the love for you to other people, which then has the resounding effect of re-affirming and increasing your love again, and around it keeps on going.

This seems a perfect time to explain how this has affected me.

When I started writing this book, I had just begun dating a lovely girl called Whitney. I had always been incredibly honest with her about how I felt and about how I compared every single relationship with the one I had shared with Hannah. Yet, Whitney didn't let that put her off, even though I know it would have sent many other girls running. This amazing girl has consistently stuck by me with a lot of personal issues and also helped me with the proofreading of this book, even though she was never mentioned properly until now.

Speaking to Hannah, as well as lifting an incredible weight off my shoulders, finally gave me the opportunity to emphatically focus on myself for the first time in many years. Whitney assiduously stayed with me throughout everything. She was enough assured of herself to help me to reinvigorate my own love, knowing full well that there was no guarantee that in the end I would want anything more than just a friendly shoulder to bear my weight.

Falling Down ♫

Although the PUA course was most probably the main catalyst for writing this book, the skiing accident certainly had a fairly large part to play in it.

Apart from the times I can't remember, because of the head injury and the painkillers I was on; times when, my mother tells me, I was often crying in agony, the only other time I am aware of crying my eyes out was when I read the hundreds of sympathy and get well cards sent to me and my parents. My mother compiled a file full of all the letters, cards, hospital notes and x-rays for me to look over on my recovery. Even to this day reading over the sentiments received from people I hardly even knew (regardless of whether or not I remembered them) reduces me to tears. The intensity of love that was sent and felt for me and my family is quite simply breathtaking. Through reading the countless cards, I am always left in a state of emotional awe over the way my accident impacted on the lives of so many people.

It is the love that was transmitted through these letters that touches me. The mail directed to me, personally, is very positive, life affirming and proactive about me making a full recovery; the letters to my parents express such heartfelt pain and anguish over the terrible situation, offering so much support, love and help with anything to make life easier for them. I may well have been an arrogant, obnoxious so-and-so before the accident but reading how it affected so many people and how much love was generated as a result, and from reading the positive comments about my life before, made me want to breathe the life back into what people thought of me and make my recovery as rewarding, meaningful and purposeful as possible, for everyone.

As you'll see in the Happiness chapter, writing a letter to express gratitude can evoke more happiness. The same goes for love. By expressing an affirmation for someone else, through writing a letter, that too can promote self-love, as well as feelings of adoration for the recipient in question.

Upon hearing the news of my fateful cliff-plummet, along with my direct family, my closest life-long friend, Will, who I have known since birth, came to be by my side. Here he was nothing but generous with his love, to support my family and me. My 'Tier One' friends, George, Tim and Ali, all boarded the next available flight and flew over to France, to be with us. Tim's girlfriend (now wife), Amelia, who was one of my closest friends at Bristol, came along, too. Bronya, who I was living with in London directly before the season and with whom I had become very close, also came out to be by my side and wrote me a letter for every single day of my recovery, which I will always treasure. The following five weeks of my stay in hospital saw countless other close friends and family make the trip to Grenoble (whose names can be found in the gratitude section at the back of this book) to offer their sincerest love and support for my whole family but mainly for my mother, after my father and sisters had to fly back to England for work. For their support to me and particularly to her, I will always be grateful. Their generosity with their own love for us has given me huge strength in learning to love myself, and to love others, once again.

Timmy's Tips

- Remember 'love brings self confidence, anger brings fear'. Recognise, appreciate and acknowledge your achievements

- Never compare yourself to anyone else and if you have faith in it, stop seeking approval from others for your lifestyle

- Reignite the affection you felt for yourself as a child. Care for your inner self as you would a child, with affection and love

- When making a decision, ask yourself how someone who loves themselves would act

- Move well, eat well and sleep well (banish electronic devices from the bedroom)

- Dedicate time to spend with yourself – go for a walk, to the cinema, to a bar, on your own

- Be honest with yourself about your mistakes; forgive others and forgive yourself: Recognise what's gone wrong; Talk about it; Understand what you want; Identify the pain; Hit the stop button; Write about it.

- Meditate

- Invest in your relationships with others

- Promote love through writing letters to your loved ones

Happiness

Smiling is infectious,
you catch it like the flu,
When someone smiled at me today,
I started smiling too.
I passed around the corner
and someone saw my grin.
When he smiled, I realized,
I'd passed it on to him.
I thought about that smile,
then I realized its worth.
A single smile, just like mine,
could travel around the earth.
So, if you feel a smile begin,
don't leave it undetected.
Let's start an epidemic quick,
and get the world infected.
– Anonymous

On the meditation weekend where I met James, most of the people who came by themselves were given shared rooms. The room mate I was assigned was a softly spoken, quiet, middle aged man named Billy. Our room, apparently, according to the person who led us to it, had once been inhabited by King Edward VII. I very much doubted his presumption, owing to the fact it was quite clearly servants' quarters, but I gleefully postulated his claims and let out some resounding ooos.

The food, completely vegetarian, was actually quite delicious. There were probably about seventy guests so every time we ate, it felt like being back at school (barring the distinct lack of greyish meat). I tried to talk to as many course delegates as possible and met people from all walks of life.

Something that struck me was that a large proportion of the people with whom I spoke had relatively recently, more or less, had a life-changing experience with which to awe me. This straightaway set alarm bells ringing in my head, leading me to assume that they were taking part in the weekend's activities as a way to help them either come to terms with a recent trauma they may have experienced, or to search for enlightenment from their pain. It worried me that this was perhaps being done through the mind of a recently bereaved or distressed individual, whose senses were not entirely harmonious. I'm not saying that it is wrong to seek solitude by whatever means possible in your time of need but, as I mentioned at the end of the Kindfulness chapter, I don't think life decisions made during times of pain and suffering can be suitably trusted.

Obviously not everyone was attending the course as a result of a recent traumatic experience, myself being one of the less dramatically-inspired attendees, having bizarrely found myself here via a course on how to pick up girls. It was quite interesting to observe the way the 'tutors' went about addressing us 'pupils'. I hate to say it, and if any of them read this they will probably refute these comments, but they almost had a doom and gloom mentality surrounding the consequences of all our actions and the way we should lead our lives. It was like they were using and transfiguring the pain built up in many of the individuals – who had attended the course in order to seek refuge from life outside of the 'commune' – to formulate some form of guilt if the pupils did not dutifully acquiesce to the course regimen.

My humour and past experiences of the Christian camp in my youth saw me dubbing the course tutors 'elders'. I automatically took a step back from the teachings, observing them with an element of scepticism. One of the main reasons I had attended the course was to develop my meditation skills. I was intrigued by everything they had to say about it and duly took notes as appropriate, to filter later. One thing I did take from this course and which, as you know from the Kindfulness chapter, I still now do every time I meditate, is to keep my eyes open and fully integrate myself in the present moment, the here and now.

For our sessions, we would all congregate in one of the large conference rooms and sit down. Once everyone was still, one of the 'elders' put on some incredibly sombre, almost depressing pan pipe music compilation and asked us to look into the eyes of a face on a large poster at the front of the hall. The elder then very quietly whispered through a microphone an instruction for us to transfix our gaze on this face, which we later found out was that of the founder of this community, back in the 1950s.

Being asked to gaze into the eyes of an individual to the sound of some melancholy musical harmony took me straight back to my teenage self at the Christian camps (with which I had already drawn parallels), trying to seek refuge in an all-loving God. The scenes in front of me put me in mind of the ways in which the tutors at the camps of my childhood seemed so determined to make us so despondent about the devilish world we inhabited, that the mere mention of a saviour would have us quaking, shaking and crying for the love of the Almighty to rescue us. But I wasn't a teenager anymore. I had become quite aware of how people use music and stories to manipulate the vulnerable.

Before starting one particular session, I had the opportunity to speak to one of the elders about their life at the stately home that hosted the retreats. I was absolutely amazed by what she had to tell me. For a start, they were not allowed to drink alcohol, which isn't exactly a bad thing but it's quite relaxing to have a glass of wine every so often.

'How do you socialise with your boyfriend?' I enquired, owing to the fact that she was too attractive to not have a man.

'Oh!', she exclaimed, 'We're all celibate'.

I didn't really know how to respond to that so I swiftly moved on to asking about any other provisions that excluded her from normal life (I don't think I phrased it quite like that).

'Well, we get up at 4am every morning to meditate, we have to clean the areas we've been allocated, and then we take it in turns to either cook, wash or tidy up'.

Where fun or even simple enjoyment of life fitted into any of this, I didn't know, but I assumed she must have been at least content with her life choice.

So there I was being advised to stare into the eyes of some hippy, to the sound of some suitably depressing music that had me welling up in misery. The elder leading us was a person who essentially lived the life of a monk. It was at that point, just before wiping the tears away from my eyes, that I realized that I was in the presence of a cult.

The weekend didn't exactly fly by but I did manage to see it through. In the final session, just after the daily depressing meditation of staring into the eyes of the revered chap, we were asked if anyone would like to ask a question. My hand went straight up and I waited.

'Yes?', an elderly monastic lady enquired of me. 'What would you like to ask?'

'Well', I said, 'why do you make every meditation session so depressing by playing such sombre music? Surely life is about smiling and being happy, so how can you expect to smile if you don't welcome in any joy?'

'That's a good question', she replied but her following answer didn't exactly enthral me. 'It's very important to focus on the founder of this faith, because we wouldn't be here without him, so it only seems right to start every meditation off with him'.

She hadn't answered my question in the slightest but I decided not to persist, because I could see she was set in her ways. I merely nodded at her and let her finish the session.

As parting gifts, we were asked to go up to the front of the hall to collect a white gown in which to meditate at home, before we went to the next elder to pick up a brownie. I wasn't overly keen on the gown, even though it was the weekend before Halloween. The brownie-giving elder said that I needed to pick up a gown before I was allowed her present but after I told her that I didn't feel ready for such a gargantuan offering, she handed me the sugary delight and sent me on my way.

Over the last few years, since attending the PUA course in London, I have tried to be as positive and upbeat as possible and to not dwell on things that are out of my control. Although this meditation weekend didn't ignite any form of heartache or suffering, it most certainly did not encourage spontaneous laughter and frivolity, especially not during meditation. Every religion and sect has its own purpose but to not support or embrace such a life-affirming and heart warming practise as happiness is surely preposterous.

From the research I've shared with you so far, and from what you are about to read, you will begin to find that happiness is by far the most imperative thing in the lives of all of us humans and has the power to end any form of suffering. I'm not saying that personal happiness can end pain for eternity (although worldwide happiness would certainly help) but in a moment of pure, unadulterated happiness, however fleeting it is, all physical, emotional and mental pain can leave you in an instant. These moments can also give you the strength to keep on trying through the pain.

Victor Frankl, an Austrian neurologist and psychiatrist who survived the holocaust, wrote an incredibly moving, poignant and uplifting account of his time in the concentration camps. In his book on the subject, Man's Search for Meaning, he notes, 'It is well known that humour, more than anything else in the human make-up, can afford an aloofness and an ability to rise above any situation, even if only for a few seconds.[1]'

Lost in Myself ♫

I have never felt irreconcilably unhappy with my life, although I can almost guarantee that had I not encountered a way to reconnect with my inner self through meditation, I would certainly not be in the same position as I am, now. The accident did knock me for six and I have fleeting memories of thinking that perhaps I would be better off dead. Luckily, I never did anything worse than just dwell on my situation and feel sorry for myself. The cliché that everything happens for a reason is very apt here and going to the PUA course, although I didn't get lucky (at the time), was one of the best decisions that I have ever made.

While I was researching this chapter, somebody asked me what it would take for me to be completely happy. There are the obvious answers like money, well-paid job, great friends, partner, marriage, children, love, popularity, health, good looks, etc. These are surely what most people desire. I must say that a lot of my friends have already achieved the majority of those goals (maybe minus the good looks) but if I were to ask most of them whether they are totally happy with their lives, I can almost guarantee that they would say 'no', because it is not quite perfect yet. That's not just my friends, though, that's almost everybody I meet. I have never met anybody who can rest their hand on their heart and tell me that they are 100% happy. But maybe this is part of what keeps us trying, stops us from becoming complacent and helps us to appreciate the good things we do have.

I have researched so much about happiness and I can now honestly say that I am definitely on the higher end of the 'being happy' scale than I was when I was growing up. Excluding the accident and the years of recuperating and recovery, and excluding my lack of girlfriend, job, money, sex, etc. at various points, there was always one condition from which I suffered, which had the ability to shut me down in an instant.

Some of my earliest memories are of experiencing this thing and although I learned how to distract myself from it, after having it in my life for so long, it never fully went away.

Before I tell you about it, I want you to understand that if this particular thing could have gone away, I genuinely believed its departure would have easily made me the happiest person, ever. That would have been very hard, though, because the condition scared me so much that I couldn't even think about it, let alone talk or tell anyone about it, for fear of its reprisal. Every time it reared its head, I would try to shut it away again by taking my thoughts off it through mindless activities.

I suffered from a condition called depersonalisation, which meant that I never really felt present, or fully alive. I felt like I was in a dream, or that there was a constant mist around me which prevented me from feeling completely involved with the present moment. A brain fog. I think the best way to describe it would be as similar to the detached feeling you might get when you have a hangover and you haven't really slept the night before. It probably first occurred when I was a young boy, so I had never experienced a hangover and I was just petrified. Although it could never hurt me physically, I was terrified of feeling completely insignificant and detached from reality, resulting in me trying to seek out techniques to keep my mind off it.

One of the most outlandish procedures that I adopted to try and divert my attention was the development of an Obsessive Compulsive Disorder (OCD), as mentioned in the Religion vs Mindfulness chapter. I think I knew, even from such a young age, that it wasn't normal to act in such a peculiar fashion, so I tried my hardest to not bring to anyone's attention my weird activities. I had always to be in the same position at the end of an event, as I was at the beginning, because otherwise I thought something bad would happen. I had to retrace my steps. I have this one vivid memory of playing rugby at school and at the end of the match we were told to go and run around a small wooded area, beside the pitch. Everyone groaned because they just wanted to go into the changing rooms and rest. We all did it and then everyone else went inside. I, however, had to tell the master that I wanted to run around it one more time because I needed to burn off some energy. He looked a little bewildered by my request but let me do it anyway. Except this time, I went in the opposite direction to retrace my initial steps.

Because I felt that it worked so well, owing to the fact I might not have had an episode for some time, the OCD became an imaginary life tool to prevent the depersonalisation from taking over. The OCD consequently became ingrained in me as a secret tool for preventing all negative situations. As a result it slowly began to evolve and I started to tap things a certain amount of times if I had a bad thought, say certain things to stop 'bad things' from happening, and write obscure miniature letters at the bottom of every page of my work, in order to right any wrongs that could be occurring and to protect my parents from any harm. I would also avoid going into certain places because the depersonalisation may have once occurred in that particular location. There is a bathroom at my parents' house, where I must have felt a little detached from myself at one point, many years ago. I think it took me about ten years, once I started to understand OCD, before I could enter that bathroom again.

My life had turned into a huge set of rules and regulations to make sure that I was able to function correctly and also to make sure that none of my friends or family suffered any harm. All of this because of a feeling that I didn't feel present in the world.

Having looked into depersonalisation, it turns out it didn't just affect me, like I thought it did. In fact, it affects a large proportion of us. I'm therefore using this one major issue of mine as an example of how something from within me was able to limit my happiness. Like the depersonalisation for me, almost everyone will have a confounding concern that they believe is restricting their access to happiness. I can tell you from experience that whatever problem you have, it does not need to go away before you are granted the love and serenity of being totally happy, because happiness is already present within everyone, you just have to know how to access it. Once you have activated your happiness, that is when all the other problems diminish and disappear.

How the depersonalization came about in the first instance, I will never know. I have vague memories of it developing at my prep school. If I had only been less afraid to talk about it, I'm sure it could have been easily rectified. That said, back in the late eighties, mindfulness was only just coming to light and I don't think children were meant to be bullishly happy. Nevertheless, it was through mindfulness, thirty or so years after it first occurred that I got the breakthrough I had been so diligently searching for. By methodically observing the detached feelings that had made parts of my life a living hell, I slowly began to see them for what they were, nothing more than a collection of thoughts. By allowing myself to befriend these feelings that I hadn't dared to even whisper about as a child, I confronted them, accepted them and then ever so slowly said goodbye to them.

Laughter is the Best Medicine ♫

There is another side to happiness, which is unbelievable to everyone who lacks faith in its true power: Being truly happy can actually save your life.

The Cancer Treatment Centre of America (CTCA) that uses laughter therapy (humour therapy) to promote overall health and wellness, using the natural psychological process of laughter to remove physical or emotional stresses and discomfort.

Humour has been in use for many years as a distraction for patients, taking their attention from unpleasant procedures. In more recent times, Norman Cousins[2], a man who had been suffering from an incurable illness for many years, devized a unique therapy involving laughter and vitamin pills, which consequently delivered him a full recovery. He mentioned that he would spend many hours a day watching comedic movies to incite laughter, taking his mind off the illness and curing him.

When it comes to people living with cancer, it almost seems nonsensical to be laughing about something so serious. Yet, at the CTCA, they have uncovered a plethora of new ways to fight the disease, through the use of laughter.

Laughter can instantly help you feel better about yourself and the world around you. When you heartily laugh (try this for yourself), no other thought comes to mind, you are, for those few seconds, free from any troubles. Genuine laughter is a natural diversion. Laughter can induce physical changes in the body and, after laughing for a few minutes, this can keep you feeling better for hours. Dopamine, which I'll keep mentioning, is also playing a role here.

There are cases of individuals who have trusted solely in the power of laughter to cure them from cancer. Most people at the CTCA, though, use a combination of laughter, positive thinking and medication to rid themselves of the disease. I am in no way advising you to refuse scientifically proven medical treatment to cure you from an ailment, that would just be foolish. What I am suggesting you do, though, with evidence to back it up, is to combine treatments. That way the two will work together. At any rate, if you're going to get through it, there is no better way than by maintaining happiness in the process.

According to the studies conducted by the CTCA, laughter therapy may also provide physical benefits. Undergroundhealthreporter.com, a great website, lists some of these as helping to: 'boost the immune system and circulatory system; enhance oxygen intake; stimulate the heart and lungs; relax muscles throughout the body; trigger the release of endorphins (the body's natural painkillers); ease digestion/soothe stomach aches; relieve pain; balance blood pressure; and improve mental functions (i.e., alertness, memory, creativity)'.

Laughter therapy may also help to; Improve overall attitude, Reduce stress/tension, Promote relaxation, Improve sleep, Enhance quality of life, Strengthen social bonds and relationships, Produce a general sense of well-being.

So basically, happiness is good for your health. So what's the prescription?

The Dog Days Are Over ♫

I came across this quote from Henry Thoreau, an American naturist poet, saying that: 'Happiness is like a butterfly; the more you chase it, the more it will elude you. But if you turn your attention to other things, it will come and softly sit on your shoulder'. I can understand that in certain circumstances but I also think that it has a very negative connotation attached to it. It effectively says that you can't will happiness into being. Of course you can. I've recently put this to the test and achieved exactly what Thoreau says would evade me. On top of this, maintaining happiness requires a level of commitment and a choice. Using the visualisation process mentioned in the Kindfulness chapter, of clearing your mind and then imagining and focusing on a massive happy smile at the front of your head, your brain will release the appropriate chemicals to inject a loving, happy feeling.

It comes down to this. There are four known naturally occurring substances or hormones that have been scientifically proven to influence happiness, which can all be activated in a variety of different ways. The names of the chemicals conveniently spell out the word D.O.S.E, which is exactly what you want. A dose of happiness: Dopamine, Oxytocin, Serotonin and Endorphins.

Dopamine

This compound is in charge of the pleasure-reward system. It helps us to plan ahead, boosting our drive, focus and concentration. It give us the immense satisfaction of accomplishing tasks, instilling the 'thrill of the chase' feeling in all aspects of life; be that in sport, business or love. It allows us sensations of bliss, enjoyment and euphoria, all of which are linked to happiness. Too little dopamine, however, instils a distinct lack of zest for life, exhibiting low energy and motivation and leading to a dependence on caffeine, sugar or other performance-enhancing stimulants. Dopamine deficiency and depression are closely linked with some obvious symptoms, so be sure to seek professional help if you are experiencing a high level of the following:

- procrastination

- apathy

- fatigue

- low libido

- memory loss

- lack of motivation

- hopelessness

- mood swings

- inability to feel pleasure

- low concentration

Individuals low on dopamine often compensate for their deficiency by taking part in self-destructive behaviours to get a dopamine boost, including consumption of alcohol, caffeine and abuse of drugs. Excessive sugar consumption, sex, shopping, video games, online porn, smoking, power, gambling or internet use are other common practises. From reading the self control chapter, you will by now be familiar with and know how to tackle this dangerous practise of transferring addictive behaviours, should you identify them in yourself or a loved one.

There are healthy ways to naturally increase your dopamine levels, for example engaging yourself in something new. So, why not learn a new language or take up the piano? Whatever you choose, the process of learning (effort+reward) will elevate your dopamine levels. You don't have to restrict your dopamine allowance to your free time, so push yourself to finish a project at work, or land yourself a new account. Any form of accomplishment that gives you that 'yes, I've done it' feeling will increase your dopamine levels considerably. Put simply, If you want to get a hit of dopamine, set a goal and achieve it.

Dopamine is made in part from the amino acid tyrosine, so eating a diet rich in this will give you a good basis for successful dopamine management. Try to manage your intake of these foods, to help increase your happiness.

- apples

- avocados

- bananas

- almonds

- beets

- dark chocolate

- fava beans

- green leafy vegetables

- green tea

- lima beans

- oatmeal

- sea vegetables

- sesame and pumpkin seeds

- turmeric

- watermelon

- wheatgerm

- all animal products

Oxytocin

Oxytocin is a hormone secreted by the pituitary gland. It has many descriptions and, according to medicalnewstoday. com, is 'widely referred to as either the love hormone, the hug hormone, the cuddle chemical, the moral molecule, or the bliss hormone', due to its effects on our behaviour. It is released in both males and females during intercourse and by mothers during childbirth. It is also a hormone that is released during close contact with other human beings and even through companionship with animals, dogs in particular (owing to the high levels of affection they exhibit towards us). It is a hormone that shows its true colours through interactions and proximity with loved ones, or through an altruistic act. If you are in need of an oxytocin hit, a simple cuddle can be all it takes. The next time you receive a gift from a loved one, your oxytocin levels will rise, which is why you feel so compassionate and loving. These feelings, in turn, help to elevate your happiness.

Serotonin

If you're feeling lonely, depressed or unhappy, your serotonin levels will be very low. Only when you feel significant and important will this compound, the absence of which is responsible for your poor state of mind. It has been suggested that the reason people join gangs is that the experiences they encounter as part of that lifestyle cause the brain to produce enough serotonin to make them feel self-worth, where nothing else in their lives does. There are plenty of other ways for you to increase your serotonin levels, however, without having to sign your life away to a bunch of tear-aways hell bent on causing misery and unhappiness for everyone except themselves. Try challenging yourself regularly and seek out situations that will emphasise a sense of purpose, meaning and accomplishment. Being able to say 'I did it', reinforces a sense of self-esteem, making you feel less insecure and creating an upward spiral of serotonin development.

Endorphins

Endorphin literally means self-produced morphine, a great thing to be manufacturing within yourself. Endorphins are mainly produced during times of pain and stress and help to alleviate anxiety and depression, preventing us from being unhappy.

The simplest way to produce endorphins is to laugh. Even the anticipation and expectation of a comedy show or a funny film, produces enough endorphins for you to have a jolly good time. With laughter comes happiness. The best way of harnessing this chemical is to exercise. They have found a way to release it through acupuncture but I've never really been into having needles stuck in me. Endorphins, like dopamine, are produced by the pituitary gland and the hypothalamus during strenuous physical exercise, sexual intercourse and orgasm. So it doesn't all have to be gruelling toil on your lonesome, you can get your other half to join in the fun. The more intense the exercise, the bigger endorphin hit you will receive.

Luckily for us, endorphins aren't just released in one fell swoop at the moment of physical stress; the hit will slowly release itself during your body's recovery, transmitting a euphoric, calm and peaceful state.

Get Happy ♫

During my research for this chapter, I came across an incredible book entitled, Be Happy! Release the Power of Happiness in YOU, by Robert Holden [3]. The vast majority of what I have experienced and researched on happiness is described in this book and so I will cover what I believe are the most important aspects for picking yourself up in this chapter. That said, I highly recommend getting yourself a copy of his book, because you can never learn too much about one of the most important aspects of being human.

Defining happiness falls into three different categories, the third of which is often seen as the most important, because it doesn't depend on an outside source to incite it. Before going any further, I will briefly summarise them.

Pleasure: A calm, loving, peaceful state. You receive pleasure from a source separate to yourself, activated through your senses. It may be the glorious smell of the pulled pork that you have been slowly cooking for the last six hours, or the fantastic sounds of the Beatles, singing about Rocky Raccoon. You might be relishing the phenomenal flavours of the sensational bottle of Côte-Rôtie that you have just opened after keeping it locked away in your cellar for the last fifteen years. Or you might be re-watching your cherished, original copy of the film Point Break, knowing that its remake has almost ruined the idea of surfing.

The one thing about pleasure, though, is that it is completely subjective. My idea of heaven could very easily be your idea of hell and you may very well not have had a clue what I was just describing. Pleasure is reliant on a 'stimulus response' variable; without the stimulus, you don't achieve any response and so pleasure is only available once certain criteria have been fulfilled. It is also very limited and it's an effect that will wear off as soon as the dopamine hit tapers away.

Satisfaction: Like pleasure, satisfaction is only activated through a cause and effect variable. It can be switched on by 'getting what you want' and is often associated with contentment and fulfilment. You can be satisfied with your life, or with your job, or with your new car.

Similar to pleasure, it is also completely subjective and so my satisfaction with last night's Indian takeaway could very easily be your dissatisfaction. To be satisfied is obviously never a bad thing and by developing and enhancing our awarenesses, and through learning and growing, we are in effect activating an upward trajectory of increased gratitude and heightened receptivity. Being grateful for something has an incredibly positive effect on how we associate ourselves with whatever or whoever provided us with the offering, so it is very important to make mental notes of all for which you are grateful.

Satisfaction only occurs when all the variables have been fulfilled. You have to be in the right frame of mind to express satisfaction, so it is dependent on your mental state, which can very often limit your access to its beneficial effects.

Joy: This is quite probably one of the hardest things to define. Only by focusing on its true meaning and accessing my past memories of pure unadulterated peace, joy and love, can I begin to unravel its essence.

I have found that, like both pleasure and satisfaction, joy can be experienced through all your physical senses. It can also be experienced both mentally and emotionally, at a much deeper and more profound level than either satisfaction or pleasure. It is peace, love, tranquillity, freedom, presence, life and laughter all rolled into one. It is the epitome of all that is good and it is something that has the power to end suffering. It is the peak of what happiness is all about.

The Oxford English Dictionary merely defines joy as either great happiness, or a person or thing that causes happiness. It goes on to exemplify its meaning by stating 'They were filled with joy when their first child was born', which, as clichéd as it sounds, and although I have not yet had the opportunity to father a child, is something I hear from all of my friends who have recently become parents. It also uses as an example, 'She wept for joy when she was told that her husband was still alive', indicating that joy is an immense feeling of relief, as well as love and happiness.

All of these descriptions and examples of joy only really touch the surface of this bountiful feeling. Although I can easily recall such vivid and insightful feelings and I am sure you can too, putting them into words is nigh on impossible. We all have these feelings, so I ask you to recall your most poignant moments of joy and create a commemorative illustration of it, through whatever means possible. Maybe write about it, or create a poem, or put it into music, perhaps draw a picture of how you see it. Once you have evolved it into something tangible, use whatever you have created as a focus point for meditating and notice your life slowly start to brighten.

By harnessing these happiness-inducing compounds, you're halfway there. But don't just count on them to make you as happy as you should be. The chemicals flow to your mind, the logical location of your happiness. Your mind then has the ability to store that happiness and dispense it accordingly to maintain your feeling of contentment. You don't always need these chemicals to incite happiness but they certainly help to give it a head start.

Before discussing how you can dissipate your joy, it is very important you first understand that happiness is already present and within you, it's within everybody. You do not need the fast cars, the massive lottery win or the perfect body before you can admit to being happy. All you need to know is how to activate it.

I read a very interesting fact in an article on happiness, about an experiment conducted with a new lottery winner and an individual who had recently become a paraplegic after being involved in an accident. The lottery winner was obviously incredibly happy immediately following the win; conversely, the accident victim was incredibly distraught following the injury. Interestingly, however, after two years, both the lottery winner and the accident victim had very similar score ratings for happiness. The lottery winner was still marginally higher but it is very sobering to know that once you have either come to terms with an incredibly positive or incredibly negative event in your life, it is your mind that has the power to control your happiness.

The fact that happiness can't be earned (by those people we all say 'deserve' to be happy) or won (by our friend the lottery winner) demonstrates that it is not limited to being a 'state of mind'. I would argue that calling it this gives it a temporary label. Happiness is, and has always been, in our true nature. It is something that every single one of us possesses and yet we keep it locked away for inordinate amounts of time because we often feel like we don't deserve it and so we don't let it out to flourish. And that's one of the biggest reasons for not allowing ourselves to be happy. We don't think that we deserve it. Isn't that ridiculous? That, or people actually feel guilty for expressing their true selves for fear of offending the grumpy old man in the shop when they go to pick up their morning paper.

Guilt and a sense of unworthiness are restricting the majority of the population from being happy. That is sad but it is so true. I am not perfect, far from it, but I remember times when my disgusting moods have brought loved ones down to my level, because they felt uneasy and unworthy of their own happiness in my presence, so decided to sink into the pits of my despair. I am not saying that you should laugh at anyone whose day is not exactly going to plan, far from it, but you most definitely should not wallow in pity of other people's gloom. Remember, happiness spreads and so does misery, so the best thing you can do is share your own happiness and resist being brought down by the unhappiness of those you could uplift.

A lot of the major points in the majority of the chapters that are in this book can all work alongside each other, to help to strengthen each part of your new inner self. Here, you will once again be able to benefit greatly from mindfulness, to raise your awareness of the pure joy that is dormant within yourself, to tap into it, and also to impart the knowledge you have acquired from this book to help alleviate the pain for a loved one, or even a stray person you notice in distress.

As I mentioned before, do not allow yourself to be infiltrated by the malaise of the person in need; instead, help them to put their problem into perspective, through mindfully explaining the techniques set out in the Kindfulness chapter. Then, allow them the space required to get control of their troubling woes. If, like most people to whom I try to introduce meditation, they tell you they're too busy to do it and their mind is way too cluttered, anyway, remind them that their troubles are only as bad as they think they are. By allowing themselves to dwell on negative thoughts, they will only exaggerate the difficulty of the situation. Explain that mindfulness is the starting point for slowly allowing happiness to take over. And explain to them about the Thought Theory Model.

I completely understand that you may very well be thinking that not all of life's problems can be solved by diverting your mind and then meditating. You're kind of right, you can't actually fix practical things through this approach. The problems I am really talking about are those that can't be put right by any force in the world: the death of a loved one; a painful breakup from the person with whom you thought you were going to spend the rest of your life. It is when facing these kinds of things that taking time out for yourself and then mindfully steering your thoughts away from the problem and back to (an albeit new) normality is imperative. Your thoughts are the issues you can fix, so remedy them.

(Focus on your breathing): your sensations, the sounds around you, and the peace you are now generating. It won't be instantaneous but utilise every bit of peace you receive, and then allow that to form a clean plate for the reawakening of your happiness and joy. It is at this moment that you can utilise the happiness you once had for whatever or whomever you have lost and then welcome that feeling into your peaceful, loving state. You must remember to only bring the joy in, though, do not allow a memory in that will encroach on your happiness.

At the beginning of your introduction to Timinology, I explained that through utilising the feeling of an intense love from the past, you could learn how to apply that love to yourself during meditation. This time, you'll be calling on the memory and feeling of happiness that resulted from that past love, rather than the emotion itself.

I want to say it one last time, because this is the only way it will work: do not bring any negative emotion into your happy place, only joy. Laugh when you're meditating, laugh when you're thinking about the joy you received, but NEVER dwell. Laughter in itself will help you feel a whole lot better; it just so happens to release a truck load of dopamine into your system, to make you even happier. You're just a happy person now. Congratulations.

Alongside the Be Happy book that I mentioned earlier, Robert Holden[4] runs an eight week happiness course, designed to teach attendees to release and embrace the pure joy that we all possess. It has received a phenomenal amount of interest from psychologists and neuroscientists, who have witnessed and recorded the incredible results that have occurred from both his writings and the course itself. They note that by simply changing the psychology of your state of mind and by thinking in a different way, you can literally alter the chemistry of your brain. Which is a fantastic thing to know. By putting your mind to it, you can completely rewrite your attitude towards life and consequently increase your happiness and wellbeing.

Thank You ♫

'The more you are thankful, the more you attract things to be thankful for' Anon.

As mentioned earlier in this chapter, the very act of expressing gratitude, or simply recognising a kindness that has been conveyed upon you, has the intrinsic power to automatically make you feel happy. As an individual, it is very heart-warming to know that one of the easiest ways to feel happy is by acknowledging kindness. That's pretty amazing.

Gratitude, like satisfaction, is normally motivated by cause and effect. An event has happened for which you are grateful. But that's awesome. You get the initial enjoyment of an act of kindness bestowed upon you by someone (let's say a friend cooked you dinner). You had a great evening and ate like a king. As if that isn't enough, you can now reap even more benefits than you had originally expected to receive, by expressing your sincere thanks and gratitude for such a fantastic evening. Not only have you relived the glory of the night's entertainment by expressing your thanks, you have also made your friend feel incredibly appreciated for their kindness and made you feel even better for making them feel so good in the process. It's like a repetitive loop of loving happiness.

Robert Holden's Be Happy book has a whole chapter dedicated to gratitude and the positive effects it can have on your life. He then sets all his readers the task of composing a list of 100 gratitudes. As a rule, I don't normally like to circumvent my reading to take part in potentially fruitless activities set by somebody who doesn't really care whether I do it or not. But if his reasoning was anything to go by, and to be believed, then I would have been foolish to have refused to give it a go. I did do it and I have benefited greatly from the undertaking.

I gained so much from writing down my own 100 gratitudes and I implore you to write your own list. Give each gratitude that you note down as much meaning as possible, note down what it is and why you are grateful for it. For example, I am very grateful for meeting Luke because he introduced me to meditation, which has changed my life inconceivably.

I have complied a gratitude section at the end of this book featuring the 100 things that I am most grateful for which have helped me to develop into the person that I am, today. A large proportion of these gratitudes have also helped me to write this book, which would have been near on impossible had they not been bestowed upon me.

Teaching yourself to be more grateful can have a huge impact on your overall happiness. Research has shown that gratitude helps us to experience more positive emotions and decrease the risk of depression. It helps you to feel better about yourself and it helps to improve your relationships with people around you. It even helps to strengthen your immune system. Recent research has also shown that it helps you to be far more sensible with how you spend your money. For such a simple act, there are so many potential positive outcomes, so it is almost foolish to not give it a go.

Please Mr. Postman ♫

100 gratitudes aside, this next practise is for every time you notice that someone has knowingly performed an act of kindness for your benefit.

You may have recently attended a dinner party, or had someone give you a small gift. Whatever the reason, however minute, I want you to write them a letter that goes in the post, to thank them. Not an email or a text, a proper old school letter. You may have problems remembering how to write with an actual pen but as soon as you've mastered it again, scribe your appreciation to whoever it is that has made you feel special.

I cannot stress how wonderful it always is to receive a personal, hand written letter in the post, just for you. I hosted a dinner party the other day and someone wrote to thank me for the evening's food and entertainment. Although I have got into the habit of doing it, myself, I am still so heartened every time I receive one, so I know that everyone who gets a thank you letter from me must also feel equally joyful. It's such a small thing but I promise that you will feel so much better for the act of writing a letter. Side note: your addressee may not express their appreciation to you for the letter itself, but I promise that it will be heartily received.

Hey Good Lookin' ♫

Like gratitude but without the cause and effect aspect are compliments. Giving a compliment is another way to make yourself, and potentially a complete stranger, too, feel great. When you meet or pass someone and you like something about them, tell them so. You might like their shoes, or their hair, the way they look, or their cheerful expression, whatever it is, tell them and I can guarantee it will make them feel happy and you too. They might be having a bad day, so what better way to help pick them up.

Similarly, you might also be having a bad day but by making someone else feel worthy and happy, you will be doing the same to yourself. Having a positive attitude will make you a happier person. Getting into the habit of being consciously receptive to and noticing positive things will also help you to maintain perspective when you are having a bad day. If you're always keeping an eye out for the good in the world, you'll see it even when the rubbish stuff happens. Giving random compliments can help change your life and maybe someone else's, too.

Money Can't Buy It ♫

Happiness is an equable footing that has the power to completely alter your perspective on life. As such an esteemed life force, you'd think there would be some long standing scientific data to back up happiness, wouldn't you? Just such an experiment was set up in 1938, known as the 'Harvard Grant Study'[5], chronologically collecting the data of 268 then Harvard students, over seventy-five years.

George Vaillant, the Harvard psychiatrist who directed the study from 1972 to 2004, wrote a book on the findings, setting out a number of notable habits that lead to a happy, meaningful life.

It may seem obvious, but love, which has already been discussed, is the optimal catalyst for reaching true happiness. A person who has a successful career, lots of money and great physical health, cannot be happy without a supportive, loving relationship. I'm not talking solely about romantic love, I'm talking about deep love for your friends, family, for your animals, and most importantly, yourself. 'Happiness is only the cart; love is the horse'[6]

The age-old cliché that stipulates money can't buy you happiness could not have been more true to its word when the results of the experiment came in. A powerful, influential, well-paid job may be a spectacular achievement but it diminishes in importance on the happiness scale when viewed in the context of a full life. In terms of achievement, the only thing that really seemed to matter was whether or not you are content with your work. If you're not content, you're sure as hell not going to be happy, regardless of the status of your job.

Irrespective of your prospects at the start of life and how well or badly you are expected to perform, only you can have the final say on how you end up. It is up to you to search for and believe that you will be happy.

Joy is related to connection with others and the more areas of your life in which you can find connection, the better. The study found that people who had strong relationships with their contemporaries and friends were happier. It also found that people who connected with their work and had a passion for it, who didn't do it purely for the money, were conclusively far happier than those who were salary-driven alone or had no real interest in their role. Social ties and connections also proved to be a fundamental aspect in reducing stress, improving overall wellbeing and leading a longer life.

As I've mentioned before, setting yourself goals and then achieving them is the fundamental basis for leading a happy, enriched life. It's getting perspective from the challenges you set yourself that can make you a happier person. 'The journey from immaturity to maturity', says Vaillant, 'is a sort of movement from narcissism to connection, and a big part of this shift has to do with the way we deal with challenges'[7].

All in all, happiness is good for your health and vice versa. A compelling amount of evidence has shown that happy people are far more more likely to live longer, healthier lives than their pessimistic peers. Rates of mortality are far higher in anxious, depressed, or simply negative people. The happier you are, the more likely you are to engage in life enhancing activities that will potentially lengthen your life span. Taking care of your physical wellbeing is the number one way to lead a happy life and in turn, a healthy one.

In the same way as with love for others and love for yourself are linked, happiness and altruism are intrinsically linked. Doing good is therefore an essential ingredient to being happy, spurring you on to do more good. How we spend whatever money we make is far more important than the actual amount we earn. Giving to others releases oxytocin, as mentioned earlier, activating the parts of the brain related to compassion, love and happiness. Being altruistic and spending money on others leads to higher levels of happiness (over spending the money on yourself) which consequently makes you feel good about yourself and will lead to more altruism, creating a positive feedback loop of giving and happiness. Just think about it – buying the perfect present for someone is often way more enjoyable than getting something for yourself.

The simplicity of it is to just be happy. You don't need drink or drugs for this – just fundamentally decide that you are happy. Smile, laugh and be happy. Make the conscious decision to be happy. Our lives are so busy and stressful that we forget to just be happy. There is no magic pill that helps you achieve this, you just have to reach the place in your mind where happiness is a constant. Find it and then bring it to life.

Timmy's Tips

- Ten things you need to take up if you want to be happy:

1. Replacing bad thoughts with good thoughts

2. Challenging yourself (set goals and achieve them)

3. Eating healthily

4. Forming close connections with friends, loved ones and bonding with animals

5. Giving yourself purpose and meaning

6. Intense physical exercise (or sex)

7. Meditation on your personal depiction of joy

8. Graciousness and gratitude (and writing letters)

9. Believing in your happiness

10. Complimenting strangers

- Ten things you need to give up if you want to be happy:

1. Limiting beliefs

2. Dwelling on the past or the sadness of others

3. Worrying about the future

4. Negative self-talk

5. The need to impress and envy

6. Complaining

7. The need to always be right

8. Resistance to change

9. Blaming others

10. The need for others' approval (see self-love)

- Happiness fuels success, not the other way round.

- Work out what it is that makes you happy

- What are your purposes for reaching this happy place?

- What are the obstacles to these purposes?

- Once you can mindfully overcome the obstacles, there will be no more barriers between you and happiness

Conclusion

I have learnt so much about myself whilst writing this book, along with benefiting tremendously from all of the material I have researched and consequently revized and integrated into my lifestyle approach: Timinology. Following on from all the fantastic tips I have set out for you to follow, I would urge anyone wishing to develop themselves to put it all down in writing. I certainly hope the life I have outlined is as captivating for you as it has been for me to write about and to live.

If you have enjoyed reading it, or even if you haven't, the strongest piece of advice I have, and which I implore you to take, is to be mindful and to meditate. It is now my mission to introduce this incredibly life-affirming, empowering, positive, depression-busting, loving, joyous practise to as many people as I can. It's not a strange, weird, hippy thing anymore, it's now a proven technique for conquering a plethora of life issues and the catalyst for making the world a better place. By all means, keep practising whichever religious doctrine you know and love, but do it alongside mindfulness. It doesn't discriminate and neither will your religion.

Don't let thoughts about not having enough time and what others may think about you prevent you from making the small change to adopting mindfulness. Whenever a negative thought arises, make it an habitual stance to constantly question why it is there and then mindfully dispel it, replacing it with positivity and love.

I must mention a few small things that have helped me get to where I now am.

When I say I'm going to do something, I'm very stubborn, so nine times out of ten, I make sure I do it. Once I had learned about meditating and decided to give it a go, New Year's Eve came around, so I decided to make daily meditation my New Year's resolution. That was five years ago and I don't think I have missed a day since. Every New Year, though, I include another thing to my list of achievable resolutions. Three years ago was to read at least one book every month, which I have strictly kept up, especially while writing this, so as to get in as much research as possible. Last year's resolution was interesting: a cold shower every day. I highly recommend it. It may have taken a lot of getting used to but regardless of season I'm now in full swing with it. I genuinely no longer get cold like I used to and every morning the exhilarating feeling of cold water over my whole body sets me up fully for the day ahead.

Like I said at the beginning of this book, I have not, through my creation and adoption of Timinology as a lifestyle choice, transformed into a beacon of spiritual light and love, who can see the peace and beauty in everything. That's a pretty unrealistic expectation for anyone. What I have done, however, is become infinitely more attuned to myself, through mindfulness. I am calmer, more loving, happier and generally a better person to be around. I love myself, which means that I can now wholeheartedly love other people and be loved in return, making me the happiest I have ever been. Please pass this book on to as many people as possible, so we can start a revolution of love and happiness.

Timmy's 100 gratitudes

I want to take this opportunity to express my sincere thanks to several people, for so many things.

To Ewan Irvine and Ryan Hodson for calmly and purposefully saving my life. I will always be eternally grateful for the extreme love and compassion you bestowed upon me on that fateful day in the mountains, and thank you both from the bottom of my heart.

For the diary that my mother so diligently composed for me in the aftermath of my accident; and for everything else they have done and continuously do, my utmost thanks, love and appreciation go out to my incredible parents and sisters.

For coming to the hospital in France to be by my family's side: Will and Marianne Allen; Charlotte and Dom Bowers; Rupert Greenish, Ewan Irvine, Karen Broom Smith and Tessa Hardy; Chris, Jo and Emily Dobson; Jenny Finch; Jane Copp; Hilary Kerrison; Barry Andrews; Matt Ruxton; Cary Norman; Tim and Amelia Knowland; Ali Paul; George Lightfoot; Bronya Hallet; Mary Allen; Charlie, Tim and Deezle Hammond; Laura Keer; Helen De Nourois; Susi Callaghan; Anne Bestler; Stephanie, Peter and Mark Leach; Sarah Brandt; Emma Lewis and Gail Palmer; Mark and Biddy Dobson; William and Charlotte Freeth; Davina Bosanquet and Johnny Morant.

Thank you also to everyone who came to visit me at Addenbrookes hospital. Every single one of you helped with my recovery and I will always be so thankful for the love that I received from all of you. I apologise profusely for not being able to name you all, my memory from that time is atrocious; my mother also tells me that she couldn't write down every name because she was often taking leave from looking after her injured son 24/7, but please know how appreciative I am for every single one of you. The small fragments of memory that I do have are recollected below.

To Celia. After reading the messages of support and love that you sent me from across the world, after our brief although momentarily deep relationship before we both set off on our different journeys, thank you for being a warm, loving memory from before it all happened, and for sending me such heartfelt love in your emails and letters.

I am constantly reminded by Ollie Embley, after he drove to see me with David Aspinall, how he had to take out a small mortgage to pay for the car parking; his generosity truly knows no bounds, so thank you.

My cousin, Dr. Lizzie Corbett, who was training in Cambridge at the time, provided my mother with so much support, which was so important for her, and me, also, because you are such a star. You were her angel in disguise.

To my dearest Olive Cox, who baby sat for me as a child, and who made the profound effort to come and care for me in hospital.

To Chinwe, my mother's incredible artist friend, who sadly died a few years ago, who visited me in hospital and helped calm my agitated mind by showing me how to release the tension through painting.

To Johnny Ferguson, one of my closest Bristol friends who was working in Cambridge at the time, I have fond memories of your lecherous ogling at all the nurses, helping to steer my mind away from its troubled state. Thank you also for supporting me ever since.

To Anthony Allen and his wife, Ting, for taking time out of their trip from Thailand to come and be by my side.

To my long lost friend (at the time), Henham Rous, who was living in Australia at the time of the accident, who assiduously stuck by me and persevered with his unwavering compassion, even though there was no assurance I would regain my former charisma of the charming Timmy he had previously known. Thank you for just being a genuinely amazing friend; alongside your amazing wife, Celia.

To all my 'Palace' friends who came to see me: Harry Meade, Henrietta Harwood-Smith Annabel Lintott, Lucy Greenish, Claire Douglas-Pennant, Johnathan Iggulden and Richard B-G (I get you weren't even at Bristol but I see you as one of us). Thank you each and every one of you from the bottom of my heart.

To Hannah Pearce for unknowingly helping me write a large portion of this book. I will never forget the impact you had on me, and I thank you from the bottom of my heart for being such an incredible first love. Your husband and children are so ridiculously lucky to have you.

To Mary Cameron, my incredible God-mother for assiduously grounding in me a spiritual awareness of all that we are. I would not be the person I am today if it wasn't for you, so thank you from the bottom of my heart.

To Luke Steele for introducing me to meditation, helping me find my inner peace, joy and love.

To Tilly (my parents' dog) for putting up with me before I found inner peace and showing me the meaning of unrequited love.

To Ickle (my parents' cat) for helping me see the misguided path I was treading, and for allowing me the dignity of seeing your final days out with love.

To Genevieve Blythe (an ex) for rather unromantically suggesting I needed therapy, which, although not previously mentioned, subtly prompted me onto this path. So thank you.

To Ben de Rivaz, for incredibly kindly giving me a place to live in London shortly after the accident, and putting up with me for over a year. All rent free.

I'm strangely thankful for the accident because I would not be where I am today if it never happened.

To Elizabeth Bowe, my 'mindful mentor', thank you for steering my mind in the right direction and teaching me the techniques needed to develop away from my mindless self.

To Katie for always trusting and supporting my every move, and for still loving me after I was such a brute of an older brother when we were growing up.

To my nephews, Charlie and Max, thank you for showing me the phenomenal ease it is to just be happy (when you're not crying).

To Rebecca, thank you for your unending love and support throughout my whole life.

To both my parents, your immeasurable love has guided and helped me to become the person I am, and I would not be where I am now if it wasn't for you. Thank you.

To Arthur Chamberlain for noticeably believing in me before I ever did, and for being one of my first friends to suggest a career in helping others. You may not even remember it but it has stayed with me ever since. To his wife, Deja, also, who epitomises joy and love.

To Giles Orford for assiduously and compassionately helping me get back on my feet through numerous acts of generosity. My sincerest love goes out to you and your amazing wife, Sarah, and your newborn twins.

To Will Hackett-Jones for his continued and virtuous support throughout all my endeavours, alongside his own battles; my love and appreciation eternally extends towards you, apace with your incredible wife, Sasha.

To Amy Hackett-Jones for showing nothing but love and support towards me and for Timinology.

To (Aunt) Penny, thank you for helping me settle into London upon my move, and for constantly supporting me with all my ventures.

To Ed Hackett-Jones, who, from living close by to my parent's house, after the accident, took it upon himself to vigilantly care for and entertain me when I needed it most. I will always remember your generosity of spirit, thank you, Ed.

To Davina Bosanquet for being one of my first visitors, upon discharge from hospital (that I remember) because you so eloquently and calmly helped me to slowly come to terms with the situation I was facing; and instilled in me the beginnings of the effort needed to rise above it.

To my brother in law (BIL) Greg. Everyone loves you for a good reason, because you're amazing. I'm so happy you and Bex found each other and I can't wait to come and visit you in Oz. Thank you for making her so happy.

To Will Allen, for always looking out for me and treating me with the same respect all the time, regardless of my lack of drive.

To Will's amazing wife, Marianne, for coming out to Grenoble to support my whole family and then help take my mother's mind off me for an evening by getting her absolutely inebriated on dodgy french liqueur – although it probably wasn't appreciated the next day, you were a breath of fresh air, so thank you.

To Ava Lightfoot, my youngest God-daughter, for so diligently showing me the beauty of life and the marvels of pure consciousness.

To Skye Allen, my incredible God-daughter in the States – you are an absolute joy to be around and I thank you for all the love you emit.

To Leo Lewis, my rugby tournament winning Godson. You are destined for great things, and I thank you for being part of my life and teaching me even more strength through your resilience.

To my closest childhood friend, Charlie Hammond. You may disagree, but I see you as such a placid, loving, easy to talk to kind of guy, which helped me reach the same state, when my path wandered. Thank you for being great – along with your amazing wife and children; and your awesome brother, Pooti, and his amazing wife, Claire.

To the boys from Tier One, thank you all. George Lightfoot, Tim Knowland and Ali Paul, for sticking by me when I hit the ground pretty hard, and then guiding and helping me to come back. I love you all.

To Ollie Embley and David Aspinall for giving life to Tier Two, I love you both, thank you.

To Freddie Lait for not actually being perfect.

To Tom Davies for his life long friendship and spiritual journeying.

To Richard and Sarah Newbery for looking after and housing my mother in Cambridge during my lengthy stay in hospital, and to Sarah for coming to visit me. Your compassion and strength transferred to my mother, so thank you so much.

To Lucy Rowan-Robinson and Sally Ellert for coming to visit me and to support my mother.

To my dearest Aunt Cary for bringing along all your puppies to help take my mind off hospital smells.

To George's mother, Hilary Lightfoot, for being so compassionate with me upon my return from France, and then assiduously supporting Tier One Clothing from the beginning, alongside her amazing clothing business of a similar ilk. Thank you, also, to Harry, her other son, for supporting me in my quest to regain my former self when everyone else had moved to London.

To all my cousins, you know who you are, I thank you for being so supportive and loving, especially Kitty Norman, Theo Black, Emily Dobson, Max Norman – for wearing a plastic glove on your head in hospital, and Mark Leach.

To Sophie Peers for her continued support and loving hand throughout my recovery.

To Charlotte Bowers for being my strength and support immediately after my return from hospital, you looked after me so well, for which I am eternally grateful.

To George's father, James, for having so much belief and support in Tier one; I'm only sorry it hasn't made it, yet!

To Janet Pearsons for helping me see the Thought Theory Model.

To my fondest University friends. Tessa Hardy and Rupert Greenish, who were working with me when I had the accident. Amelia Knowland, Bertie Kerr, Harry Meade, Marta Wilkins, Sam Burrell and (sometimes) Charlie Hagan – I don't see nearly enough of you now but however long we spend apart from each other we will always begin where we left off. So I thank you all for demonstrating true friendship and love.

To James, for so kindly sharing his addictive behaviour and resolution techniques with me, something that helped develop the self-control chapter into its present form.

To Emma Close-Brooks for editing this book from the start. Your ability to get into my mindset helped further the explanations and ease of reading, which I hope everyone can attest to.

To Johnathan Iggulden, Will Allen, Alice Hobday, Penny Ferguson, Sarah Leach, Amy Hackett-Jones, Leila Stocker, Biddy Donson, George Lightfoot, and Whitney Simpson for generously giving their time to proof read this.

To Ali King for his genuine support with all my ventures and for making Sundays so scary; alongside his dearest girlfriend, Lucila.

To Mike Dickson for his support and experienced hand in guiding me.

To all my amazing Uncles and Aunts, every single one of them (of which there are quite a few).

To Bronya Hallett for writing me a letter every day I was in hospital and then tirelessly helping me every step of the way during my recovery, thank you for being so ridiculously loving and amazing – your husband and twin boys are very lucky to have you.

To Whitney for putting up with and sticking with me throughout this whole process, thank you for your unending love and support.

It runs slightly over 100 but it could easily reach 200, so if I haven't mentioned you, please don't take it personally, I hit my head pretty hard. I genuinely love you all, so thank you.

Throughout the book I have mentioned that alongside my writing I also offer several online group and one-on-one courses, which can be accessed through my website: www. timinology.com. If you want to learn more about mindfulness – or kindfulness, as I like to think of it – I am a trained instructor and offer eight-week courses online and in person for groups of up to thirty people. Similarly, if you think you'd benefit from a more tailored course, I also offer one-on-one mindfulness and life consultancy classes, details of all of which can again be found on the website. Don't be put off by the idea that I am a scary author – I'm just another person like you. Get in touch.

The content of this book is drawn from life experiences, case studies and a lot of research. Some of the stuff that's informed my thinking happened long before I came to write it all down. I've read, researched, chatted, hunted, called and dug for all the references you'll find in the bibliography but if you notice any oversights, please do contact me without hesitation and I will unreservedly update the bibliography to include them in any subsequent editions of this book.

Bibliography

Introduction

(1)   Neil, Michael, *The Inside Out Revolution: The Only Thing You Need To Know To Change Your Life Forever* (London: Hay house, 2013)

(2)   Hadley, Kathy, www.hadleykathylifecoach.com/put-the-glass-down [accessed 11 December 2017]

Kindfulness

(1) *Trust me I'm a Doctor, What's the best way to beat stress*, Jacqueline Smith. BBC 2017

(2) Kabat-Zinn, Jon, Medivate Quote Database (2017) < "www.medivate.com/quote/122/jon-kabat-zinn/mindfulness" www.medivate.com/quote/122/jon-kabat-zinn/

mindfulness-means-paying-attention-in-a/> [accessed 21 November 2017].

(3) Higher Perspectives, https://themindsjournal.com/pain-linked-emotional-state/ 2017. [accessed 20 Novermber 2017]

(4)   Gibson, Andy, *A Brief History of Mindfulness* (2010) <www.mindapples.org/2010/03/15/a-brief-history-of-mindfulness/> [accessed 01 February 2017].

(5)   Foer, Joshua, *Moonwalking with Einstein: The Art And Science Of Remembering Everything*, 3rd edn (United States: Penguin Books, 2011).

(6)   Alidina, Shamash, *Mindfulness for dummies*, 2nd edt (United Kindgom, John Wiley & Sons Ltd)

Religion vs Spirituality

(1)   Chopra, Deepak and Mlodinov, Leonard, *Is God An Illusion?* (United States: Harmony Books, 2011), p. 14.

(2)   Ghose, Tia, *The Science of Miracles: How the Vatican Decides*(2013)   <www.livescience.com/38033-how-vatican-identifies-miracles.html> [accessed 22 April 2017].

(3)   NIGHTLY NEWS, San Francisco Schools Transformed by the Power of Meditation (2015) <www.nbcnews.com/nightly-news/san-francisco-schools-transformed-power-meditation-n276301> [accessed 15 March 2017].

(4)   Chopra, Deepak and Mlodinov, Leonard, *Is God An Illusion?*(United States: Harmony Books, 2011), p. 14.

(5)   Weisberg, Josh, *The Hard Problem of Consciousness* (2017) <www.iep.utm.edu/hard-con/> [accessed 01 May 2017].

(6)   Miller FG, Rosenstein DL, *The nature and power of the placebo effect.* (2006) <https://www.ncbi.nlm.nih.gov/pubmed/16549251> [accessed 05 May 2017].

(7)   Spira, Rupert, *The Absolute Happiness of Pure Consciousness* (2015) <www.oceanandwave.tumblr.com/post/87924904360/the-absolute-happiness-of-pure-consciousness-only> [accessed 15 August 2016].

(8)   Kornfield, Jack, *The Wise Heart: Buddhist Psychology for the West* (United States: Bantem Dell, 2008)

(9)   Chopra, Deepak and Mlodinov, Leonard, *Is God An Illusion?*(United States: Harmony Books, 2011), p. 264

Nutrition

(1)   O'meara, Cyndi, *Changing Habits, Changing lives* (Australia: Penguin Books, 2007)

(2)   *The truth about healthy eating*, dir. by Paul Barnett (BBC, 2016)

(3)   Bajpai, Prableen, CFA, *Is Quinoa Destroying Bolivia's Economy?*(2015) <www.investopedia.com/articles/investing/083115/quinoa-destroying-bolivias-economy.asp> [accessed 4 May 2017]

(4)   Shepherd, Mark and Waterhouse, Andrew, *Journal of the Science of Food and Agriculture* (2017) <www.onlinelibrary.wiley.com/journal/10.1002/(ISSN)1097-0010> [accessed 21 September 2016].

(5)   Yorke, Harry, *Brits spending more on vitamins than painkillers due to health craze surge* (2016) <www.telegraph.co.uk/news/2016/06/13/brits-spending-more-on-vitamins-than-painkillers-due-to-health-c/> [accessed 2 May 2017].

(6)   By Dr. Mercola, *Will Eating Meat Really Increase Your Risk of Heart Disease?* (2013) <www.articles.mercola.com/sites/articles/archive/2013/04/22/eating-red-meat.aspx> [accessed 4 May 2017]

(7)   Panaman, Roger (Isacat, Ben), *Meat Consumption Statistics* (2008) <www.animalethics.org.uk/i-ch7-6-meat.html> [accessed 5 May 2017]

(8)   Simon, Stacy, *World Health Organization Says Processed Meat Causes Cancer* (2015) <https://www.cancer.org/latest-news/world-health-organization-says-processed-meat-causes-cancer.html> [accessed 5 May 2017]

(9)   Phares, Emily H, *WHO report says eating processed meat is carcinogenic: Understanding the findings* (2015) <https://www.hsph.harvard.edu/nutritionsource/2015/11/03/report-says-eating-processed-meat-is-carcinogenic-understanding-the-findings/> [accessed 5 May 2017]

(10)   Merrill, Jamie, World Health Organisation places bacon and ham in the same category as cigarette smoke and formaldehyde (2015) <www.independent.co.uk/life-style/health-and-families/health-news/processed-meat-and-

cancer-link-just-two-rashers-of-bacon-per-day-increases-risk-of-bowel-cancer-says-a6709811.html> [accessed 5 May 2017]

(11)   Professor Andy Salter, The truth about meat. (BBC, 2016)

(12)   Haspel, Tamar, *The decline of the (red) meat industry* — in one chart (2015) <www.fortune.com/2015/10/27/red-meat-consumption-decline/> [accessed 5 May 2017]

(13)   Evans, Terry, *Poultry industry analyst, Terry Evans, explores the trends in chicken meat consumption in the Americas.* (2014) <www.thepoultrysite.com/articles/3324/global-poultry-trends-2014-growth-in-chicken-consumption-in-americas-slows/> [accessed 4 May 2017]

(14)   Cambridge university, *Saturated fats and heart disease link 'unproven'* (2014) <www.nhs.uk/news/2014/03March/Pages/Saturated-fats-and-heart-disease-link-unproven.aspx> [accessed 01 December 2016

(15)   Greger, Michael M.D. FACLM, *Disclosing Conflicts of Interest in Medical Research* (2016) <https://nutritionfacts.org/video/disclosing-conflicts-interest-medical-research/> [accessed 02 February 2017].

(16)   O'CONNOR, ANAHAD, *How the Sugar Industry Shifted Blame to Fat* (2016) <https://www.nytimes.com/2016/09/13/well/eat/how-the-sugar-industry-shifted-blame-to-fat.html?_r=0> [accessed 02 February 2017]

(17)   O'CONNOR, ANAHAD, *Coca-Cola Funds Scientists Who Shift Blame for Obesity Away From Bad Diets* (2015) <https://well.blogs.nytimes.com/2015/08/09/coca-cola-funds-scientists-who-shift-blame-for-obesity-away-from-bad-diets/> [accessed 03 February 2017]

Self-Control

(1)   Peele, Stanton, *The Truth About Addiction And Recovery* (New York: Fireside, 1992)

(2)   Wheeler, Mark, Study shows that chronic grief activates pleasure areas of the brain (2008) <www.newsroom.ucla.edu/releases/study-shows-that-chronic-grief-52217> [accessed 07 March 2017]

(3)   Benuto, Lorraine, Ph.D, *Sexuality and sexual problems*   (2017)   <www.swamh.com/poc/view_doc.php?type=doc&id=29704&cn=10%5C%22> [accessed 22 February 2017]

(4)   *Everything You Need To Know About Addiction*, dir. by Hari, Johann (Ted Global London, 2015)

(5)   *A Simple Way To Break A Bad Habit,* dir. by Brewer, Judson (TED MED, 2015)

(6)   Rhodes, Alexander, *Get a grip on life* (2017) <https://www.nofap.com> [accessed 01 August 2016

Self-Love

(1)   Holden, Robert, *Be Happy: Release The Power Of Happiness In You* (USA: Hayhouse, 2009), p. 56.

(2)   Fromm, Erich, *The art of loving:* (Harper & Brothers, 1956)

(3)   His Holiness the Dalai Lama (TED Vancouver, 2014)

(4)   Swan, Teale, *365 Days of Self Love* (2017) <www.tealswan.com> [accessed 17 January 2017]

(5)   Kogan, Sam, *The Science of Acting* (Oxon: Routledge, 2010)

(6)   Michaud, Ellen, *12 ways to forgive yourself, no matter what you've done* (2015) <www.prevention.com/mind-body/how-to-forgive-yourself-no-matter-what/slide/1> [accessed 17 FEBRUARY 2017]

Happiness

(1)   Frankl, Victor, *Man's search for meaning: Rider,* 2004 (new edition)

(2)   Cousins, Norman, *A Laughter/Pain Case Study* (2017) <www.laughteronlineuniversity.com/norman-cousins-a-laughterpain-case-study/> [accessed 1st March 2017]

(3)   Holden, Robert, *Be Happy: Release The Power Of Happiness In You* (USA: Hay House, 2009)

(4)   Holden, Robert, *The Happiness Project* (2017) <www.robertholden.org/the-happiness-project/> [accessed 04 May 2017]

(5, 6, 7)   Gregoire, Carolyn, *The 75-Year Study That Found The Secrets To A Fulfilling Life* (2013) <www.huffingtonpost.com/2013/08/11/how-this-harvard-psycholo_n_3727229.html> [accessed 05 October 2016]

Index